CW01623512

PLAYING FOOTSIE

First published in Great Britain in 2003
by Artnik
341b Queenstown Road
London SW8 4LH UK

ISBN 1 903906 33 4

Printed and bound in Spain by Bookprint

PLAYING FOOTSIE

JIM PARTON

ARTNIK • LONDON

This book is dedicated to

Chris Lawless

CONTENTS

CHAPTER 1

I couldn't see the point of suffering in the City of London if the sums I earned were only mildly revolting, as opposed to completely obscene. It was make or break: either up or out. I'd been a stockbroker for five years and I really wasn't rich enough. I was doing well at UBS Phillips and Drew, then a respectable if crumby firm, but not well enough.

It was 1990, a little over three years after a major stock market crash. UK and US shares had more or less recovered and it seemed to me that here was a window of opportunity that led to the financial stratosphere. But soon it would close. My clients were Japanese investment institutions who had trillions of yen available to pour into European stock markets and were optimistic after the tumbling of the Berlin Wall, on November 9th 1989, that the unification of Germany would lead to a new economic miracle. I should be able to trade myself up because a lot of broking firms saw these trillions as just the start of the arrival of a Wall of Money from Japan or, to mix metaphors, like the Great Wave in the famous *Hokusai* print that characterises the *Ukiyo-e*. Sorry to show off, but you see, I knew a little about Japan, at a time when the mere ability to handle a pair of chopsticks made you an expert on the place.

Japanese money came from twenty years of raking it in from the bullish rise in their stock and property markets. In early 1990, however, the Nikkei had collapsed and it seemed to me that their property market could not be far behind. The domino effect would soon hit other asset markets strongly influenced by the Japanese. The evidence was there for all to see in the plummeting values of second-hand Van Goghs, Ferraris, golf course developments in Esher and condominiums in Hawaii. Second-hand Jim Partons would be next. I was a 'sell' and had better put myself on the market immediately.

A broker in my position, sensing that he could squeeze more money out of a situation, would normally stride into the boss's office and threaten to leave if his pay were not upped immediately. The trouble is that in my case they would probably have said 'Fine Jim, go'. I had an enemy in Tokyo; he was doing very nicely out there on a tax-free salary and saw me as a threat, because I could speak Japanese and he couldn't. It would have made sense for us to swap jobs. He was senior to me and made sure it didn't happen by sending hostile faxes to my boss every so often about my ineptness. He had a point, I was a lousy broker. But such footling considerations had rarely held back a career at UBS, so I felt quite hard done by.

With the road to riches at Phillips and Drew blocked I was more than amenable to a discrete suggestion from a friend at Merrill Lynch that I should consider an interview to work there.

I had been at P&D for almost two years – a long time by the standards of the City in the late Eighties. There were still a few fuddy-duddy ex-partners who'd been there thirty years, but most of us younger brokers had been part of a City merry-go-round, jumping ship every few years as a good way of getting a pay rise without the bother of negotiation.

P&D was an extraordinary firm. With a reputation for blandness even before the Union Bank of Switzerland bought it, it was amorphous, inchoate – a vast blob of ectoplasm smothering and suffocating all the young men and the handful of women in its path. The dealing room – with the UBS bond floor downstairs – had all the excitement of Heathrow Terminal 4. Salesmen, analysts and dealers sat in six or seven forty-yard rows watching their screens and talking into phones. Stockbroking by the Henry Ford method: you could have any colour you wanted – provided it was grey. Even the corporate Swatches I gave my clients at Christmas were grey.

As a financial institution P&D's chief merit was that it was enormous. If you wanted to find out about almost any listed company in Europe, somebody there would been able to tell you something. It was unlikely the analyst would be full of analysis, but the chances were that he would have a set of earnings forecasts and a competent understanding of the key financial ratios.

P&D pundits were often interviewed on telly and quoted in the papers, a sure sign of mediocrity. When I was at Citicorp Scrimgeour Vickers, in its period of steepest decline, its analysts used to appear with increasing frequency in the market reports of the *Financial Times*. If Scrimgeour (RIP) had actually been doing the business, it would have been the last place they would want to have appeared – their clients would be furious at the indiscretion. I didn't have to trawl through many copies of the *FT* to find this example: 'British Steel...' (RIP) 'edged ahead 1½ pence to 68½ pence after its broker, P&D, turned buyer of the shares.' Sixty salesmen, on a day the market rose 26 points to 2,516, could only push up a major house stock 1½p.

Times have changed a little. I notice that these days the reassuringly stripey-shirted and red-braced well-spoken City guru they wheel out on the telly tends to be from a private client firm or, perhaps, the subsidiary of a high street bank. Or it is a unit trust manager or a personal finance advisor. Sending your staff on telly is a legitimate enough marketing tool, given that your client base is made up of the likes of the widowed Mrs Bloggs of Bognor Regis – an old lady with pots of money who is anxious to invest wisely, so that she can leave even more to the local cats' home or a charity for distressed donkeys. But if the expert is stuck doing private client work, basically it means they're not much cop.

As I see it, there was absolutely no way that P&D made UBS any money. My computer system, flashing telephone board, floor space, company car and share of deal settlement costs must have cost them at least £250,000 a year, of which my salary was a mere £35,000, a rather quaint sounding figure these days. Did I really earn so little? Multiply my salary by 300 people, add in the cost of all the hospitality suites upstairs, plus the salaries of half a dozen burghers of Zurich called Rudi, and you get some pretty big numbers. Take a look at commission income from a typical salesman such as myself and you get some pretty paltry numbers.

> 'Logically', I wrote, somewhat presciently back in 1993…
>
> 'UBS should close P&D down, although it would be an expensive process, entailing the loss of a large amount of face back in Zurich, not to mention London. But there may be entirely different reasons as to why it has been kept going. Who knows? Certainly not I.
>
> 'There is a rule in Switzerland that deposits unclaimed after fifty years belong to the bank that holds them. About that length of time ago rather a lot of wealthy Middle-Europeans lost their lives unexpectedly. Many of them would have put their

> money in numbered Swiss accounts for safety. In the 1990s many Swiss banks' capital ratios may improve substantially, at a time when economic fundamentals suggest they ought to be deteriorating. If such a Swiss bank had a subsidiary that loses lots of money, that process could be made to look a lot less embarrassing.'

What I was trying to insinuate, without risking a libel suit, was that UBS might be sitting on a lot of Jewish money, effectively stolen. And so it turned out to be. Compensation has been demanded, although they are not exactly racing to pay it out.

As for P&D, the name has been quietly dropped following a 'merger' with S.G. Warburg. That is to say, P&D were crap and Warburgs were OK, so having failed with P&D, UBS took over Warburgs to have another go at messing up a good broking firm. Who knows, perhaps they're doing better this time.

Swiss bureaucracy had taken hold at P&D, and management was chaotic. I used to reckon that if I were to stop phoning clients altogether, it would be at least three months before anyone noticed. Never a workaholic, I was not far from putting the theory to the test – not on purpose, but because I felt unenthusiastic about my job and unenthusiastic about what the analysts were telling me to tell my clients whom I didn't call all that often.

Though I was neither a behind-the-bike-sheds kind of person, nor even a smoker, nonetheless, I occasionally nipped to the smoking room for a coffee in a corner of glass overlooking the Broadgate ice rink for a chat with Yvonne, an old friend from when we used to teach English in Japan. She'd turn to me and point at all the people still arriving at work at nine in the morning – an hour or two after us – and say, 'Look at all those people who hate their jobs...' She's now married, has kids, lives in Hertfordshire and, sensibly, sends her husband to work in the City instead.

There were frequent changes and the creation of new responsibilities. A new memo would arrive on my desk each day along the lines of: 'Smith will spearhead the marketing of Belgian equities into Andorra. Smith's duties will be taken over by Jones, our new hiring from Warburgs.' If Jones was leaving Warburgs it was because he was not such a high flier and had realised that UBS was one of few firms in the City still coughing up inordinate sums for his low-flying work. Which made it ironic that I would need to leave P&D to earn my fortune.

The head of equities at P&D was Hector Sants who, despite being no older than most of the staff, was a somewhat remote figure. It was usually his signature on the memos about Belgian equities.

One should not despise mediocrity, as the purveyance thereof undoubtedly fills a market niche; a lot of fund managers don't like razor sharp stockbrokers because they feel intimidated by them. It is comforting to be brighter than your broker, which is perhaps why people with first-class degrees almost never make good salesmen.

Another factor might be that if you understand too much about what you are saying, you spot the contradictions and find it difficult to continue. Sadly, I can't cite a 1st as an explanation for my shortcomings as a salesman. I have a solid 2:2, an honourable degree. Anything more is usually evidence of having tried too hard. A 3rd shows you couldn't even get your act together for the two weeks of revision before finals. The only other meaningful degree is a 1st awarded for natural brilliance.

My boss – who had no degree – was an effective salesman. I was more snobbish then than I am now and regarded him as a thick, ignorant, abrasive, card-carrying, nasty bastard. But he did have that kind of intelligence not often possessed by chaps with degrees. He could see the wood for the trees. And explain things in a simple way, without jargon or circumlocution or repeating himself or going on and on. In his way he was probably too good for P&D. He told me he thought I was 'crap'. He couldn't manage much, but he did manage to spot the one thing that I'd hoped would go unnoticed.

There was one black person on the entire UBS trading floor. Of course, occasionally there were other black people in evidence (Somali cleaners and the like, and from time to time a black person would appear to fix the computers), but Sharon was different. She worked on the economics team and fancied transferring to sales.

I met her on the Northern Line tube home one evening where she explained that she'd asked my boss whether she could join his team, and he'd said 'No'.

'He was very honest about it,' she said without rancour. 'He said he knew it was wrong, but he couldn't help himself, he didn't want a woman on his team. I respect him for being so up-front about it.'

I'd heard a different explanation. To me he'd said, 'Sharon, she's quite good, but I could never have her on my team. She's black.'

I should emphasise that when I refer to 'my boss' I am not talking about Hector Sants, but the manager of my sales team. *The Independent* newspaper got the wrong end of the stick on this point and wrote a jokey piece about *The Bucks…* and how it had described him as 'thick, ignorant and abrasive'. Hector was nice, remote and unimpressive. Or so I thought until I heard that he'd been boasting at a dinner party that he'd threatened *The Independent* with a libel suit over the piece and been paid off with £5,000. 'That financed the holidays,' my informant reported was his comment. With the passage of time, however, I heard a new version of how he spent the money. At dinner parties he claims that he paid for a plot of cherry trees at his local church.

Whatever. The sad thing is that his libel pay-off was as big as my advance.

I think it unlikely that my thick, ignorant and abrasive boss (with wood-for-the-avenue-of-trees intelligence) would have fired me, but it was clear that I was just as unlikely to get richer at UBS. At least, it would not happen quickly enough through either an increase in my salary or promotion into management, where I could assist in the setting of my bonus. I rang up and accepted the Merrill Lynch interview offer.

When I went to see my future boss Alick, at Merrill's, it was clear that he had more or less made his mind up to offer me a job. This was despite the fact that the friend who had tipped me off about the job in the first place had overheard Alick making inquiries about me via someone he knew at P&D. That someone had unkindly warned that I was a 'low energy individual'.

But Alick had his idea and it was a brilliantly original one, so whatever the warnings he wanted to hire me. Stock sold by British and American clients, he thought, could be bought by the Japanese and vice versa, thus improving his distributive power. There was this Wall of Money arriving from Japan, he said, like the famous Great Wave print by Hokusai…

I exaggerate: I doubt he mentioned Hokusai.

The only question in his mind was whether a catch like me would accept their offer. I was, after all, fluent in Japanese, with five years' broking experience and a great facility with chopsticks. Presumably I could pick and choose.

The first interview, therefore, went swimmingly and I was called in for another to meet the 'rest of the team'. This meeting took place over a few pints in a pub with Alick and his two colleagues Henry and Charlie, the latter eschewed pints for rather effete bottles of tasteless Mexican lager with lime sticking out of the top. In those days the height of fashion. Some prats still drink their lager like that. In fact, I now part-own a restaurant called Cubana, which sells it that way. I said I would like the idea of working in a small team of four as opposed to the team of fifty or so at P&D, but made sure they understood that the Japanese money earmarked for overseas was still mainly tied up in Tokyo, so they shouldn't expect too much of me in London immediately. The Wall of Money, the Great Wave, would take a while to break. They assured me that they understood and took a long-term view.

So far in the interview process I had been protected from senior management. After the pub I was taken in to meet Michael Hewitt. Mike Hewitt! I had been at school with him. He was a year below me, so it was sort of surprising that he would now be my senior. He'd been something of a rebel. In 1977 he wore the broadest bell-bottoms you could get away with without expulsion, but unlike most teenage rebels his hair, jacket and, indeed, the bell-bottoms themselves were immaculate. He used to glide, ineffably smooth, on highly polished illegal cowboy boots, with ridiculously impractical forward sloping heels.

Thirteen years on and the hair was still as immaculate as

the Virgin's Conception, but bell-bottoms had given way to another form of rebellion, this one against City pinstripes. I was all for rebellions against the City dress code – this was before the arrival of '*dress-down* Friday' as the shift to casual was called in the countdown to the weekend's exodus – but I found Mike's olive-green suit from Milan with brown Guccis a bit off-key.

It was not entirely clear to me what his role was – something to do with management – but he filled me in on Merrill Lynch and its ethos. He went on and on, seamlessly and I soon lost track, which he didn't notice. They had something called 'matrix management'. Mike was a smoothie and had clearly mastered matrix management – or at least talking about it, which is the key in these things. He could even manage the plural of matrix correctly. We'd been at a good school.

The three pints I had had with Philip, Henry and Charlie were beginning to percolate through my system and I wished he would hurry up.

Mike might have had me confused with an older brainier brother who used to win the Smedley-Turgess Latin-Unseen Prize and the Pratt Greek Poetry Prize every year by being the only person in the school to go in for them. As my brother went up for his tenth academic prize one Speech Day somebody could be heard from a few rows back saying, 'My God, is that Pongo Parton's son? He must have married somebody clever!' Sadly I inherited my father's brains not my mother's. A similar genetic mischance must have happened in the Hewitt family, because he apparently recommended to Alick that I should be hired.

I had also inherited my father's bladder – my entire family suffer from a high metabolic rate combined with low capacity

– necessitating visits to the loo at short intervals. Hate to think what it will be like when my prostate hypertrophies and puts a stranglehold on the urethra.

Final hurdle: I met the Americans. Along with other US firms like Salomon Brothers or Morgan Stanley, Merrill Lynch had the reputation of being lean, mean, keen, thrusting, determined, ruthless, tenacious, assertive, sharp, not to say aggressive, so I was on my guard. But this interview too was a pushover. I had a pleasant chat with a nice grandfatherly man, who was in charge of sales, and a nice, short, rotund, grandmotherly lady from the Bronx who ran research. She was clueless, but had a kind of acidic charm. An even uglier, older version of Bette Midler. I noticed she had a rather intriguing little gold anklet under her stocking dating presumably from svelter, sexier days.

After all these meetings I just had time for a further brief meeting with Alick who was thinking in terms of £45,000 a year, which I would gladly have accepted. My bladder was killing me by this stage, so I just said, 'I'll think about it, goodbye.' And then dashed back to P&D.

In the evening I was phoned at home.

'£55,000,' said Alick tentatively.

We settled on sixty. I promised I would try to persuade UBS P&D to reduce the three-month notice I was on.

As I handed in my letter of resignation the next day, the head of overseas equities at P&D said, 'Jim, I think you've made absolutely the right decision,' which was definitely not in the script. When a high-flier resigns, he is supposed to be 'kept out of the market' so that the firm he is leaving can nick his clients. I'd been thinking of three months paid leisure on a yacht in the Mediterranean. 'I expect you'll want to start as soon as possible, so we'll reduce your notice period to a month. You can leave immediately.'

I visited Merrill Lynch towards lunchtime.

'How did it go? asked Alick. 'Did you have trouble persuading them to let you leave?'

'Yes,' I replied. 'But they gave up when they realised how determined I was.'

CHAPTER 2

For my month's notice period I booked a flight to Egypt with Gen, my three year old son, pronounced with a hard 'g' as in Genghis. People always ask what it means. Nothing to do with the great Khan. It means source, fountainhead, origin, which may sound a bit silly but it's a handy name, easy to pronounce by both sets of grandparents. Ryutaro wouldn't do.

My wife Saeko couldn't come because of the pressure of work. She said, 'If anything happens to Gen, I will kill you,' which was fair enough.

Her job was to help out Japanese TV companies when they came over to make documentaries and, when she was busy, she was very busy.

In Cairo we stayed with an old friend called Andrew, who had done a Cat Stevens or a Cassius Clay.

He'd gone to Cairo to teach English, developed a bit of a dope problem then solved it by getting God, 'same God, different One' as his postcard about his conversion had explained.

When I met him at the airport, I noticed he had on one of those crocheted hats that Muslims wear, then I had to come to terms not only with calling him Osman but also with being greeted with a bearded kiss on both cheeks.

Gen had to be dissuaded from jumping on Osman's back when he prostrated himself five times daily, but Andrew-Osman didn't mind, indeed was delighted with Gen's wailing of the Islamic call to prayer, perhaps seeing it as a leading indicator of future piety. I was relieved at his tolerance as one was all too aware that in some parts of the Islamic world taking the piss was a beheading offence. This wasn't so long after the death of Ayatollah Khomeini and when al-Qaeda was only a gleam in Osama Bin Laden's eye. But let's be straight up about this, Gen, in his childish way, thought he was being very amusing about something most Muslims do not find funny.

Overall we had a tremendous time. Gen shouted his head off inside Tutankhamen's tomb. Inside the Great Pyramid of Cheops too. Both have sensational echoes and at three feet tall, he could charge up the tunnel inside, while I, at six foot four, was on my hands and knees. He might also be the youngest person ever to have illegally been to the top of one of the great pyramids. Our snakehead was a young man in flowing robes who took twenty Egyptian pounds to guide us round the tourist traps. Our private pyramid wasn't as big as the ones you commonly see on the posters but it was still bloody big when you got up close.

The only hazardous moment on the trip came when we got lost in a Nubian village on Elephant Island in Aswan, trying to find a short cut to the five star hotel to watch England vs West Germany on the lobby telly.

Another young man (in more flowing robes) approached me and, seeing Gen perched on my arm, pointed at some mangoes in a tree.

I thought, 'Third World interacts in harmony with First World – we are going to have a beautiful experience.'

These days, of course, I wouldn't have thought that. I'd have thought Developed World interacts in harmony with Developing World, because apparently the term 'Third World' is no longer politically correct. I don't know why. Nor do I care.

When he got me round the corner he leant on my

shoulder and gave me an enormous kiss. A somewhat moister one than I was used to from Osman. To my shame – because one should be able to receive every culture on its own terms and not bring to bear Western values, which may not be appropriate or superior, to other peoples' customs – my first reaction was not 'When in Nubia, do as the Nubians'. I did not reciprocate. After all, I was still holding Gen but I did not spurn his advances either.

To make his intentions explicit the young man then attempted to mount my leg, like an untrained male Labrador excited by the sudden arrival of, say, a doggy JoJo Lopez. I should say too that, despite the flowing robes, one could tell he was excited and that it was clearly no gun in his pocket.

He was pleased to see me.

I didn't stay to discover where the mangoes fitted into the man's imagination. Gen and I made it to the hotel where we settled down with a group of brickies from Hackney to watch the match. West Germany beat England on a penalty shootout. Gen was not as concerned as I was when, first, Southgate missed and then Waddle ballooned his one over the net. Instead he chose this moment to keep asking in a loud voice, 'Daddy, why did the man in the nightie kiss you?'

I had a one-day attack of the Pharaoh's Revenge, but Gen, fed for his health on Fanta, bananas, peanuts and crisps was fit throughout. It was several years before he stopped asking to go back.

I started at Merrill Lynch in the middle of July.

Two weeks later, on August 2nd, 1990, Saddam Hussein sent his armies into Kuwait. It was also the day of my great aunt Gwen's funeral. Gwen used to take me out from boarding school for lunch. The Pratt Prize-winning older brother always used to make an excuse, but I loyally endured the ridicule of friends as I was driven off in her rusty Hillman Avenger, which she wasn't very good at steering. Then we'd go to an Aberdeen Steak House, naff even in the seventies. It was her treat and it brought out the caring person in me and made me feel good to let her buy me a slice of fat and gristle garnished with button mushrooms.

In the interests of professionalism – all hands to the pump, there's a war on, investment portfolios need rearranging – I skipped her funeral and have felt guilty about it ever since.

Especially as I didn't even deal that day.

CHAPTER 3

A huge wave of relief might have been expected to sweep the financial markets with the Gulf war cease-fire. Instead, it was the signal for a return to stock market torpor. The start of the war had got people frantically dealing. As it was obvious early on that the Allies would win quickly, the end proved to be an anti-climax. It was already too late to buy.

It was the first telly-war. Very few had cable and only working class people on sink housing estates had satellite. But we could watch Stormin' Norman on CNN in the Merrill Lynch dealing room, and see as it happens folks the 'smart' missiles home in on their targets. 'That's the Iraqis Chief of staff's Headquarters taking a hit now,' said Stormin'. Although the pictures were a bit green and fuzzy, it looked more like Hiroshima than a gangland murder to me.

More recently, I was indulging a displacement activity from my current career – anything but write my next book. I was varnishing the rotting doorframes at the back of my house, when the radio news announced that one of the World Trade Centre towers was on fire. Early reports were that a Learjet or small private aircraft had gone into it. So I dashed upstairs to watch Sky. I'm afraid the BBC took at least an hour to get a picture feed, so while the first tower collapsed live on Sky and CNN it stood for another twenty minutes or so on the BBC.

Tragic though it was, the event was remote: a smoking tower is not that interesting, especially as the ad-libbing Sky presenters still thought it was a small executive jet that had crashed into it because of a ghastly air traffic control mishap. So I nipped to the loo, preparatory to going back to finishing my varnishing.

Having relieved myself, I went to turn off the TV. While I was peeing another aircraft had crashed into the second tower, very obviously not an errant private jet. So I missed one great event of history. Where were you when you heard President Kennedy was assassinated?

Taking a leak.

But more interestingly, my ex-stockbroker's brain began functioning. A monstrous bubble had just burst. In this bubble, internet shares – the dotcoms – had acquired extraordinary valuations on the basis of future promise and no track record. Moreover, Chancellor of the Exchequer Gordon Brown, had been boasting for some months that the cycle of boom and bust had been broken forever, a dangerous and stupid thing to say. So, even before September 11 2001, you knew that financial markets were at risk.

I was in the process of re-mortgaging my house. Immediately I began to think where interest rates would go – down. But why? Because already fragile confidence would be damaged further and no one much would want to borrow money to invest, so to get them to borrow make it cheaper. Within fifteen minutes of the collapse of the second tower I was already thinking 'Yippee, cheap mortgage'.

Another fifteen minutes and I was thinking 'Economic confidence damaged, equals less advertising in newspapers, equals less work for freelance writers'.

I'd need that cheap mortgage.

Another fifteen minutes, and by this time I'd given up all thought of anymore varnishing or writing that afternoon, I was thinking 'no confidence equals plunging house prices equals they wouldn't even give me a new mortgage'.

It was still too remote an event to get personally upset. I'd also begun to think that, if 25,000 people had been killed, as they were saying on the TV (the final toll seems to have been around 3,000), the chances were I had lost acquaintances. They were beginning to show pictures of people waving from the windows, and you knew all these people were now dead. Perhaps my thick, ignorant, abrasive but genial boss at P&D had been posted to New York? I seemed to remember that his brother had been there.

But sorrow didn't come into it yet. Shameful to admit it remote horrors in this telly age are - come on everyone be honest – entertainment. 9-11 was like the Gulf War, live on telly. Incidentally, another of my market thoughts as it happened was they'll have to re-brand the Porsche 911 for the American market.

I do feel sorry for Jo Moore, the hapless Labour party spin doctor, who issued an email saying, 'It's now a very good day to get out anything we want to bury.' If you have certain training, you can't help certain thought processes, and when she sent her bad-taste email, only one tower had been hit, it wasn't obvious that it was an ongoing terrorist attack and that a large number of people were about to die. It looked like a couple of hundred. If you were a Bangladeshi, say, tens of thousands of whom die in any given cyclone, or closer to home for me, a Japanese, 6,000 of whom died in the Kobe earthquake without much notice taken in the West, a legitimate response might have been, 'Don't make me laugh, that's "Not Many Dead"' as the famous headline had it.

My son Gen and Saeko were fifteen miles from the earthquake in Osaka. He slept through it, but she was woken by the tumbling of bookshelves all over the house. Heavy life-threatening ones too, because my father-in-law was a bit of a scholar and owned some mighty tomes.

The spin doctor's mistake was to put her bad taste in an email. Email is like electronic DNA; lawyers regard it as an inviolable smoking gun. Thank goodness email was still in its infancy when I was in the City otherwise my career would have been even shorter.

Something called EC is replacing PC. Emotional Correctness. It may have started with Lady Di's death, when an entire nation went mad. It was another one of those President Kennedy questions: 'Where were you when you heard about Lady Di?'

Thankfully the City is except from any form of Correctness. Wits are quick in the City and usually the jokes would start to pop up within minutes of a disaster. The trading screens would fill with sick jokes. E.g.:

Q: What does NASA stand for?

A: Need Another Seven Astronauts.

(A joke recycled for the Columbia exploding shuttle).

But we could all see that the World Trade Centre disaster was a bit closer to home. Still, jokes did begin to appear after a couple of weeks, but generally quite safe ones. Composite pictures of Osama Bin Laden with a cruise missile up his bum, and 'Bin Laden Found' with a picture of him shagging a donkey, as my Nubian might have done, after he had failed to relieve his frustrations on me and Gen.

I digress. Back to the Gulf War. With its end the grim reaper moved from the Iraqi slit trenches and visited the equities trading floor at Merrill Lynch, where a market-maker, a salesman and the two most attractive girls in the office were made redundant. (Dear me, what an un-EC sentence: comparing World War I-style death of an Iraqi foot soldier to redundancies at Merrill Lynch.)

The salesman was delighted because he had taken out redundancy insurance that, for surprisingly modest premiums, would pay him more than he had been earning anyway for two years.

In his spare time he had been contributing to the Jewish hour on Spectrum Radio (RIP) and he could now pursue his ambition to build a career as a disc jockey or TV presenter.

The thought had crossed my mind that I should investigate this insurance before the underwriters started to run up huge losses and the premiums either rocketed or the schemes were abandoned.

The girls were tearful and, being 'foolish virgins', they had no insurance. Neither had I. They were going to be a great loss to sexist bastards like me who enjoyed looking them up and down; but, apart from the intangible economic benefit of keeping morale high with male staff (the overwhelming majority in any City office), they were an obvious area for cost-cutting.

Market-maker Ron, trying to look brave and not unmanned, was ashen-faced.

'You'll get another job with your experience, Ron.'

'Not so easy at my age, especially in this economic climate, Jim. But I'll be all right.'

Since the 1987 Crash, mass redundancy had been a feature of City life but virtually everyone who lost his job soon found another, frequently better paid. I feared that for solid, competent, but unexceptional people like Ron, such times were running out.

Last heard of he'd done 'the Knowledge' and was driving a black cab.

On the other hand I was slightly envious, having had no holiday in the eight months since joining Merrill Lynch.

Egypt was a distant, fond memory. A skiing holiday was coming up soon but a decent spell of redundancy would not go amiss, if healthily under-written by a Lloyds syndicate. Insuring myself would be prudent; my Japanese clients had been decidedly quiet, thanks to Saddam Hussein, and although I was in constant receipt of assurances that Merrill Lynch were Here-For-The-Long Term, the place had the feeling of Bomber Command circa 1943. There was a pervasive, if forced jollity, as people failed to come back from sorties into the boss's office. At the back of most people's minds was the thought, 'Ron bought it in the last lot, who next?'

Despite the change of firm I still didn't like stockbroking. I was like a Norwegian Blue parrot pining for the fjords. From where I sat it was impossible to tell whether it was a sunny day outside the airless room in which I squandered my disappearing youth, but much as I'd have liked to have been doing something else, I was in a trap. I couldn't afford to give up. Of course, I hadn't realised at that time how many of us distort the meaning of the word 'afford'. But as I saw it, in that time of negative equity, when house prices could go down as well as up, my mortgage was larger than the value of my house in Camberwell. Camberwell – too South-East London for many, though handy for the City and the Temple – is pretty in parts and has been up-and-coming for thirty years but had still not up-and-come. I had the habits of my free-spending wife to consider, a fearsome Japanese of Korean decent, and four year old Gen who would start to absorb school fees soon, plus an overdraft that seemed to grow in direct proportion to the amount of money I was earning. It's not uncommon for big earners to have burgeoning overdrafts. Banks love lending to us. My earnings were scarcely stratospheric by City standards, even if, aged thirty or so, I was earning roughly the same as the

Chancellor of the Exchequer.

I glanced at my Reuters screen in an attempt to piece together clues as to which way the dollar might be going and what effect that would have on European company profits. It didn't take long to decide that I didn't care.

At times like this, when the stock markets were quiet – which despite the image in the public mind of young men in bright red braces yelling 'Buy, Buy; Sell, Sell' was almost all of the time – I would ring up a tame client called Mr Hoshide. I had no sensible advice to offer him and he had only a tiny fund. The importance of the relationship lay in the fact that we could engage each other ad nauseam in inane conversations about interest rates or interim results, thereby looking busy and professional to our respective colleagues. I could speak Japanese to him and, thus, appear to be working when in fact we might be discussing sumo or rugby. If I called him five times it would look as if I had called five clients.

Mr Hoshide worked in the tiny London investment office of a giant life assurance company. A charming and amusing man, he had the very Japanese fault of being meticulous and pedantic. But at heart he was a long way from the stereotypical workaholic, being comfortingly idle.

The stereotype is wrong in any case. Idleness is a trait you find in more and more Japanese, particularly of thirty or under. As a people they were bombed to oblivion in World War II, then, by dint of extraordinary, hard working self-sacrifice, created an economic miracle. Many have predicted they'd become the pre-eminent economic and global power, replacing America. But I don't think so.

This is not a judgement made with the benefit of ten years' hindsight at a plunging Nikkei index. It's the observation that the Japanese have gone from diligence to decadence too quickly.

Their office workers put in fabulous hours, but they don't work hard. They're just there, if needed. A bit like us stockbrokers…most of the time our day's tasks could have been accomplished in two hours flat.

Japan is beginning to suffer from advanced country disease with a real option, on leaving school, of decadence rather than work.

The ordinary Japanese people suffered mightily at the end of the war, then suffered building what, for a time, became the world's mightiest economy. Many parents and grandparents of the current generation of young adults didn't want to put their children through what they had gone through. People like Mr Hoshide were thus thoroughly spoilt and pampered as kids. So was my wife.

They are a nation of nouveaux riches, which explains their execrable taste. I still cherish a moment in my marriage when Saeko, who by and large had good taste, rounded on me accusingly because some really over-the-top, flouncy braid cushions had appeared on the sofa. I was not guilty; they were the work of my visiting mother-in-law who didn't like me much.

Mr Hoshide was a on a two-year stint in London. He was thrilled to be away from the one-and-a-half hour each way journey to work that he had in Tokyo, and the long, long hours in the office, a lot of them spent reading cartoon books to pass the time, followed by the duty of going out to get pissed with workmates. Mrs Hoshide liked London because she didn't have to put him to bed drunk so often, then kick him out of bed at seven in the morning., still stinking. I'm sure she also enjoyed the proximity and cheapness of the Burberry shop and Harrods.

As a salesman the best use I could be to him was to supply easily re-workable reports from our analysts that he could send back to his head office, passing them off as his own work.

Most evenings, there was no tarrying at the office for me, I followed a complex routine of picking up Gen from his friend Rory's nanny, whipping round to Tesco, then processing him for bed, my wife usually being busy until late with her Japanese TV people. I don't think many male stockbrokers have to contribute quite as much to the child care as I did. Submissive Oriental wife chasing around behind me with my slippers she was not.

Normally I would have to read him half a dozen *Thomas the Tank Engine* stories. I'd really looked forward to this part of parenthood. As a child I'd so loved the books. But they're boring to the point of torture for an adult. Unreadable. That night I had an excuse not to read them, with the Gulf ceasefire just announced, Gen and I opted to watch the nine o'clock news in the parental bedroom; he loved all the burnt-out tanks and lorries on the road to Basra, and the sand reminded him of Egypt.

'When can I go to Egypt and have Coca-Cola and krrips again?' he asked.

Eight o'clock was his scheduled bedtime, but not a target ever attained.

I have no recollection of the end of the news, only of being shaken awake by my unaffectionate wife with a perfectly reasonable requirement to expel Gen back to his quarters (though she could have done it herself). The television was still on. We then went to bed where I attempted to cling to consciousness for a little while in the hope of getting lucky, but the telephone went. Knowing it would be a Japanese colleague freshly-squeezed from his morning train with an earnest desire to talk up the market for high-definition TV screens…I went to sleep.

Friday's morning meeting, being the last of the week, would normally have been greeted with more enthusiasm than most. In this one, however, the news was that German truck sales were weakening, the dollar was basing, East Germans were going on strike. *Dullsberg*, Schleswig-Holstein.

I battled manfully, by taking frantic notes, to stave off sleep as half a dozen stock analysts talked us through their ideas of the day. Later on I rang up my Japanese clients and bored them rigid with what I had heard. Unsurprisingly I received no orders that day.

Talking to the Japanese is an activity that requires specialists at the best of times, because their English is usually so dire. Things have improved since I taught English there in the early nineteen eighties when they treated our language in the same way as we treat Latin (or, for that matter, any foreign language). There is now a new generation of bilingual little Gens coming along, but at the time when I used to talk to Mr Hoshide, the job still required a specialist.

There was also the prejudice that the Japanese have no sense of humour and are just a tiny little bit mad. Madness can not be held against them, after all, the British are palpably a bit mad, too, and in my opinion a degree of madness is healthy. Imagine what it would be like to be Swiss. All that sanity would turn me into a psychopath. If I were Swiss I'd end up deliberately dirtying other people's cars so that their owners got fined for not cleaning them.

The perception that the Japanese have no sense of humour is wrong. Humour is language-based and sadly a lot gets lost in translation – even with me doing the translating –

so proving my thesis that the-Japanese-can-be-witty is tricky. It's an understated, ironical sense of humour; yet, ever a nation of contrasts, they are into very unfunny slap-stick too. Still, Japanese fund managers unite with British fund managers in being just as dull, just as much of a chore to talk to.

My job was made doubly difficult by the mess Japanese financial institutions had begun to find themselves. This resulted from their belief that their stock and property markets could defy financial history and rise forever. Even after falling by a third, Tokyo's stock market in 1991 continued to look very expensive by Western standards; for example, asset valuation anomalies remained, such as the grounds of the Emperor's Palace continuing to be worth more than the combined real estate value of the entire state of California. That really was a bit rich.

We Westerners could congratulate ourselves on our prescience in spotting this over-valuation, if it weren't for the fact that less than a decade later we allowed the dotcom bubble to swell then burst. It's astonishing how quickly lessons get forgotten. And they aren't new lessons. The crash after Tulipomania – speculation in the value of tulip bulbs: a single bulb could be worth more than the farm on which it was grown – destroyed Holland as a mercantile force in the seventeenth century. And there have been regular booms and busts ever since. The 1929 Wall Street crash saw a 90% melt-down. Truly over-bought markets fall by as much 90%, as happened with the dotcoms. The Nikkei fell from 39,000 to 7,000, nearly there.

Apparently the price of a sheep in 1830s Australia fell from 60 shillings to 1 shilling in six years. Bet you didn't know that. Some markets, like tulips for example, never recover; you can buy a dozen bulbs for £2.50 at Homebase, which I still regard as a bit pricey.

I remember attending an investment seminar in about 1988, at which the hosts Yamaichi Securities (RIP) came up with the preposterous suggestion that the Nikkei index would rise from 18,000 to 24,000 that year. We Westerners scoffed at how expensive the market would then be. But we were wrong. It got to 28,000 and later peaked at 39,000. It's difficult to know whether it was us who were wise and they who were stupid or us who were stupid and they wise. If you'd got your timing right, on the way up and then on the way down, you would have made a killing.

I do believe you can predict trends in markets. You can say with a degree of certainty that something is cheap or expensive. What you cannot predict is when everyone else will start to agree with you. 'The trend is your friend' as they say, but you can lose a lot of money waiting for the future to dawn.

In 1991 enough people were saying that if anybody should undo the bits of string and sticky tape holding the whole Japanese economic miracle together, the collapse would be spectacular. Preventing this was where Japanese financial fire-power was concentrated, so there was little spare cash for investing overseas and enriching the likes of me.

I was aware of such apocalyptic views, but obviously my employers were not. After all, they had hired me a mere eight months previously when such things were already being mooted.

But then, perhaps, I should have paid more heed to the fact that very bright people often don't get to the top of stockbroking because they offend too many stupid people on the way up, and end up being stabbed in the back. This could be true of any profession – politics springs to mind. Our managers were all Americans in their mid-fifties who had got to where they were by offending nobody.

Perhaps that is unkind. Some UK fund managers were convinced that Japan was over-valued for all ten of the ten years of their 1980's bull market. They were thus wrong for a whole ten years before finally being proven right, but in stockbroking terms being right for one year in eleven is a sackable offence.

The grandfatherly head of sales had told me when I arrived that it would be not too long before the Japanese became a force to be reckoned with in European equities. His experience of the Japanese and European equity markets had been garnered selling US equities to American private investors for thirty years in Peoria, Pennsylvania. I hoped that he would keep thinking bullishly about Japan a little longer, because my personal view was pretty cataclysmic. I reasoned that the Japanese were in such shit that it would perhaps be five years before levels of activity made a decent recovery (generally an under-performing sector or market under-performs for at least that long). But with luck it would be a couple of years before Merrill Lynch realised this, so that I could continue to earn as much as the Chancellor for producing next to nothing. Merrill would continue to travel hopefully rather than arrive. By the time they realised that with me they would never arrive, I would be on my way to yet another firm.

Selling on hope had been a speciality of mine. With my reasonably fluent Japanese, it was assumed that I would be able to communicate very efficiently with Japanese investors and persuade them to put their investments through me. In five years I had worked for five companies. The first three, Laurence Prust, Vickers da Costa and Scrimgeour Vickers have now all been first wrecked, then closed down by the foreign banks that bought them. That sounds xenophobic. British banks are just as good at wrecking broking firms.

Banking and broking are two colliding cultures: the former about being cautious, the latter about risk-taking. I remember one of P&D's few good stock analysts recommending the stock of Lloyds Bank on the basis that they were 'the bank that likes to say *No*'. They're my bank and they say 'no' to me often enough. 'No, you can't have a bigger overdraft.' So they must be good. And they never made the mistake of buying a broking company – unlike NatWest, the Midland or Barclays – where in each case the adventure has been, to varying degrees, a failure.

Though latterly, Lloyds took over Scottish Widows (an apparently solid life assurance) the thinking being that Widows' portfolios were worth a fortune, markets would go up for ever (so the fortune would be worth more and more) and the life assurance products themselves could be distributed through Lloyds' branches.

Unfortunately markets didn't go up forever. They never do.

I was the eternal trainee, always promising lots but in terms of revenues delivering nothing. Each time I came under pressure to produce, I changed jobs, switching from selling UK equities to the Japanese, to selling UK equities to the Japanese, then selling finally Europe to the Japanese. I was well into my third year as a stockbroker before getting my first order, yet my salary nearly doubled each of those years.

I started on £11,000 at Laurence Prust. I was found this job by Chris Lawless of the Bloomsbury Group. I mention Chris now because I recently promised him some product placement in this book in exchange for a good lunch. That's how easily bought I am. Back then, he'd sent me on various interviews and one bond brokerage wanted to offer me a job at the startling starting salary of £25,000, which would not be bad even two decades on. He only told me about this later, which is lucky, otherwise I'd have become a bond dealer and, who knows, I might have been a success, in which case, horror of horrors, I'd probably still be doing it. I'd be grey, fat, permanently tired, prematurely aged and, OK I agree, rich, which has its compensations.

I accepted the Laurence Prust job because a Colonel Arthur took me out for lunch and filled me with a bottle of Port. This made me feel wanted and, at the start of my City career, I was idealistic and believed that happiness was worth more than a fat pay cheque.

They assigned me to an engineering stock analyst. A nice man, but I think I spent most of my time in *Jane's Book of All The World's Aircraft* looking up how many executive turbo-props were made by British Aerospace. Well, that wasn't wildly interesting or even terribly relevant to BAe's share price, so I left Laurence Prust eight months later for £17,000 at Vickers da Costa (RIP), then the pre-eminent Far Eastern broking house, a partnership that had seen a sucker coming and just sold itself out to Citicorp – now called City Group (I think, I lose track).

Almost exactly a year later there was a massive storm in London, the 1987 hurricane. I was one of the few to make it to work, ducking the fallen trees and cycling to work as always, arriving to get my suit out of the filing cabinet where it spent the night. My boss was a serious man and nothing would have stopped him from making it in. I had announced my intention of transferring internally from the Citicorp Vickers da Costa part (where I was a trainee Japanese equity salesman) to become a trainee UK Equities salesman in the Citicorp Scrimgeour Kemp Gee bit, selling to the Japanese. My idea was that I would be one of the few Brits able to talk to his clients in their native language.

The Wall of Money was coming.

My boss tried to dissuade me. He pointed out that commission rates were lower in the UK market. I hadn't quite worked out the direct link between commission earned on the one hand, and salary and bonus received on the other. These things were just paid to me, without my having the slightest idea why.

With the benefit of hindsight, I can see that my failure to spot this crucial relationship was responsible for my never becoming obscenely rich. If only I'd stuck with Japanese equities or, better still, done some serious insider dealing in Japanese warrants like everybody else did.

My boss gave me a £10,000 pay rise. It was Friday 17th October 1987. That afternoon certain perturbations began to occur over on Wall Street and by Monday markets worldwide were in free fall. I still made the transfer to Scrimgeours, but they paid £10,000 more for me than they would have. I wonder how many other people got a £10k pay rise the day of the Crash.

At this stage, I had never had an order as such. I had offered stock once.

'Where is it?' the client asked over the phone.

'I don't know, I'll go and ask someone,' I volunteered helpfully, leant across to ask a colleague who informed me that 'where' in City parlance means 'how much?'.

At this stage in my career, having never received an order, not understanding that 'where' can mean 'how much', I was worth £27,000 a year to my employer.

By the time I had three years on my CV it was a bit difficult to disguise the fact that I might actually have accumulated some experience, so rather than promising what I would become, I promised what my client base would become.

The Japanese had scarcely diversified a fraction of their mammoth portfolios into Europe; so far, surplus investment cash had all gone to the US but the great Wall of Money was confidently predicted. The terrific thing about the Wall of Money was that nobody knew when it would arrive. You had to be prepared, because by the time it did arrive the Japanese, with their notorious love of long-term relationships would only give business to the brokers they knew and trusted. Therefore you had to employ Jim Parton. The consequences of missing this bonanza were too terrible to contemplate, so even if for the moment I produced little in the way of commission a great day would come…it was imagined… when I and my team would support the rest of whatever firm I worked for.

You do get little bits of companies supporting the rest, tails wagging dogs. It's what happened with Nick Leeson and Baring Securities in Singapore. His little bit made so much money that everyone was very happy, and nobody ever asked *how*.

So far, of course, the Wall of Money had never arrived and to me, at least, it was obvious that it never would. But I felt pretty safe. Management at Merrill Lynch was as chaotic as at P&D. Since my arrival, Mike Hewitt, plus the grandfatherly head of sales, who had been my ultimate boss, and the rotund Jewish granny from the Bronx with the sexy gold anklet had all gone on to different things. Furthermore, whilst New York or Tokyo Merrill Lynch might have sounder views on Japan's economy, inter-office rivalry would prevent such knowledge ever reaching my new boss's ears and poisoning his view of my long-term worth to London.

However, the new boss, Kelly Martin, was some thirty-five years younger than the grandfatherly head of sales and keen to make his mark, so I would have to be on my guard. Chopping non-revenue earners is an easy way to demonstrate corporate machismo, even if it is at the expense of the Long Term. Martin – when last heard of – was on the main board of Merrill Lynch, so he did well.

For me though, the strategy was keep a low profile, draw that fat salary and survive. A Little Oscillating Dick, as opposed to a Big Swinging one.

CHAPTER 4

At the end of a week it was amazing how tired I'd get, given how little I'd exerted myself. All stockbrokers believe they do a hard, stressful job…it justifies their grotesquely inflated salaries. There is no doubt that a certain amount of discipline is required, to get in at 7.45 a.m. and survive until 5.30 p.m., and read the *FT,* which would be the world's dullest newspaper if the *Wall Street Journal* were not duller. I used to enjoy *The Economist* too, subscribed to it from the age of eighteen; it used to be quirky. My theory is that it's been wrecked by market researchers. It has that stamp of blandness about it, you get the impression that market researchers have told its editor 'This is a serious newspaper, drop the jokes', so it's been blanded down. It began to drop through my front door too often, a pile of unread ones began to accumulate in my loo, and I've not renewed my subscription, especially as I'd filled in their market research questionnaire to no avail.

It doesn't take long to read the three articles a day in the *FT* that are relevant to you. I doubt that more than two per cent of brokers or fund managers ever read the editorial. Why would you read any Comment in the *FT*? By the time a story has interested the leader writers of the *FT*, it's dead. Meanwhile it costs more than any other broadsheet. The *Daily Telegraph* sports section alone gives better value for money.

Some people do work long hours in the City – corporate financiers frequently work into the night on deals such as a take-over – but most long hours are explicable only by some macho staying-on-at-work competition instigated by those with more ambition than sense. That's one reason I left Vickers da Costa. Even though the Japanese markets we served were already closed by the time we arrived at 7.30 a.m. at our work stations, we stayed at work till half six. The UK guys, who'd been in a live market all day, were out of the door by 5.30 p.m. Far more civilised. At Vickers da Costa we could easily have had some sort of gentleman's agreement whereby we waited for the opening of Wall Street, around 2 p.m., and if nothing too globally exciting was to occur, such as a key economic announcement from the Federal Reserve Bank, to take our end of day orders off the clients and be home by three. We'd have been so much fresher, and been better brokers and investment advisors. Goodness, I might still be doing it. It wasn't just Vickers, it was Barings and the whole Japanese equity industry had this weird butch attitude to staying on at work.

Very few jobs in the City require you ever to have two telephones strapped to the ears à la financial soap, bellowing 'Buy, Buy; Sell, Sell' and the infrequent bursts of frenetic activity are interspersed with very long periods of profound tedium, sometimes – no often, no usually – lasting weeks on end.

Stockbrokers do not have notably stressful lives and, in good times, it is easy for incompetent people to avoid being fired. It was sometimes said that we deserved our high pay because like female tennis stars burn-out comes early. This argument is pretty specious. As for the high pay being compensation for low job security, I fail to identify a correlation between low pay and high job security. Somewhat the reverse. Much easier to fire a burger-flipper at McDonalds than me.

I guess that getting up at 6.30 every day did take its toll, but the main stress generated came from trying to work up enthusiasm for the machinations of the Bundesbank or the business prospects of some Swedish rock tool manufacturer day in, day out. The compensatory buzz of dealing in huge sums of money and calculating the percentage that would accrue to my bonus was not one I often had.

Weekends were spent recovering from the Bundesbank or the rock tool manufacturer. It's a shame to waste one's precious days off, but usually I achieved nothing beyond a bit of supermarket shopping. Saeko would give me inviolable instructions to dust mantelpieces, change sheets, wash them, hoover upstairs, put the rubbish out, clean the stove, buy some new shoes for Gen and other exciting leisure-time activities. I violated them, I rebelled, I did nothing.

On Sundays, if nothing had been organised, Gen and I would walk round the corner to the local car boot sale to marvel at the array of merchandise on offer, most of which would be thrown away by Oxfam. I always came back at least a fiver poorer to the despair of Saeko, who had a tendency to be less optimistic about the investment potential of my restoration projects. Also there was a bit of a culture clash there. The Japanese prefer things that are new, whereas I was bought up to value second-hand or antique. Probably because my parents were bought up in the war. Mind you, so were hers.

With the junk we bought Gen could recreate the road to Basra on *News at Ten* or, by the imaginative removal of tyres from toy cars and juxtaposition of Lego, an authentic Camberwell street scene. The fact that he possessed only broken toys made trips to Rory's house, with its expensive kit from the Early Learning Centre, all the more exciting for him.

As Gen's toys didn't measure up to Rory's, we rarely had

to reciprocate hospitality. Rory loved Gen's broken toys, but Rory's parents wanted him on the Early Learning Centre programme. It really is a very clever name for a toy shop. Takes all the guilt out of spoiling an infant. You can't help wishing a child with 'learning difficulties' on parents like Rory's. They were also very keen for Rory to grow up as liberal as they were on the subject of race. Gen, being of yellowish hue, was a gentle initiation before exposure to the really hard stuff you get further along our street in Camberwell.

The tyranny of the Sunday papers was one of the worst things about being a stockbroker. It was dismal to have to plough through all that dreary analysis on company results and contract on one's day off, in the vague chance that a journalist had come up with something that we didn't know or fabricated a week before.

I nearly always cycled in to work. In the world of the company BMW this marked me out as eccentric, but I did it because it was the only regular exercise I got, and public transport was so hopeless, and, even on my wages, I balked at the cost of parking in the City. 'But you don't get rained on?' I was often asked. Although it rains often in England, it's surprising how infrequently it rains between 7 and 7.30 a.m.

My colleagues Charlie and Henry shared a car from near Camberwell, but that would have meant getting to Charlie's house by 7, which was about half an hour too early for me (or two and half hours lost sleep a week).

I kept three suit jackets on the back of my chair with their matching trousers in my European equities filing cabinet, filed somewhere between Chemicals and Consumer Goods. This was necessary to avoid the tiresome ritual of having them hidden for me each day by Charlie; proof, perhaps, that the

British are not necessarily endowed with more sophisticated senses of humour than the Japanese.

At 7.30 a.m. there were few people about other than my colleagues, mainly ex-Army officers used to communal life in a tent, so rather than walk all the way to the gents I'd glance up to ensure any women about were looking the other way, drop my jeans, and whip on my suit trousers in the middle of the room. I suppose this may not have been normal corporate behaviour.

At one morning meeting we learnt that l'Oreal might take over Revlon, that there were some important employment numbers coming up from the United States on Friday, that Heineken's earnings per share were up, as expected, by 12.3%, that Ericsson had won a small order from Kuwait to help rebuild its cellular phone network, and that was it. You could glean as much from a careful read of *The Sun* and, for good measure, get a peep at Page Three.

Alick, our chief and mentor (ex-Guardsman, Old Etonian), therefore, spent the morning writing a stiff memo to New York demanding that the lazier analysts be sacked. They were in a different league from the analysts at P&D in terms of their industry knowledge and experience, but Alick did have a point that some were not great producers. The nice, grandmotherly head of research from the Bronx with the sexy gold anklet had let them become very un-American in their working habits.

To New York head office, the European equities sales team (only four of us) was just a pimple on the butt of Merrill Lynch, and Alick its suppurating centre; so this memo was unlikely to have anymore effect than the previous twenty-five.

Meanwhile, Henry (ex-Guardsman, wife's brother went to Eton while he himself was educated at mere Charterhouse) went round to the research department to photocopy that day's *Telegraph* crossword. I suspect he had been a more sybaritic officer's mess kind of soldier than Alick. He may also have had a degree. He definitely hadn't answered a 'Join the Professionals' ad. On days like this he would do about half of the puzzle then ring up clients and flatter them by asking their help on the clues he couldn't do. He gossiped that a former officer colleague of his, James somebody or other, was having an affair with the Princess of Wales. A spectacular name dropper, none of his clients believed him.

His pace of work drove Alick spare but, so long as a large order from one of the flattered clients arrived once a fortnight or so, there was not a great deal he could do about it. It was as reasonable a means of achieving sales as any other.

Charlie (very minor public school, Dad in the RAF, straight into the City, children will certainly go to Eton – though these days they test that you are bright enough before admitting you) was, at twenty-five, the youngest team member. He got directly on to the phone and didn't get off it until he had told all his clients about the Kuwaiti phone order and Heineken's earnings-per-share, even though all this mundane information was freely available on the Reuters screen.

My three colleagues had all come from Swiss Bank Corporation (RIP), then the Number One in Euro equities, where Charlie had been the most successful of them. His 'This is the News' service was important to fund managers because they needed to know what SBC was up to. The sad fact was that no European fund manager needed to know what Merrill Lynch was doing, so Charlie's commission figures had slipped somewhat. Merrill Lynch, then as now known as 'the Thundering Herd', is not a small institution, but our little group was the equivalent of what is known as a broking 'boutique'. Charlie's figures were still in a different league from mine, but then I was Building-For-The-Long-Term.

Self: Can't bring myself to admit minor public school, but it was a shock to discover, after I left, that most people hadn't heard of it. Famous old boys: Clement Attlee, and ex-Beirut hostage John McCarthy. I can't remember him, although my older brother, when he was a prefect, the one who won the Pratt Prize for Greek Prose, claims to have busted him for smoking.

Things brightened considerably with the arrival of a new trainee, a lovely Italian girl. She wore a contour enhancing dress, a sculpted masterpiece of Milanese haute couture, with a zip all the way down the back which somehow seemed to say 'undo me'.

She introduced herself. 'I am juicy,' she said. I and several others tried not to gasp too visibly.

'I'm sorry?' I muttered.

'I am juicy,' she repeated, and the truth gradually dawned that that was what she wanted to be called. Nobody could quite cope and variants on Josie and Jessie were tried. It turned out that her first name was Giusseppina or Giussi for short.

Giussi was just off the Merrill Lynch MBA training scheme in New York and, therefore, knew next to nothing about economics, companies or broking their shares. Ultimately she would be joining us on sales but first she would have to tour the desks learning the job. She was to replace a nice, clean-cut Dane entrusted to us from the same source, who in the few weeks he'd been with us had got us down with his sincerity and enthusiasm.

Giussi had an alluringly naïve, doe-eyed way of asking

questions and of perching herself on the end of one's desk in a way which enchanted most men. She'd been instructed to get experience where she could and would arrive at the market-makers' desk, generally unsentimental East End barrow boys, and say, 'I am Giussi. Please let me revolve on your desk. I want to learn something.'

In England we were probably unfamiliar with the expression 'intern' – this was pre-Monica Lewinski – but I suppose that was what she was. Eurotrash is also a new expression, well-heeled Eurotrash, she was definitely that too.

Henry and Charlie were soon eating out of her lap or would have been if they'd had half a chance – Giussi was a good girl, no Monica – and even Alick found time away from harassing American senior management and the research department to give thoughtful answers to her queries.

Around this time, Alick told me he'd discussed with his boss Kelly Martin the strong possibility of posting me to Tokyo where business was said to be still brisk (or so I did my best to make everyone believe). Actually, my Japanese clients had been disquietingly quiet of late. Of course, Saeko would be delighted to be nearer home but I had severe misgivings about working twelve-hour days and being in close proximity to my mother-in-law. Against that there was a nice tax-free expatriate's salary, through Guernsey…

The next day I drove to work because it was raining. My car had an immoderate number of valves, went 135 mph and from 0-60 mph in 6.9 seconds. Not bad for a family runabout in London, even seen from a decade later, though in retrospect, a Citroen BX 16v may not have been the coolest car around. I thought it was fantastic. As it was a company car I never cleaned it and the insides had eight months of biscuit and crisp crumbs pressed into the crushed velour of the back seat. In Camberwell there isn't quite the pressure to wash a car that you get in, say, Purley.

I parked it on a very handy parking place, just outside the office, where the workmen had obliterated the yellow lines.

In the morning meeting we were told that despite the dramatic pictures of burning wells in the ravished oil fields of Kuwait, the world was awash with the stuff and its price was likely to weaken for the next six months. Merrill had predicted a collapse in the oil price almost as soon as Saddam Hussein invaded Kuwait, a brave forecast. At the time the almost universal view was that oil would jump further from forty dollars to sixty or even a hundred, not fall back to twenty dollars as we were saying. It was very pleasing for a salesman to have taken a strong contrarian view with his clients and proven to be right: oil down = inflation down = interest rates down = markets up. Contrarian, incidentally, is a very City word.

That prediction was now a 25% fall ago, but even with that proof of accuracy I could not press my clients into buying anything. The Japanese had a pathological distrust of stockbrokers, having been so comprehensively and continuously leg-overed by the likes of Nomura and Yamaichi (RIP). We were little better than yakuza gangsters. Some Japanese brokers no doubt were yakuza. For example, political campaigns in Japan were commonly funded by ramping shares owned by politicians.

So if a broker came on with a well-argued story, inevitably they'd assume that there must be some sort of catch. In early 1990, the Japanese had been relatively big buyers of Europe just before the Saddam crash. Because of their losses from this, some had gone as far as to ban their fund managers from investing at all during the war. They made the same mistake during the 1987 crash, thereby missing an opportunity to buy at the bottom.

The xenophobic politicians and protectionists who have complained about the ravages Japanese manufacturers have inflicted on our industry should reflect gratefully for a moment that Japanese investors have always been available to buy at the top and sell at the bottom of our financial markets (a similar role to that fulfilled by private investors). This, I suspect, amply redresses the trade imbalance.

Though if the theory has a flaw, it is that this inept selling and buying by the Japanese should reflect itself in superior performance by British and American fund managers. In truth, though, with all their fabulously expensive and complex methods of prediction, they did no better in the run up to the Gulf War. They were just as scared to buy anything as the 'amateur' Japanese.

The moral for an investor used to be to watch what the Japanese did and do the opposite. I am not sure how this investment strategy operates in the new era in which they have no spare money to invest overseas and when many of their financial institutions are owned by foreigners.

After lunch, Wall Street opened strongly. Somebody from the New York office rang in with the information that there was massive buying of US shares and the largest number of small buys for four years. I called some of my clients but couldn't panic them into purchasing anything. I ought to have been telling them to sell, as small orders = private individuals = unsophisticated investors = top of the market. There was no point though – as they hadn't bought at the bottom they could hardly sell at the top.

At the next morning meeting I passed the time doing an audit of Hermès ties. Six out of nine men had them, a not untypical score. Giussi had a Hermès scarf. The three without them were myself, the electronics analyst, making a rare appearance at the meeting to tell us about one of his companies and an exponent of 'the dismal science', an economist from the bond department. Analysts would compromise their credibility if they dressed fashionably. They need to look gritty and industrial and as if they went to Northern grammar schools and studied chemistry or engineering at university. It was always curious to see men on £100,000 a year wearing polyester shirts and ties with gravy stains down them, but it undoubtedly helped clients take them seriously. There must be an Old Etonian ex-Guardsman working as an analyst somewhere in the City, but I have yet to meet him.

By chance I was wearing one of my Hilditch and Key shirts and an Armani tie, bought for me several Christmases previously by Saeko in a last ditch attempt to smarten me up. If I had one sartorial weakness it was Hilditch and Key shirts. This is mainly because they're so well stitched they took the strain of biking to work and, as their cotton hardly creases, enabled me to arrive looking ironed. So with my cool tie and shirt, I felt I could announce the results of the survey without the regular jokes about my dishevelled appearance diverting us from the point of the meeting. In a confident mood, I began by pointing out that the numbers of Hermès ties on display showed how common they were becoming.

This sparked an animated conversation about whether you could get Hermès ties cheaper at JFK, Heathrow or, closer to source, at Charles de Gaulle; I advocated Hong Kong's excellent forgeries. American employment numbers, looming the very next day no less, temporarily took a back seat, despite the presence of the dismal scientist to explain them to us. Charlie said that he knew a little man who could turn a soiled Hermès tie inside out or back to front or whatever was necessary to re-stitch it as new, for as little as thirty-five pounds.

I got three orders, all about £100,000, so it could be said that I was busy. It didn't really compare with the nine million pound order Henry had been working on for Barings over the last few days or the two million pound sell order in a defence contract Alick had been eking out into the market for Bernie at the Kuwait Investment Office. The latter may have been in a position to make some clever guesses as to who would replace all that Arab hardware lost in the Gulf War. One day the Japanese in London would be BIG in European equities and the market would tremble every time it got wind of an order emanating from Jim Parton. Sadly, not yet. Still, Merrill Lynch was there for the long term.

Giussi's father turned out to be the president of the chamber of commerce in Naples or some other Mafiosi-ridden city. It was only a few days into her job and she had her first order, not bad for a beginner. She hadn't associated the name Daimler-Benz with the maker of the smart motor cars, but with half a dozen panting men helping her it was soon traded.

It was one of my duties to do the shopping at Tesco having picked up Gen. I liked the Brixton Tesco; they had lots of ethnic food, though Saeko still had to travel to Chinatown to get the right brands of soy sauce and sesame oil.

As a stockbroker I could keep the shopping process under control, because I was fully conversant with tricks supermarkets play to improve profits, mainly because in City presentations the heads of Tesco and Sainsbury's boast about them. Tricks like placing high-margin products at the end of aisles. As you slow to go round them, you see Blanquette de Veau Provencal aux Champignon (Medallions of Tasty Veal in Savory Mushroom Sauce, Provence Style). And because it seems a good idea at the time, you buy.

Gen always insisted on driving the trolley, so at the end of most aisles I was usually apologising for a collision, rather than loading up with high-margin products. Gen was not a victim of the great capitalist conspiracy, until we reached the check-out counter where Tesco, like all supermarkets, cynically stash all the Crunchies and Smarties, knowing that harassed parents are more likely to give in to their children there than in the aisles.

My skiing holiday was on the way to being arranged, although, as every year, Saeko complained that pressure of work would prevent her from going. This was a kind of brinkmanship designed to force the rules of the trip, i.e. I would not abandon her in a cloud of powder snow to make her own way down the black piste. I had been skiing since I was six, she since she married me. It was a source of tension, made worse by the fact that we stayed every year at my parents' rudimentary ex-ruin near Val d'Isere. Unfortunately, it is not self-effacing modesty that makes me describe it as such.

As a concession and an incentive I allowed her to ask Chip, an American friend of hers who had been angling for an invitation.

Alick had been unable to get in a skiing holiday, so a few weeks previously I had invited him. It could do no harm to my career, I reasoned; and he was a nice enough chap apart from a slight intolerance of Henry for doing the crossword, the analysts for not doing enough work and the Americans for being American. His wife was about to drop mewling puker number three, so his usual annual skiing plans were quite literally up the spout.

Part of the attraction of inviting him was that he said he was a very good skier and had never skied with anyone better than he, so he might be fun on the slopes. I had also invited Niall, fellow stalwart of the St Andrews University ski team, and completely fearless madman, who used to do scree skiing down slag heaps (i.e. with no snow on). I had a lurking fear or, let's be honest, hope that Alick would be shown up. And not only by Niall, but also by me, formerly officially seeded Number sixty-three in Great Britain in slalom, and in 1980, the fastest through the bumps at the British Freestyle Championship by six whole seconds (worst points for style – result: second from last).

Alick had grown markedly less bullish over the weeks about his brilliant skiing. He hadn't had time to get fit and, because his wife had developed the habit of having a baby at this time of year, hadn't had a decent holiday for several years. I was gently disabusing him of the notion that he would be staying in my parents' *chalet* or indeed in any kind of Gallic rustic idyll surrounded by lots of cheery yokels with bloodshot cheeks from drinking too much vin rouge. He was going to stay in a converted cowshed, the most picturesque parts of which still contained fossilised cow dung.

CHAPTER 5

On Friday evening Saeko and I went round to dinner with Rory's parents. Gen and Rory cavorted upstairs until about eleven o'clock. Rory had got a massive Scalectrix for his fifth birthday.

'That's not a bad present for a such a young child,' I remarked to Rory's dad.

'Oh, it was only ninety-three pounds,' he replied. It must have taken considerable negotiation with Rory's mum to have got away with not getting something wholesome and wooden from the Early Learning Centre for about the same money.

Rory's mother was adamant that Rory would not be allowed to play with guns, a disappointment to Gen who was heavily into the Gulf War at the time. He became quite adept at smuggling arms into Rory's house. I got a bit of an earful from her about the secret arms factory discovered under Rory's bed. Rory had said Gen had made them. I tried to explain that boys play with guns, cars and bicycles and girls play with dolls and prams, but she would have none of it.

Rory's dad was a partner in a big City law firm: a plutocrat, but slightly embarrassed about it. The kind who, these days, would downshift to more work with a social conscience by accepting a New Labour life peerage. The other guests were selected to offset capitalist pig-dogs like me: a teacher, a conceptual artist, a doctor and his wife.

Why was it that when asked my profession on occasions like this I always found myself saying 'investment banker' rather than 'equity salesman' or even plain 'stockbroker'?

Next morning Gen woke up at around 8.30, something

of a result from an exhausted parent's point of view, but still far too early for me. He acceded to my exhortations to go downstairs and play with his toys for about five minutes before coming back up alternatively to bounce on my head and try to force my eyes open with his fingers. For some reason I lost the battle to have a lie-in, so ended up giving the urchin his breakfast while his mother snored on upstairs. In any case now was the time for sycophancy, if I wanted her to come skiing with me. In addition to getting up early I dusted the mantelpieces, changed and washed the sheets, hoovered upstairs, put the rubbish out and on Sunday even bought Gen some bootlegged shoes as instructed (Reebok, five pounds, apparently new, reduced from thirty-five, as smart as Rory's) from the car boot sale.

On Monday I was late to work because, as usual, I had forgotten to iron a shirt. Saeko had embraced with great enthusiasm those parts of the Western feminist canon that suited her and had never been known to do one for me.

My brain was already on holiday. Had it not been, I would have noticed the car pulling out in front of me on the Elephant and Castle roundabout. I had read some reassuring statistics saying that only eighteen Londoners had been killed on bicycles that year, a highly acceptable rate of attrition, making it much safer than the tube. I executed a neat, if involuntary somersault over the bonnet before landing on my feet unhurt, thereby avoiding becoming the nineteenth. More importantly my bicycle was also undamaged,The only casualty was a limp looking wing mirror on the car.

I recounted my tale to Alick who said,'I bet he was black.' Irritatingly, he was right.

The morning meeting was dominated by some

unpronounceable Swedish company's results: Rock Tools good, Cemented Carbide weak, Special Stainless poor, Wire and Strip poor, but Tubes OK and the tax charge respectably low and no Exceptionals. Earnings per share would fall a touch in 1991, and probably be lower still in 1992 because of exposure to the US car industry. A bunch of Swedish speculators had been ramping the shares recently, so it was an obvious sell. I wondered how I was going to explain all this in Japanese.

Mr Hoshide took the plunge and bought some of the unpronounceable Swedish tool maker; he was humble enough to admit that he had been a bit of a turnip not to follow my advice on the oil price and made this order as a sign of trust. £500,000 was large for him, indeed, it was the biggest order I'd had in several months. I didn't have the heart to tell him I had been recommending a sell. Fund managers are grown people and can make their own decisions, I reasoned. Who cared anyway, when the money belonged to a group of policy holders in Fukuoka, a group whose existence was entirely abstract to me.

After getting Gen to bed at the unheard of early hour of nine o'clock, I enjoyed a lovely romantic candlelit dinner cooked for me by Saeko, who was free, for once, of the exigencies of her jovial Japanese workmates and their requirement to wind down from their documentary on the Changing of the Guard in a karaoke bar.

Over dinner she told me she would probably be able to come skiing but on certain conditions.

1. I would carry her skis.
2. Every lunchtime would be spent in a restaurant.

3. I would never abandon her at the top of the mountain and say, 'You know the way down, meet you by the car.'
4. I would devote time to teaching her how to ski.
5. She would not have to do any cooking, washing or cleaning. (This was not so different from the way things were at home.)
6. On the other hand, she wanted to be in charge of the shopping. (I would say 'spending' not 'shopping'.)
7. My mother would look after Gen. (Mum would be delighted. Saeko and Mum didn't always see eye to eye and, thus, she didn't get many goes with her grandchild. I looked forward to turning Gen into a champion skier, but though Rory's parents might start their child off at four, I felt Gen could wait a year.)
8. She would sleep in a single bed, because she knew what too much vin rouge does to me. (My father, in his concern over the decay in morals coincident with his children's late teens and early twenties, had built only bunk beds and designed them to make it impossible to push two together. But there was one double bed…I still had hope.)

Normally Monday evening would be early-to-bed night – when I caught up on the sleep I had failed to catch up on at the weekend. But with a holiday looming I was feeling a bit demob happy, indeed a touch reckless. I had survived a near fatal bicycle accident, got some decent business off Mr Hoshide and the wife was coming skiing. I reckoned I might get luckier still, provided, of course, I disabled all Saeko's telecommunications equipment so that nobody would ring from the Tokyo morning in the middle of the English night.

Tuesday morning passed in a haze. I was tired but happy.

I didn't even notice what Giussi was wearing. My wife was not the easiest of people – what spouse is? But I loved her and, when she was nice to me, I could look at no other woman.

Mr Hoshide rang up very excited. His unpronounceable Swedish stock had risen five per cent already. 'Thank you Parton-san, very good recommendation, you are a very good broker. Why is it so strong today?' I modestly admitted that we'd been doing some buying. The fact that it was his own stock purchase pushing the price up in a thin market was neither here nor there. Well, it was but I didn't tell him. He gave me an order to buy 3,000 Deutsche Bank, another million pounds or so. More than adequate recompense for a profitable recommendation.

My skiing holiday was virtually arranged, which was just as well with only a few days to go. I always left it to the very last moment in the belief that people would fall over themselves in gratitude at being invited – which is how it was when we were all penniless students. But any card-carrying plutocrat had already booked a fully serviced chalet in Val d'Isere, leaving me with no choice but to invite people like Alick and the wife's friend Chip.

Dramatis Personae, skiing holiday. (Provisional.)

1. Me.
2. Saeko (possibly/probably).
3. Chip, American friend of above.
4. Niall, lunatic Scotsman.
5. Alick, boss. He would join us in the middle of the first week some time.
6. Verona, twenty-seven, the youngest ever director of Breese, Spotch and Betts, advertising agency.

We were still short of a car and it occurred to me that Verona probably had a nice company car. A quick telephone call and a Maserati Biturbo convertible had been made available, but could she bring her sister Sienna too? That would be jolly, so why not.

Mr Hoshide's Swedish stock went up another seven per cent, making a total of twelve in two days. I advised him to take profits, which he did. I liked Mr Hoshide, he was the only client of mine who did more or less what he was told, unless over-ruled by head office, as had been the case with our oil recommendations. There was a chance he'd miss a further rise – the stock had a bit of momentum – but from my point of view it was a risk-free recommendation. If he didn't take my advice to take profits and the stock fell I'd look clever again. If it went on up he'd pat himself on the back for knowing more than his broker, so he would be pleased with me either way.

He told me that he had no plans for the Easter holiday other than to relax, go to the park and visit Burberry's and Harrods with his wife. I persuaded him that as he was in Europe for only short while he should get out and see some of it. Buy Armani at source in Milan for example. Or Vuitton in Paris. I even got him to agree that it would be a good idea to take a couple of extra days off. 'When in Lome, do as the Lomans.' Result: an afternoon on the phone to various travel agents trying to arrange an Easter break for him and Mrs Hoshide.

Since the end of the Gulf War all those wimps who had been too scared to get on an aeroplane for fear of meeting an untimely death at the hands of Saddam's terrorists had been making up for lost time. As if terrorists would have had any interest at all in nonentities like senior Merrill Lynch management, who were re-emerging from under their stones in New York to take their wives shopping in London and prune some 'cost centres' as opposed to 'revenue earners', by enacting some delayed redundancies in London at the same time. They had probably missed the safest travel conditions ever, with all that hysterical extra airport security, and far fewer travellers.

Ten years on, after al-Qaeda had driven two aeroplanes into the World Trade Centre and a new Gulf War had erupted, the phenomenon repeated itself. Never had air travel been safer, security more stringent. And there were some great deals around.

This pent-up demand for travel meant that organising an Easter break for Mr and Mrs Hoshide was next to impossible. Preferred destinations of Venice, Barcelona and Prague being unavailable at any price, I eventually got them on a coach tour of East German industrial installations, topical if nothing else. They would be able to buy themselves a chunk of Berlin Wall, some nice Dresden china to bring back home, and have themselves photographed next to a Trabbie.

Giussi got some more orders. Her Italian clients were turning out rather well. It all goes to show that it is not what you know, but who you know…looking like her is not handicap either.

One excitement at the time was that Alick, Henry and Charlie had been interviewing a Nordic person, who had impressed them a great deal. 'A bit of a bandit,' as he had been described. When asked his salary he had named successively higher figures to each of them as his confidence grew.

Logistically, I wondered how this was going to work, because there weren't any spare workstations in our area.

Nordic people are staid and dull on paper, but the variety

that end up working in the City can out-spiv any East Ender. Scandinavian institutions, out of naïvety one assumes, were used to paying far larger commissions on international stocks than others. You could often make them pay 0.5 % commission on a UK stock, for example, when a UK institution might pay 0.2% or nothing at all.

I had an exciting time picking up Gen from Rory's. I double-parked, as usual, leaving the keys in the ignition, as usual. When Gen and I turned to walk to the car, only ten yards from the house, there it was, gone. Nicked, purloined, schnaffeled, rustled, misappropriated. I had had my back turned for a maximum of a minute. Rory's mum saw a man take it as she was talking to me.

'Oh, I didn't realise it was yours.' Her description for the police was particularly useful. 'Man in a green sweatshirt', censoring – because of PC-ism – his salient descriptive characteristic, that he was black.

I dialled 999 for the first time in my life.

'Police, fire or ambulance?'

'Police, quick.' Three-minute wait before the service I wanted answered.

Any chance of heading the car off evaporated. I had to give various fatuous details like my name and address to some police message clearing centre. By the time an alert reached Camberwell the car would be in Croydon. Imagine if it were more serious: 'I Jim Parton, no, not Parsons, Parton as in the buxom singer, ha, ha, ha, of twenty-eight Dunbrokin' Villas, yes, *n* apostrophe, am fending off a frenzied axe murderer, could you come and save me?'

Having the same surname as Dolly Parton is quite handy. For some reason, certain types of people find it hilarious to call me Dolly. For my part, I find this tendency a useful and infallible index as to whether or not my interlocutor is a prat.

It had only been a company car, but its theft was a serious blow to the skiing holiday.

It was Friday and the last morning meeting before freedom. The disappointing demise of my car didn't stop me making some brilliant remarks about Hermès ties and the ex-Army officer's need for conformity. The electronics analyst with the gravy stains found me amusing, and I even raised a faint titter from the exponent of the dismal science.

There was news that Ron the redundant market-maker had got another job already and would be starting with a Japanese securities house on Monday. That made just two weeks unemployed. I thought he was off his head; I could never understand the urgency some people had to pile back into work when they had just received a fat redundancy cheque and could, therefore, take a nice long holiday.

Giussi asked why it was that the unpronounceable Swedish stock, which had risen another eight per cent since Mr Hoshide's sale, making a total of twenty, was going up when our analysts had said it was a 'sell'.

'More buyers than sellers, Giussi,' came the irony-laden chorus from around the table. This is stockbroker-speak for 'We don't know'.

It would take Giussi about a year to work out that stock analysts' earnings forecasts are rarely right and that, even when they are, it is just as rare for the shares to react in the way predicted. There are just too many unpredictable variables such as Berlin Wall falls (shares rise, peace loving West German celebrant gets crushed), Saddam invades Kuwait (shares fall, plump Arabs flee to the Edgware Road), unemployment increases for the tenth month running (shares do nothing at all), general panic occurs for no identifiable reason (shares crash or, just as likely, soar).

Many stockbrokers are vain enough to believe that they might be capable of supplying correct recommendations. Equally, many fund managers think they can act correctly on the recommendations or cleverly disagree with them. There is a compelling argument for saying that a dartboard is a more valuable tool than a fund manager's judgement, because at least then you save his monster manager's cut of your money.

This was proven beyond reasonable doubt by a small child called Tia Laverne from Peckham in 2002.

She was pitted in competition against a financial astrologer whose star-crossed choices fell 6.2% while the FTSE index had fallen 16%. Not bad. At least the astrologer out-performed, doing better than a professional stock market analyst whose portfolio plummeted by 46.2%.

Little Tia made her random portfolio selection by catching pieces of paper with company names on them as they fell from a balcony. She was just four. A year later and her shares had risen 5.8%.

One Henk Potts of Barclays Stockbrokers was quoted in The Times saying that she had done well to avoid the telecoms sector. 'Tia would be a welcome addition to the City, school work permitting of course,' he said, with a chuckle.

(He might have added with a similar chuckle, 'If she weren't black.' A headhunter friend said to me that in twenty years he had only ever placed one black person in a City firm. The City has a nasty, entrenched institutional racism, which curiously enough is ignored by the Anti-Racism Industry.)

If you think about it, almost by definition, if 50% of fund managers out-perform the market, 50% must under-perform.

Not quite by definition, because there are other investors, but there's not much evidence that old ladies with hunches do notably worse than the pros.

So 50% of the pros don't do terribly well. Until, that is you factor in their management fees that come out of the funds, then, obviously, the proportion doing badly rises. Professional fund managers are bad for your wealth.

Some recent research quoted in Prospect magazine found that 90% of 'buy' recommendations under-performed the market while 60% of 'sell' recommendations did better. Doing the opposite of what you're told is known as being a 'contrarian'. Few manage the strategy: it's against human nature to do what everyone else is not doing.

Our nature and so the nature of markets is to behave like sheep.

The discreet use of insider knowledge is the only sure way of beating throwing darts at the dartboard blindfold. Contrary to popular opinion, insider knowledge is surprisingly rare. I don't think I was ever in possession of this kind of information – maybe I moved in the wrong circles, I was never a corporate financier – certainly I never had it in a form where I could act upon it and make myself a fortune. I did once act on a sure-fire tip that a company was going to be taken over, but it turned out to be an ugly rumour that turned me into a sucker.

The law that makes unit trust ads mention that 'the value of investments can go down as well as up' ought to be extended such that they carry the warning that seventy per cent of professionally managed funds under-perform the indices they are trying to beat.

Ask a professional stockbroker if he owns any unit trusts. Or ask a fund manager for that matter. Especially one who manages unit trusts himself. The answer will be 'no'.

In Tokyo things were different. Japanese brokers were only a step away from the Yakuza. 'Front running' – a surer way of making a certain profit than insider trading – was rife. A fund manager would be encouraged to place a large buy order in the morning, and plenty of Western fund managers did this. If, by the time it came to be settled, it had gone up then he could sell, book both transactions to his own personal account and pocket the profit. If, on the other hand, it went down he could book it to the fund as long as the fund manager was in on the swindle, which a lot of them were. The percentage made would not be enormous but risk free. Once so corrupted, the fund manager would put more business the Japanese broker's way.

The slicing of tiny percentages is pretty much how the City works. But overwhelmingly, outright theft of the type mentioned above is not necessary. Honesty pays well too.

If an equity deal of £1 million is done on a commission of 0.2% the percentage is nothing, isn't it? £2,000. A good equity salesman might turn over stock worth £500 million in a year. That's £1 million in commission. Then there's the fact that the broking firm's market-makers buy the stock off the client for one price, and sell it on immediately for a higher one, a half or even a whole percent higher. The salesman gets a profit credit for a slice of the market-makers spread, the profit from buying at 99p and selling at 100. That could add several more millions to his commission of £1 million. Obviously the bank gets to keep most of it – it's the bank that takes the risk.

In bad years when market volumes are low, commissions and market making profits will be well down. If market-makers are caught holding stock in a falling market they will make a loss, if they have sold stock they don't own when the market goes up, they can make a loss by getting 'caught short'. I imagine that's the origin of the expression for not making it to the loo in time.

Even so, on the basis of tiny percentages it shouldn't be a wonder that stories abound of £1 million bonuses. They'd be top end of the scale, but even if you do a fraction of that, an extra £50,000 in the pay packet once a year isn't bad, is it?

Beating the markets through analytical success is not unknown. Derek Terrington at UBS Phillips and Drew was famously not allowed to express his fears about Maxwell Corporation because the corporate finance department were touting for some merger and acquisition business from Robert Maxwell. Instead he wrote, 'Can't Recommend A Purchase – hold,' a euphemistic way of telling his clients what he really thought.

It's harsh to say the City is not smart in its valuations. The City as a whole got Maxwell dead right. The stock's rating made it look incredibly cheap, a price earnings ratio of a mere 7 times earnings per share when the market average was 12 times, and a notional yield of 13%, when the market yielded only 4%. The fact is that 'the market' didn't trust Robert Maxwell to pay a dividend.

It's like the rule that you should never back a horse at 100-1. The horse is priced like that because real punters know you will always lose your money. Whispers abounded that Maxwell was a crook and you have to say that the City rumour mill did its job. Terrington was right about him and his stock – the stock was CRAP.

There is a grey area where gossip becomes Insider Knowledge. Without gossiop, though, markets wouldn't be efficient and prices would be wrong. Beyond reproach, for example, is the way, once the rules changed, stockbrokers sold their own broking firms to banks and it became possible, indeed necessary, for banks to own brokers. All the brokers up to the 'Big Bang' of 1986 were partnerships owned by the people who worked for them.

I'm simplifying a lot, but The Big Bang resulted from changes in the law that allowed banks to get into broking from which they'd been banned previously. The banks went berserk buying out brokerages, seeing it as a one-off opportunity. It was buy now or be left out forever. The brokers understood that the value of what they owned was less than what the banks were offering and were thus willing sellers.

Almost the only brokers to remain as partnerships were Goldman Sachs in America and blue-blooded Casanove in London. Goldman did eventually sell themselves out at the peak of the 90s' bull market, Casanove got the timing slightly wrong and, at the time of writing, are still in the unfortunate position of owning themselves.

The City and Wall Street certainly understand value. I have yet to see a study that proved that professional fund manager 'A' or his company consistently turns in superior performances in all market conditions. 'I have yet to see...' sorry, modify that, there is no such study, because such a thing has never been achieved. So any fund manager with a couple of years at the top of his performance table is sensible to use the opportunity to move on to a higher-paid job, because it is improbable for his luck to hold. Or, if his method is that good – or hers, many fund managers are female – the rest of the industry will start to copy it, nullifying any out-performance.

The chances are, though, that he will move onwards and upwards, not through a cynical understanding of what little value his abilities add to a portfolio, but through a genuine belief that he is worth more than he is paid. And brokers, of course, encourage the vanity of the recent winner: if they can get a client working for a bigger institution, he may deal no more often but the deals will be bigger and so more commission for them.

The fund manager himself spends his whole working life being fawned upon by brokers and ends up with the genuine belief that he is witty, companionable and highly analytical, which more often than not makes him arrogant and tyrannical. Any given stockbroking salesman actively dislikes nine out of ten fund managers, frequently his best clients most of all.

Alick used to put it this way 'Would you invite your client home for dinner?' And the answer, in his case, was affirmative for only two from a list of twenty or so. I don't think I'd damage his business prospects with such a revelation; each of the blackballed eighteen would believe they were one of the chosen two.

It is a funny relationship. Fund managers look down upon brokers because they believe themselves to be brighter. And in their way perhaps are. Brokers look down on fund managers for being so dumb as to be fund managers and are, therefore, paid considerably less.

Until the first Gulf War at least, Alick's biggest and best client Bernie was a no-flies-on-me Essex boy – complete with a teenage conviction for manslaughter – at the Kuwait Investment Office. The KIO had massive funds until the first Gulf War, oil money reinvested for the benefit of future generations of Kuwaitis; so even when the black stuff ran out, they could continue to be fat and feckless, run Ferraris and exploit Filipina maids. Am I sounding racist? Oh well.

For the KIO's investments to be invested meaningfully

they had to be big. Meaning no point in putting money into an interesting little start-up. It was 10% of ICI or nothing. At Christmas Alick sent Bernie a book, *Blood in the Streets* by Lord Rees-Mogg. It turned out to be rather prescient, predicting crashes and the early nineties slump. Bernie rang back and said, 'I don't want a fucking book, send us some wine.' Alick sent him some wine.

Because of the size of the orders, and the ferocity of Bernie, each time he struck one Alick would run around like a headless chicken, in a panic that it wouldn't be executed properly by the dealers. I lost count of the numbers of times that Alick was threatened with being struck off Bernie's small list of preferred brokers. I think this salesman-client relationship worked because Bernie, the barrow boy, got a kick out of pushing Alick, the Old Etonian, around.

Fund managers got paid bonuses in relation to performance against a yardstick, such as the FTSE 100 index; whereas brokers got a bonus related to the amount of commission they made, which was unrelated to the performance of any index, only their level of activity. We brokers could develop selective memories if we had the misfortune to recommend the Maxwell Corporation, say, shortly before its corrupt chief executive fell off his yacht, leaving his company to collapse. To recommend Maxwell carried few personal risks, whereas for a fund manager to follow the advice could set his career back quite severely. Giving advice is risk free, taking it is fraught with danger.

I assume that all this is pretty fundamental stuff to anyone who works in the City.

But maybe not... I was constantly surprised at brokers who were genuinely indignant at fund managers who didn't give them business despite 'brilliant' recommendations. If they really knew what stocks were going to go up they wouldn't altruistically pass this information on. They would all be retired millionaires.

For the record, in my time, apart from getting the oil price right in the Gulf War, I have earnestly recommended the fugitive Asil Nadir's collapsed Polly Peck (my employers, UBS Phillips and Drew, PP's brokers, were particularly keen on it at the time), even the Maxwell Corporation (when it did seem cheap and P&D were keen) and other disaster areas, all at their peak.

A decade on, only indolent failure to ring my broker prevented me from buying Railtrack shares on my own account. I was convinced that rail privatisation would one day deliver a better rail service. In fact, I still am. But it's one of those investments where you really do have to think long term, and remember all those nineteenth-century investors who lost fortunes investing in the railways. Those who do not read history are condemned to repeat its mistakes.

In 1989 I bought an expensive house in Camberwell, thinking it was near the bottom of the market, when in fact it was not the bottom, nor even the start of the bottom. It was the top of the beginning of the bottom, as Churchill might have put it. Nonetheless, the smile has returned a little. Camberwell, up-and-coming for the last thirty years but never-up-and-come has finally a decade or so later begun to show signs...

Probably a leading indicator of the next recession... When Camberwell begins to look cheap, sorry, good value, it may be time to sell your house in Knightsbridge and Chelsea, where investment bankers are losing their jobs.

My major City market choice had been to back the Japanese and their Wall of Money in 1986. This decision had served me well, but by 1991 time was running out.

On hearing the sad fate of my car, Alick asked his usual, 'Was it a black man, Dolly?' As somebody who occasionally smuggled a copy of *The Guardian* into the office in a brown paper bag to read in the loo, it irritated me to have to reply in the affirmative.

Fortunately half a dozen people in the bond department had been fired recently, so the company car man was able to offer me an immediate replacement. He was very understanding about my having left the keys in the ignition. 'Would have done it myself, mate.' His pay was obviously not linked to insurance premiums for his cars.

He offered me the loan of a Vauxhall Astra GTE, one year old, lots of valves, 8,500 miles. But what miles they must have been, driven, self evidently by a twenty-four year old from the fixed interest desk, who had sidled up to every Porsche or Ferrari at every set of traffic lights, then raced it. I used to do that when I had a Citroen 2CV (600 cc), which because of its low gearing in first could beat any car away from the traffic lights…well up to fifteen miles an hour. Still fun beating a Porsche with a 2CV even if it is only up to 15 mph.

The Astra had seen better days, with jagged holes for the various stolen radio components, scrape marks from parking misjudgements or errant supermarket trolleys, a forlorn stump of an ex-wing mirror and doors that could only be opened from the outside. The ashtrays were full, so the floor had been used instead.

A typical company car!

CHAPTER 6

I assembled my ski team and two cars at home in Camberwell, minus Alick, who would be joining us a few days into the holiday

Dramatis Persona: Skiing Holiday (Final).

1. Me. Brilliant skier.
2. Wife. Rotten skier.
3. Niall. Ski should mate of old. Brilliant skier.
4. Alick. Friend and boss; in which order, unsure. Claim to be a brilliant skier as yet unaudited.
5. Chip. Young American disco-soul-mate of wife. Unknown quantity.
6. Verona. Beginner. Extremely glamorous if tired-looking, youngest ever director of Breese, Spotch and Betts. Terrifying advertising exec.
7. Sienna. Beginner. Sister to the above. Willowy tennis pro, too British and not butch enough for Wimbledon.

By 1 a.m. we were south of Reims. Driving through the night was gruelling, but it's fast as the autoroutes are almost deserted. We had a deal whereby if one car was stopped by the police for speeding, the on-the-spot fine would be divided across all passengers in both cars, which enabled us to drive at 120 mph. March is not too bad a time for French speed cops, though. The real danger time is around Christmas when they need a bit of pocket money for presents for their mistresses.

But this all changed when we changed drivers and Verona refused to let Chip drive her Maserati at anything other than a very un-Italian 85 mph. By then, though, the Astra needed a top-up of oil every petrol stop, so it was just as well. I suspect it had never been serviced by its Merrill Lynch salesman or, not to be sexist, saleswoman.

Arrived at the Cowshed at six in the morning, knackered. Outside it was minus five degrees Celsius.

Step One: I spent ten minutes while everyone shivered introducing the key to the lock, which was obviously frozen. I suggested using duty free Scotch to thaw it. Niall objected on the grounds of economy and sacrilege. The girls started to cry. As team leader, I took command and we compromised on gin. Inside it was minus ten degrees Celsius.

Step Two: Referred to Major Parton (Dad's) Cowshed operating instructions. We had owned this property for ten years, in which time it had expanded into a monster of Byzantine complexity as a result of my father's DIY fantasies fused with his concept of military precision.

Step Three: Chip moved all the gas heaters into one bedroom. The girls all went to bed as did Chip. Niall volunteered to help me but, realising that we were dealing with Parton technology, I sent him to bed too.

Step Four: Turned on the water system which had been carefully drained to avoid the problem of frozen pipes. Opted for option E. 'Kitchen with all three bathrooms; for larger and/or richer parties.' We fitted into the latter category. 'Open stopcock A, close stopcock G (in hole in panelling between lavatory and basin in far bathroom, ensure stop cocks C, D, and E are open, close system draining taps (behind a hole in the back of the kitchen unit behind sliding door).' Simple. Water now flowed into most basins, although not all, implying the odd ice blockage somewhere.

Step Five: 'Section C, Annex A. Please ensure that all members of your party read this section of the instructions and follow them to the letter.' I hadn't the heart, it could wait till morning, not least because there was a block of ice in each of the loos. I let the girls sleep.

The time was about half past six.

It was two hours later, half past eight.

'Hey, man, let's kick butt.' Chip was up brewing coffee. Keen, enthusiastic, American, only twenty-three – he wanted to go skiing.

Immediately.

'Up yours,' said Niall. Some delicate Scots irony was not entirely lost on him.

Two hours later. Half past ten.

'Hey man, let's kick butt.' Chip had been out, collected wood, found the chain-saw, cut it into even lengths (the wood that is), built a fire and, as an enticement to emerging from under warm duvets into the cold air of the house still hovering around zero, was brewing some more coffee. He had discovered the local shop and bought a baguette and some croissants. Keen, enthusiastic, American, only twenty-three, he wanted to go skiing.

Immediately.

I would have just said 'Go skiing then', but the resort was five kilometres away, so he would need a car.

Niall emerged, as did I. The girls remained in bed.

An hour later, half past eleven. Chip, whose enthusiasm could not be faulted, was beginning to foam quietly at the mouth. Keen, enthusiastic, American etc… He wanted to go skiing.

Immediately.

I didn't really see this as my problem. Ten years earlier I might have had some sympathy with Chip. But I was a grown-up now and, as he was my wife's guest, I hinted to her that she ought to get up and look after her young beau. She and the two sisters dragged themselves out of their warm pits. Before they were fully awake I thought it safe to inform them about the block of ice in each loo, and also issued a military briefing thereon.

Section C, Annex A. Lavatories.

1. Please ensure that all members of your party read this section of the instructions and obey them to the letter.
2. If a lavatory bowl fails to drain, the septic tank is: either (a) frozen solid or (b) temporarily blocked.
3. If (a), there is nothing you can do except consider the alternatives laid out in paragraph (7) below.
4. If (b), take action as given in paragraph (5) below.
5. The tank is designed to cope indefinitely with the output of four people. For limited periods (two weeks) it will cope with larger parties (10) provided that the following points are rigidly observed:
a: Minimise amount of paper used. Single thickness, not double. Use only lavatory paper, i.e. not newspaper or kitchen paper.
b: Under no circumstances should it be used for disposal of any kind of rubbish whatsoever. Not even paper handkerchiefs. Not items of personal hygiene. Nothing. GEDDIT?
6. Provided any blockage has been reported to the head

of the household immediately, and you have not got a blockage on top of a blockage, you should be able to free it with copious amounts of cold water and a plunger. In a 'bad case', try several times. On no account flush during this procedure if you are keen to avoid an environmental disaster.

7. If this fails you are left with the following choices:
a. Use the emergency Racasan bucket.
b. The river.
c. Hang on until the bottom of the telepherique.
d. If frozen, wait for a thaw.
e. Go home.
8. See also Annex A to Section A.

Annex A to Section A. The downstairs Bathroom.

1 This bathroom is below septic tank level and so has an electric pump and shredder to raise solids to the right level at the appropriate consistency.
2. The shredder will cope with all normal lavatory solids but not with plastic or rubber. You must tell your guests about this and be utterly explicit. Experience indicates that euphemisms pass over most people's heads. The shredder is a very expensive piece of equipment. (That's enough plumbing – Ed).

Having drawn this, euphemistically, to the attention of the party we were about ready to go skiing, except for a need to equip Verona and Sienna. I took them to Monsieur Noz, a wizened old man of the mountains, where I explained that they were debutantes. Noz was deeply suspicious of the new fad for shorter skis. Small details like the fact that they are easier to turn were nothing against la stabilite. Verona and Sienna were issued with monsters.

Beginners at skiing are not merely beginners at skiing; they have to learn how to walk with ski boots, how to carry planks and sticks at the same time, and tricks like remembering that they stick out at the back when you put them on your shoulder, so that if rotated through 180 degrees the bit sticking out invariably decapitates a passing Frenchman. Or so it used to be in the early 1990s. Nowadays even World Cup skiers prefer the stubby little skis knows as 'carvers' which I think is cheating. Or thought so until I tried them… Certainly a 'carvers' skier would never have met Pascal, who had been looking at Verona's bum, when her skis swung through 180 and caught him a glancing blow in the face. It didn't take too much mountain craft for Pascal, with his roguish Alain Prost good looks and short stature, to realise he was confronted by potential students. Having looked them up and down and especially from the front, he volunteered to teach them.

The other thing about beginners is that they take for ever to assemble themselves, adjusting boot clips, bindings, getting snow stuck under the boot, falling over when they try to knock it off. 'Lean on me,' said Pascal.

To kill time Chip had bought lip salve, mirror sun glasses, a new pair of gloves and a coloured scarf to tie round his knee, had gotten the bottoms of his skis hot waxed, the edges sharpened and, having ascertained the correct local frequency for his avalanche bleeper, was saying things like 'Let's kick butt' with the time lag between each utterance diminishing like the minor shocks before a major earthquake.

It was well past one o'clock by now, so Saeko suggested that it was time for lunch. A nice restaurant with a sixty-seven franc menu, including half a bottle of wine, beckoned. I was in a dilemma because I had signed a charter to do whatever my wife wanted but, on the other hand, her friend, if he didn't get skiing soon, would start having some kind of seizure. Although I was now thirty-one, I still remembered the frustrations of being twenty-three. I ordered us up the mountain.

On the first day of a skiing holiday a series of 'species recognition' dances take place, which are much worse than the strains one's unfit body is subjected to. The women had already eyed each other's anoraks and admired various features in the way only women can do when they have a point to make.

'C & A (RIP) are making some lovely things these days,' said Saeko. Pretty hard-hitting stuff showing a sophisticated grasp, for a foreigner, of how the British middle classes don't want to be suspected of dressing.

Verona's riposte of 'Gorgeous design, lovely feel, but you must have had to take a mortgage on it' was water off a duck's back. It is a peculiar British virtue to be seen not to be trying. Large sums of money spent on clothes were not something my wife had difficulty coming to terms with. That was left to me and my bank manager, a sympathetic fellow who recognised that my earnings made me capable of supporting a high maintenance wife.

We men eyed each other's skis. No contest there. Niall's were two metres fifteen centimetres long. He had bought them from a member of the British ski team who had blagged some spare ones from his sponsor. Chip's were not especially long, but they were made of Kevlar by the Box Torsion Zeta method and matched the scarf round his knee. He pressed the bottoms lovingly to his cheek as we went up the cable car. Mine were a good second hand pair bought off some flash bastard who had wanted to graduate onto that year's colours.

Chip flew neatly down the mountain with a cry of 'Hey

man, let's kick butt'. An alarmingly good skier. Niall eschewed style; he could afford to because he had the longest and most manly pair of skis, too massive for threading through the bumps, he bounced over them, touching only where gravity dictated. He had the assurance of somcone who didn't need to show off.

As for my classification, kind people called it 'spectacular' – legs and arms everywhere. I don't see how you can be six feet four, possess size thirteen feet and be elegant. Purists have trouble coming to terms with this style, but it works for me.

It is extremely galling to report that Chip was better than me. Saeko viewed the battle from the side of the piste having taken the blue run down, satisfied that her protégé was humiliating her husband.

We only managed a couple of hours before it was time to go in. Verona and Sienna were looking flushed with success. Pascal had told them that they had natural talent, apparently referring to their skiing.

Back at the Cowshed, things were not quite as they might have been. Water cascaded down the stairs and through the floors. Carpets, upholstered furniture, bags of sugar, lentils, all saturated, rivers of Weetabix on the floor along with soggy baguettes floating like escaped turds at the Thames Barrier.

It was of course immediately evident to me – how could it be otherwise? – that I had overlooked Annex P (3) of the Cowshed operating instructions and failed to close down system draining tap G. Also a block of ice in the upstairs lavatory cistern had melted sufficiently to allow the ball-cock to descend and supply it with water. This would have been fine if the aforementioned block of ice had not cracked said cistern thereby making the supply of water everlasting. The only double bed was soaked, a severe blow to a working man now too tired to do anything but sleep in it, still clinging to the vain hope of luring wife to join him. It would take about a month to dry.

There is a myth that Orientals are inscrutable. Saeko speaks very good English, particularly when roused, and handles certain idioms skilfully. I think she caught the mood of the occasion perfectly when she described me as a 'Fucking idiot'.

None of the women were of the tough outward-bound variety, so I realised it was in my interest to suggest that they spent the night in the local auberge while we men sorted things out. Chip volunteered to help them with their bags and skis.

The temperature inside had crept up to about three degrees Celsius, enough to melt the plug of ice leading to system draining tap G, but not exactly what was needed after a vigorous day's exercise in the cold. Still, Niall was a genuine Scotsman, who had learnt his skiing in blizzards in the Highlands and whose *bothy* was, if anything, colder than the Cowshed, and I, as team leader, had no choice.

We had supper at the auberge; Chip and the girls looked refreshed after long baths. Then it was early to bed having scotched a move by Chip to 'kick butt' at a disco.

CHAPTER 7

Outside it was ten degrees, bad news for the snow, inside still not quite as warm, but getting there. A charming feature of traditional Savoyard properties with four foot thick stone walls is that they retain the temperature of the coldest snap that winter.

I had a depressing day on the slopes. My body wouldn't do what it was told, whereas Chip's appeared to do everything demanded of it. Age? What was I? Thirty-one, still young surely; but shocking to think how a desk-bound job eviscerates physical stamina. Niall was still the great skier he'd been at St Andrews, smoother actually: the only thing dividing us then was that during slalom races he used to fall a lot more than me. He said he hadn't fallen for the last three years. Clearly he hadn't been trying hard enough. I was reduced to lying to Chip that I used to be better than Niall at university. 'Yes, I can see that you were a very good skier once, James, but you are looking a bit stiff. Try leaning forward a bit more.'

I stifled the wish to say 'Chip, my name is Jim'. I associate *James* with being in trouble with my mother.

We met Verona and Sienna in the cafe drinking vin chaud and genepi with Pascal, who reaffirmed that they were 'very good', still apparently referring to their skiing. They had an air of contentment.

Physically speaking, the end of the second day is always the worst, but taking ski boots off is still a torture. Can't the manufacturers do something? So all the passengers opted to get into the cars with them on. Verona's Maserati, being a convertible, was ideal for piling skis into.

Verona demonstrated why her rise at Breese, Spotch and Breese had been so meteoric. She ordered us and skis out.

'These seats are leather,' she said.

'But it's a company car,' I remonstrated.

But she couldn't be persuaded to see that a few scuffs and some melted snow could scarcely matter, especially as she never sat in the back anyway.

I did manage to persuade the women and Chip that the Cowshed was now safe for occupation, which it was, give or take the odd pool of water and a pervasive smell of damp mingling with pine smoke from the fire.

Even Chip had his uses. He was very good at hewing wood and building fires and soon had one big enough to roast an elk.

It was the last day for honing skills before the arrival of Alick. I was convinced that I was as good as Chip, it was only my body holding me back. I'd lost my nerve. I thought twice about doing things, quite a shock to me who had hitherto been fearless. I was held back by an inability to commit myself and by knees without the correct shock absorbing qualities. Not being able to hold my own against a twenty-three year old was an unexpected blow. When I got back I promised myself a new regime, squash twice a week at Slim Jim's gym in Broadgate, running, sit-ups and press-ups before bed.

I offered to teach Saeko, whom I had more or less ignored in the battle to beat Chip. She couldn't fail to be delighted. 'Chip's much more stylish than you and Niall,' she opined, rejecting my offer. I was beginning to hate Chip. What did she know about my style? She was a beginner on skis for goodness sake.

The snow was getting distinctly patchy: roots, rocks, myrtle bushes all appearing, so the final ski down was really for the foolhardy only, which included all of us men who were trying to prove things to each other. Saeko went down on the chairlift. Only those of us who had skied a lot in Scotland would regard the conditions as good. 'Hey, man, this is really different,' said Chip, before regaling us with tales about heli-skiing in the Bugaboos. I had provided him with a pleasant part of rural France to stay in, sorry I hadn't been able to arrange the helicopter or the snow.

Verona and Sienna had had another successful day and had invited Pascal to dinner the following evening.

In the evening we prepared a cauldron of boeuf bourguignon. The only thing that anyone could remember about the recipe was that it required a lot of red wine.

Outside, rain was gently falling which was likely to be disastrous for the snow unless the temperature dropped suddenly.

8.17 p.m. I went to meet Alick's train from Lyon, but he wasn't on it.

9.17 p.m. Neither was he on that one either.

10.47 p.m. Nor, come to that, on the final one. I concluded that Merrill Lynch must have got busy or that Bernie the barrow boy had thrown a fit, having given him a large order that the dealers had messed up, and he had been unavoidably detained or that perhaps his wife had sprogged.

Just as I turned in for bed there was a loud knocking on the door. 'Ah, Alick,' we thought. It turned out to be a drunken Pascal who had inexplicably lost his way to the village. We sent him on his way. 'Demain, Pascal.' I politely but firmly told him that he had already exhausted our womenfolk, who had gone to bed, although I said Chip was available for the disco.

Five minutes later, Pascal was again at the door, muttering something about his *voiture*. It turned out that he had driven it off the road above the house and been very lucky to avoid a cold, premature death in the River Isère. In a way he had my sympathy – I once drove my student Deux Chevaux containing Niall and others of my ski team into the River Spey, shortly after a trip to the Tamdhu Distillery. These things happen. I borrowed the Maserati and drove – ignoring the 'other drivers' speed limit of 85 mph – Pascal to the village where his mate was woken to retrieve it with his tractor, before the arrival of the flics, not that I had ever seen a flic in this part of the valley.

(They've woken up: ten year later I was fined 1,800 francs (£180) for pulling out without stopping and then immediately over-taking across a solid white line).

Four a.m., I think. Further loud knocking on the door, this time angry and insistent. *Va t'en, sale grenouille*, I thought.

In fact it was Alick. The poor fellow had misread my instructions and got off at Bourg St. Maurice instead of Landry, the station before. He said my directions were very ambiguous. When he'd started on his quest to find us there had been a few taxis about, but towards midnight he'd run out of transport, so laden with skis and bags he'd spent a few happy hours waking up Frenchmen asking, 'Ou est la maison de Monsieur Parton?' in his army officer French (similar to my father's) before he'd had the good luck to fall in with a jolly chap with a bruised face muttering something about his voiture and resembling Alain Prost. Later, after a large quantity of eau de vie from an unmarked bottle later, it emerged that we were well known in the area. 'Ah, oui, les Parton, la-bas,' at which the jolly man had collapsed. Alick walked in the direction of the prostrate figure's arm and eventually found us. He said he had already walked past three times earlier in the evening because it had looked too agricultural.

8 a.m. Chip was noisily making coffee and building a fire, muttering 'Let's kick butt'. He was only marginally less irritating than Gen of a morning. I wondered how Gen was. Would he have discovered that bouncing on Grandpa's head at 6 a.m. was not allowed?

'Powder snow', said Gen senior/Chip. And sure enough the apple trees outside had acquired a gentle dusting of the fluffy stuff, meaning that higher in the resort, conditions would be great. Early though it was, I felt galvanised. I felt a bit sorry for Alick who, on five hours sleep and a hang-over, must have been knackered; but he would understand.

Alick brought me up to date on developments at work. Amongst other things, he was pleased to say that they had been able to hire that Nordic person, the one they had described as 'a bit of a bandit'. High praise. Being on holiday, I wasn't terribly engaged by this conversation, but it did cross my mind that there would be some upheaval on the seating front. If I played my cards right I might end up sitting next to Giussi.

Seven people, two cars. Not an unmanageable equation in normal circumstances, but Verona was adamant that ski-booted men would not be allowed in her car. Three women got into the Maserati (by now rechristened Masturbati by its growing number of detractors), four men into the Astra. With the ban on skis in the Maserati, the four men were made to share their space with seven pairs of skis, which stuck out of the sun roof.

The Maserati set off first. The Astra was delayed by the difficulty in finding a configuration for putting the skis through the sun-roof, so that they didn't interfere with the gear stick and hand-brake. We encountered the Masturbati halfway up the mountain, stuck in the new snow. Masturbatis don't go up icy mountains very easily. Verona had no chains. Neither did we, but being four heavy men and seven pairs of skis and having front wheel drive, we gripped very nicely. I impressed upon Verona the importance of correct weight distribution, dodged the ensuing slap, explaining that I was referring to the car. I succeeded in having two men and seven pairs of skis transferred into the back. We made it to the slopes, hee, hee…

Pascal was still pissed, concussed, or both and therefore hors de combat, which meant we were stuck with two beginners – we agreed to meet them for lunch at the top of the mountain. Chip was under strict instructions not to ski better than Alick. Overnight there had been two feet of powder and at the top, we came through the clouds into the sun to look down onto valleys filled with cotton wool. Chip weaved perfectly regular, rhythmic, snake-like tracks down the mountain. He was kicking butt. Niall did the same, except that his tracks had gaps because he spent so much time in the air. The two feet of powder was on a base of rock hard ice and I couldn't take the strain – it was my thirty-one-year-old stock-broker's knees playing up again.

Alick attempted to weave similar tracks to Chip's. He was in first day species recognition mode. He took a purler and got up looking like an Old English sheepdog. He roared with laughter, but a vein throbbing in his forehead told of deeper seated angst. I went to cast Chip a sharp admonitory glance but he was already 500 yards down the slope kicking butt.

Arriving at the top again I had just about recuperated

enough for the next run. Having established that Chip was fitter and generally a better skier than me, I thought I might as well allow Alick to discover the same thing for himself before showing him that he was not first in the pecking order, as he was apparently used to being, but a devastating fourth.

The usually ebullient Alick was oddly quiet at lunchtime. He started going on about being a qualified army ski instructor and volunteered to give the girls a lesson. There was as yet no sign of them: "The best laid plans of mice and men gang aft a-gley", as Niall might have put it were it not gobbledegook and were he not from Kelvinside, one of the few (only) refined parts of Glasgow.

Having colonised a nice patch in the sun with a splendid view, fought through the queue, purchased saucisses, frites and, as they say in Kelvinside, an elegant sufficiency of wine, we waited. And waited. Scrounged some abandoned wine from the next table then waited some more. No Verona and Sienna.

Chip began to get restless. He wanted to kick some more butt. Me too. I felt fortified. Saeko was content to lie in the sun; my wife was very attractive and it wouldn't be too long before some unctuous Frog tried his chances with her.

Back on the slopes Niall and I pulverised Chip, while Alick was left standing. I had discovered the missing *je ne sais quoi*. Wine. All the old skills came back, the ability to turn a seemingly lost situation into a spectacular recovery, to spray passing Germans with snow. The Box Torsion Zeta method was no match for me.

The two sisters had arrived by the time we regained the top. There was no sign of Saeko, who was probably queuing for the ladies. This always takes a good half an hour in ski resorts because there is only ever one cupboard sized loo. Saeko used to explain that spectacular gymnastics were required to undo the salopettes and get into a decent squatting position without getting them wet in the melted snow on the cubicle floor.

The sisters were distinctly unimpressed by our non-presence. They had just spent two and a half hours trying to find the restaurant. I had given them unambiguous instructions to take the chair lift up on the left, and they had taken me at my word, except that they had been coming up when they followed the instructions and I had been pointing down when I gave them, so our understanding of the word *left* was not the same.

Alick was not in butt-kicking mode, not surprising given his troubled time the night before. Butt-stroking was more his thing, so we left him doing his army ski instructor thing with the girls while Niall, Chip and I had a fabulous 'boys only' burn up off the pistes.

Later on, following Chip and Niall down a steep and narrow slope, I lost control. I can remember going too fast, then waking up in the snow with only a partial idea as to where I was or what had happened. I was way behind my companions who had disappeared in a cloud of snow. I could see the chair-lift I'd directed Verona and Sienna towards and knew it led somewhere important but whether to home or to lunch I had no idea. I remember thinking in the lucid part of my brain that it must feel like this to be a stroke victim or a confused old lady with Alzheimer's.

I knew enough to understand that I should find Chip and Niall, and that I should ski downhill, which I was able to do.

'Chip, where are you?' doesn't have the resonance of 'Heathcliffe'. The only clue as to what had happened to me was a bruise on my nose (not bleeding) and a dent in my side.

I found Chip, 'Chip where am I?' By this stage events were coming back to me: I could remember Alick's throbbing vein but I couldn't remember whether I was in Les Arcs or La Plagne.

Chip took me to a clinic to have my head X-rayed and my memory gradually began to seep back. The doctor said I needed constant observation and should be woken at regular intervals in the night to check that I was still alive. We paid him an outrageous sum of money for this advice, then paid a taxi driver another outrageous sum to drive me back to the Cowshed, Niall being despatched to the other side of the resort (La Plagne, by the way) to tell the others what had happened and not to wait for me but to drive the cars back.

Basically I was alright. The worst thing about it was being looked after in a considerate but patronising way by Chip, and the vindication of Alick's decision to duck out of our testosterone contest and give the girls a ski lesson.

Back at the Cowshed everybody was knackered. Not even Chip was campaigning for a trip to the disco. People either had their noses in bulky novels or were dribbling into them, having fallen asleep. On doctor's orders I wasn't allowed to go to sleep in case I didn't wake up again.

Verona had volunteered to do the cooking. I think she had only ever opened a Marks & Spencer's packet and popped it into the microwave and she clearly regarded the whole process as a bit of a joke, never mind a novelty. Eating is one of the things I do best and commensurate with that talent is an enthusiasm, I wouldn't say talent, for cooking. I made sure there was loads of mince in the spag-bog she was preparing, and enjoyed her expression when I told her it was horse.

Pascal arrived. We had forgotten about him – after all he had been too unwell to make it to work. However, after a day in bed, he was fully recovered. I too had fully recovered my faculties by this stage, but had a splitting headache and an incomplete set of stigmata, namely what felt like a hole in my side, not from a Roman legionary's spear, but something that may hurt nearly as much – a ski binding. Pascal produced an unmarked bottle of eau de vie as a gift and aperitif. 'Cadeau de mon grand-pere,' he said, before pouring himself a large slug and passing it around like a cigarette with illicit substances in it. The local moonshine.

It turned out that Pascal had lived in this very house when he was small, or rather, smaller because, like Alain Prost, he was still small. It had belonged to his extended family until we had fetched up and bought it from his grandfather for £4,000 twelve years before. He had lived here with grandparents, parents, four brothers and two sisters. He was very complimentary about my father's DIY efforts. In his day the cows had been the central heating system, kept directly beneath, in the place where we now stored skis and wine. Once the family had become well-to-do in the ski boom it had moved into a well insulated modern building made of concrete, faced with wood for authenticity. Only the English are interested in old properties like this one.

Fascinating though all this social history was, I got the impression that Verona was losing interest rapidly. I don't think she had had too much to do with genuine peasants in her life and was beginning to regret inviting him for supper. She must have been taken in by his ski clothes. Even Johnny Europeasant knows how to dress up: it is difficult to imagine Eddy Grundy in Armani. (You haven't heard of Eddie! He is one of characters in R4's *The Archers*, the world's longest-running soap. He is not exactly cool.)

I helped her unstick the spaghetti and suggested a few herbs to add to the Bolognese sauce. '*Àtable*, dinner is served.'

Noses emerged from novels, bodies from beds. Pascal was in tremendous form, having spent the whole day lying in bed. Bottles of plonk were distributed around the table. 'Produit de plusieurs pays de la communauté européenne.' Not even the local plonk.

After a day in the cold doing unaccustomed exercise everybody was ravenous, so it didn't matter that Verona had scorched the horse mince a la Bolognese to the bottom of the pan. It was head down, nose in trough, revolve jaws, remove nose briefly from trough for a swig of wine, nose down again. Pascal was irrepressibly cheery, and seemed to have been hair-of-the-dogging since well before he arrived. 'Putain', (local argot for 'Gosh' and not a reflection on the women assembled before him), 'delicieux.' He complimented Verona on her kitchen, 'Tu cuisines bien.' Bovine grunts of approval from around the table. Verona looked at Pascal with renewed appreciation of his Alain Prost-like good looks.

He turned to me. 'Elle parle francais?' indicating my wife with his nose.

'Non,' I replied.

'Ca baise bien, n'est-ce pas, les Japonaises,' he opined, somewhat impertinently, given that we were dealing with my spouse.

'Yes, they kiss very well,' I replied in English.

Saeko smiled benignly. She'd had three glasses of red, and was not entirely with it. Everything one hears about the Japanese not being able to take their alcohol is true, except that in Saeko's case, she didn't get wild and silly, she'd go quiet and silly, then fall asleep. And anyway she was Korean not Japanese. But I gave her about fifteen minutes.

Sure enough she was soon collapsed into her spaghetti at the end of the table. A combination of altitude, alcohol, skiing and the irrepressible Frenchman. I gave her a fireman's lift up the stairs. Pascal winked knowingly, unaware that I might be suffering brain damage, could incur a fatal or disabling brain haemorrhage at any time, never mind the design of the bunk beds and the sodden state of the one double one. My wife was completely safe from molestation.

The stairs were apparently original and used to lead to the hayloft where Pascal avait souvent fait dans le hayloft ce qu'on fait dans le hayloft (or so he claimed).

By the time I got downstairs again Pascal was virtually alone, having bored everyone to bed, with the exception of Chip who appeared from the cattle byre below clutching his skis with the intention of having an animated discussion about wax and edges, and whether Kevlar was as good as Teflex. Pascal decided it was time to leave – the women were all in bed and talking skiing would remind him too much of work. Probably he had a secret yearning for a job on a bond desk somewhere.

My night's sleep was broken once every two or three hours by Chip, worried that I might die, asking how many fingers he was holding up. My joke of looking puzzled then saying 'Four' when he held up two backfired on me because he then started waking me up once an hour.

8 a.m. Chip was up making coffee, with the rest of the party determined to lie in. He told me I wasn't allowed coffee, which was a blessing because I could lie in. I was beginning to realise that it was in everyone's interest for him to be encouraged to go out to the disco and twitch away till dawn.

8.15 a.m. Everybody was up, woken by a combination of file rasping along edges and the smell of molten ski wax.

I had a day off before rejoining the circus. Alick drove off to Courchevel to look at a new development of flats on which to spend his bonus. Lots of guff about needing to be right on the slopes, so that his children could pitch in and out. This may have been so – there's great skiing for beginner through to advanced – but the real reason, if you ask me, was that in Courchevel there's an air-strip and a cup of coffee costs three times what it costs in neighbouring Meribel, which keeps out the riff-raff.

A few days later a telegram came for Saeko summoning her to Venice (or was it Cannes?) for some must-do filming. We didn't have a telephone in the Cowshed. Some members of my family thought the Cowshed should have modern telephony available to its occupants, but I was definitely in the no-phone camp. Imagine being called by the office about some settlement problem? Could ruin your holiday.

Mobiles were useless as there was no GSM signal in Cowshed valley. This was still an innocent time when mobile phones were big clunky things that often didn't work abroad and were generally derided as the territory of yuppie show-offs. Indeed the word 'yuppie' itself seems to have died a death. Maybe the British chippiness and scorn for success has finally died too.

No telephony was a problem for Alick who had to trudge off to the village to check whether his wife had sprogged yet. But no bad thing in that the office couldn't catch him either. I digress. She hadn't, but anyway her pregnancy was probably a elaborate set-up to escape to the trip. She never was much into skiing or the privations of the Cowshed.

Our skiing was developing a pattern. I was pretty much

rehabilitated and, after ten days or so, was skiing well. On the one-franc-in-the-slot automatic slalom machine at la Plagne I reigned supreme. Chip might be able to beat me down something requiring nerve but on something where skill was the criterion I could kick the younger man's butt.

His holiday was at an end too, and we said goodbye to him. In the visitors' book he wrote 'Hey, man, sure as hell liked your cowshed!! It's kinna neat?!? Apart from the dung!! James, kick butt, but mind your head!!!!'

Prat.

My father had a pathological dislike of people who write comments in his visitors' book, and I guess I can see his point. I have a dread of visitors' books of other people – especially the exclamation marks that they attract. When you are confronted with that blank column at the end, the pressure to write something witty and apposite invariably leads to it coming out merely idiotic. (Signing copies of my books is just as bad – 'You're the writer, you think of something' they always say).

At the Cowshed, under Section D(5) of the operating instructions it says, 'Under no account will you allow your guests to write comments in the visitors' book. This is reserved for items of historical interest only.' Entries are restricted to 'Upstairs back room sex-proof bunk beds completed, 3/6/81.' When my father visited he would solemnly go through Tipp-Exing out all other comments.

The snow was fast melting and again some runs were only for the foolhardy like ourselves. Niall had a distinct advantage here. He was used to Aviemore, where you bounce from heather to sheet of ice taking in the occasional patch of snow, usually during a blizzard. In France the problem is more likely to be warm weather. It was the end of the day and we were near the bottom of the resort. 'Och, I remember this bit', he said, pulling up ahead of a patch of snow, rock and semi-submerged logs with the piste forty yards beyond across the slush.

He couldn't possibly have remembered 'this bit'. It was a good ten years since we'd skied here together and, in the early eighties, there was always loads of snow, so falling didn't hurt. Or perhaps we were younger and more athletic. He turned over the first rock, landing briefly on the patch of heavy slush beyond, hurdled a felled pine tree, strung together three deft turns over obstacles out of my view and landed on the piste in a flurry of wet snow.

If he could do it so could I. And by luck as much as skill, I did. Looking back at what I had just done and seeing some of the lurking dangers I had unknowingly avoided I realised what a nut he was – in a different class from Chip. I would not have done that if I'd known. Mind you, Chip probably would.

For Alick the rhythm was never quite established. Happens to the best of us. He got over the rock but misjudged the hurdle, and the three deft turns were never there. We looked up to see him in an intimate embrace with a fir tree, shouting, 'My knee.'

The lifts were closing anyway, so we went down.

Next day Alick had a rest day and borrowed a car to go and have another look at apartments in Courchevel. The swelling on his knee looked ominous. I knew the outcome of this, having done it myself – I can bore for Great Britain on the subject of anterior cruciate ligaments. I did mine skiing, then playing rugby, then skiing, then playing rugby…and I've needed surgery to reconstruct it for the last twenty years. But as the operational techniques get better and better, I keep putting it off. Meanwhile I wear a massive knee brace with a metal hinge in it. Alick's holiday was finished. He decided to go home early to be with his pregnant wife. In the visitors' book he wrote: 'Dolly, shame you can't broke shares as well as you broke your head!!' Quite witty…for Alick, but two exclamations marks.

I was sad to see him go. We were all just getting into it and I was regretting not having taken the chance to have a frank man-to-man with him on the chair-lift about what sort of pressure he might be under to have me let go. The 'long term' for Merrill Lynch is an expression notoriously fluid in meaning.

From there on in, the holiday started to wind quietly down. The girls disappeared to Paris in the Maserati. Verona had a Trans Manche link with a young French broker there and needed a service. Her contribution to the sale of Tipp-Ex was: 'Jim knocked himself out; of historical interest!?!' Yes, more E marks.

Niall and I were left for a final blast down the mountainside, unfettered by the need to show off or be shown off to. I was thoroughly wound down from the City pressure cooker and in no mood to crank myself up again for it. I hadn't thought of the markets once, hadn't bought a newspaper and was only dimly aware of the date.

In the visitors' book Niall wrote: 'Jim, you're a head-case on skis!' One E.

We had a relaxing drive back through France on side roads, loading the car with all the kinds of things that cost half of what they did in England and that were utterly unavailable in the hairy wastes of Glasgow – these days a former 'European

City of Culture' but in those days just 'miles better' according to the slogan and the originator of the deep-fried Mars bar. I mean good coffee, Belgian chocolate, olive oil, gourmet cans (cheaper than the take-away), smoked ham, donkey salami, really smelly cheese and, of course, a sufficiency of elegant red wine (right thinking plonk drinkers only drink red – these day Australian red). Niall says that in recent years it has become possible to buy olive oil in Glasgow. Apparently it is really quite a sophisticated place nowadays. There are even places where balsamic vinegar gets drizzled onto rocket salad.

As we approached Calais it clouded over, then the wind started to buffet the car, then it actually started raining. By the time we were on the ferry it was a full-scale tempest. The rain continued to London. Somehow this seemed to happen every time I made this journey, and I told myself that I must give up living in London and working in the City. I would have a suntan for two weeks, after which no one would even be able to tell I had been away and neither would I feel as if I had.

Niall went back to Scotland. We promised each other we would do the British ski championships next year: it was a long-standing ambition to do a real downhill before the biological turned past the skiing hour.

I spent the next day recovering. At no stage of a skiing holiday does your body fully recover from all the bruises and strains. Thank God for God. It was Easter Monday and there was no need to go to work.

CHAPTER 8

I knew I was back from my holiday when I made the usual demoralising discovery of no ironed shirt.

I felt unenthusiastic about work so I passed the day calling no clients whatsoever, using the excuse of catching up on the two weeks of economic and company news I had missed. In my absence, my desk had been relocated out of the group of four salesmen. I was now next to the settlements girl, Mimi. This was, it was explained, so that Giussi could sit closer to the other three to learn the ropes more easily. Mimi would shortly be found a place nearby on her own to accommodate the Nordic bandit. This seemed a bit unfair on the diligent, hyper-efficient girl who, while a 'cost centre' as opposed to a 'revenue earner', was a far more crucial member of the team than me. After all, settling large deals inefficiently is the quickest way to lose a good client. Mimi was particularly good at disarming Bernie the barrow boy from the Kuwait Investment Office with her pukka Benenden vowels, before he had a chance of alleging that Alick had ripped him off with a price.

Alick himself was still limping but seemed in good humour.

'New baby?' I asked.

'Still not. She's about nine and half months.' (Phantom pregnancy?)

On the second day I grasped a few nettles – like calling clients and telling them I was available for business. Overnight the Dow Jones index had closed up sixty-four points, a sizeable move, at 2945. I looked at my diary and discovered that on the last day before going on holiday it had been down three points at 2946, which shows how futile all the intervening activity had been.

I was to meet Alick's boss in the afternoon to discuss a game plan for dealing with the Japanese on their own patch. My view was that Tokyo was the best option, despite the long hours and the proximity to my mother-in-law.

'Did ya have a good vacation, James?' he asked, when I went to see him at about five in the afternoon. Kelly Martin was relatively new in our office and had replaced the grandfatherly head of sales. He was probably younger than me and out to make his mark. I'd been vaguely conscious that he'd been floating around my desk a bit while I was catching up with the markets. The word 'vacation' doesn't have the same friendly, cuddly connotations on Wall Street (where they take two weeks a year if lucky) that the word 'holiday' has in the Square Mile.

A few pleasantries were exchanged and mention made of the sad end to Alick's holiday.

'How's business going, James?'

Well, being only just back, it had to be said, not at all. But in any case, right from the first interview eight months ago, I had been dead honest about this. It would not be possible to make money from the Japanese in London on European equities for quite a while. The money was in Tokyo. But we were professionals, we knew this, and Merrill Lynch were building for the long term. That Wall of Money was delayed but, like an avalanche, like a tidal wave, it would break over us, unstoppably, soon.

'Not very well,' I answered and explained about the deleterious effect of the Gulf War on biz and the fact that it was not immediately obvious why my Japanese clients should trade European shares through an American broker.

'How do you think it is going to develop over the next six months, James?'

'Not very well.'

I explained how the Japanese financial system was in deep shit as a result of borrowing money and speculating with it. Kelly – not exactly an old hand – would nevertheless understand the mechanism. Value of shares or property rises à bank happily lends money on the back of the new valuation à borrowed money invested in shares or property à which then go up further à bank lends more money...it's what is known as a 'bubble', though it was still a year or two before the Japanese would begin to acknowledge that this had been driving their economy. For Jim Parton, what this meant was that shares and property were weak in Japan, so there was little excess money to spare for investing overseas, although they still did a reasonable trade in Tokyo itself.

So I should go to Tokyo.

Kelly Martin explained that he had costed sending me to Tokyo and decided it was too expensive. He admitted candidly that Merrill Lynch, an American house, was having trouble selling US equities out of Tokyo, let alone European ones for which they had no obvious franchise.

He looked out of the window at the view of sheet glass opposite. 25 Ropemaker Place was not a building into which much light penetrated. 'In these circumstances, James, we feel your activity needs refocusing.'

Refocus? yes. I could not but agree. For the time being what I certainly seemed to need was a little more focus, given the troublesome market conditions. We must tackle this problem.

He said that for a US firm it made more sense to spend

money improving their hitherto weak attempts to sell European equities to the Americans, before bothering with the Japanese. 'We have decided that you need redirecting, James.'

The logic of this, too, was inescapable. Direction was just what I needed and New York sounded fine. The wife would love Macy's, 5th Avenue, Broadway shows, the feeling of being at the pulsating centre of twentieth century culture (and some great shopping). We could hire a nice Latina girl to look after Gen; probably it would be good for Saeko's career too. It would be an adventure, the escape from London I'd been thinking of as I drove back across France with Niall. Never skied in America either, though they say upstate New York can get a bit icy and wind-swept. Still, Vail or Aspen would be a cheap flight away, the Canadian Rockies, too...fun.

'Your area of expertise, for the moment, is redundant James,' he said.

Quick on the uptake these Americans – it was more or less what I had been explaining to him.

Because I still didn't seem to grasp what he was telling me, he was forced to stop looking out of the window and glanced briefly at me with an are-you-understanding-me-or-are-you-dumb? or a Jesus-who hired-you? look. He handed me a piece of A4 Merrill Lynch headed paper and added, 'You are redundant – here is your termination letter.'

The perception dawned that I was about to have an unscripted encounter with a P45. Unscripted as far as I was concerned, anyway. He was handing me a prepared script.

'What are my termination terms?' I asked. I was too shocked to be angry.

'It's in the letter and there's some more paperwork waiting for you down in the personnel department. We don't have to pay you anything as you have only been here for eight months, but we want to look after you.'

A letter already! So why all that discussion about prospects? It must be so much easier in New York where they just say, 'You're fired.'

Back at my desk, my colleagues already knew. Alick must have been in on the decision and had told them. He said that I could come in any time over the next few days and pick up my stuff and have free use of the phones to ring a few headhunters – Chris Lawless and the Bloomsbury Group sprung to mind – and broking contacts in Tokyo. Obviously no need for an unseemly stampede to round up my clients.

It was all very gentlemanly. In the late nineteen-eighties you and fifty others might first hear of your redundancy by reading the business pages of the *Daily Telegraph* over somebody's shoulder on the Northern Line. Then you'd arrive at work to find your personal belongings handed to you in a black bin-liner by the security guard at the door. This method caught too many unfavourable headlines, which brokers now avoided because it undermined confidence both for the survivors and the clients. Just as many people were being 'redirected', but they were being dribbled out slowly.

I had just been dribbled.

CHAPTER 9

Saeko had not come back from Cannes (or was it Venice?) so I had time to psych myself up for confessing that I was redundant. She came from a job-for-life culture so it was not necessarily going to be easy. When the Japanese started to lose their jobs-for-life in numbers, redundant men would sometimes leave home in their business suits at the usual time so that the neighbours wouldn't know. One heard of cases where they deceived their wives this way too, though I don't see how they could have got away with such deception for long. In Japan the custom is for the man to hand over his entire wages cash to his wife and draw a little pocket money from her for karaoke nights with the lads. It took Saeko a while to come to terms with the fact that I wasn't prepared to go that far, though we had much the same thing: a joint bank account. Cynical advice to married people: always have separate bank accounts.

I picked up Gen from Rory's and got him ready for bed. The urgency to settle him down quickly, so that I could have a bit of the evening to myself, had somehow gone.

I slept soundly and decided not to go into Merrill Lynch the next day. I needed time to myself to think things over. While I was at home I had no fewer than three telephone calls from headhunters wanting to see me. It seemed that there was demand out there for somebody like myself. I spoke fluent (for CV purposes) Japanese and French, and had five years experience. I'd had a reasonable pay-off – about three months wages – and had time on my hands. I would play the field, recognise that I could no longer play the Japanese-Wall-of-

Money lie and make sure I got a good job for the genuine long term.

That night I was already drowsing in bed when a taxi from Heathrow decanted my wife.

I told her that I was redundant. She said that she was tired, didn't feel like it, added that she had a headache and was asleep almost as her head hit the pillow.

I tossed and turned through the night rehearsing brilliant business plans that would make Merrill Lynch come to their senses and realise that they were discarding a source of massive future profits.

The theory remained good. We British and the Americans had invested massively abroad for years. ICI might nominally be a British company, but much of its stock was owned by foreigners and even that owned in Britain was often owned by British funds owned by foreigners. The Japanese had barely begun diversifying their massive wealth out of their own shares into ours, although they owned massive amounts of American treasury bonds. They'd been a bit cocky about the lack of need to invest abroad; they hadn't needed to, when all that their own markets did was go up and up.

I was further kept awake by the realisation that, although it made perfect sense for the Japanese to invest abroad now, that logic had no application if they didn't have money to invest. I achieved oblivion towards the small hours.

I lay in until Gen came into the bedroom to bounce on my head at around 8.30. I had no excuse not to give the urchin his breakfast. Saeko remained fast asleep.

It suddenly came to me that 8.30 was cutting it a bit fine. His nursery school started at nine. I force fed him two pieces of Weetabix, Strasbourg goose style, put a school sweatshirt and tracksuit over his pyjamas, did similar for self and got him there only ten minutes late.

I bumped into Mr Gibbon from next door on his way to get his old age pension. Trotsky, his Doberman, sniffed suspiciously at my trouser legs and growled.

'You still on holiday then?' he asked.

'In a manner of speaking, yes,' I replied enigmatically.

On my return Saeko was rolling balls of rice round pickled plums then coating them in sheets of dried seaweed. Normally she ate a good Western breakfast of toast and coffee, but at times of severe stress or fatigue reverted to traditional fare. This put me further on my guard…I had some explaining to do.

'Why aren't you at work? You having it off today?' she asked. Her English was excellent, but she'd still slip up on the occasional phrasal noun. *Having it off* today might have made a pleasant change from calling Mr Hoshide.

'In a manner of speaking.'

'Haven't you had enough holiday already?'

'You can never have too much holiday.' A controversial statement perhaps. I wondered if I should have put on a suit and hidden in a pub somewhere. But then Gen would have been late for school. Honesty is always the best policy: 'I told you last night, I have been made redundant.'

'Oh,' she said, looking thoughtful. 'Does that mean more pay?'

'In a manner of speaking yes', (pet phrase of the morning) 'but only this month. Treble pay.'

'Congratulations,' she said. 'Did you make a lot of commission?' A misunderstanding had evidently occurred, which for reasons of personal safety it might have been worth prolonging, but it was prudent to pre-empt palpitations later developing in her Harvey Nic's loyalty card. I could imagine a dreamy mist of descending Hermès scarves that might be already blurring her vision.

'Redundant means I have lost my job, I am no longer employed,' I said nervously.

'Typical. Still, you never did like it,' she said and went on preparing her seaweed. And that was where the discussion remained. I'd got off lightly.

I drove in to Merrill Lynch to pick up my things, ring round my clients to explain what had become of me and go for a farewell drink with my ex-colleagues. I decided to keep quiet about the car. I knew of several people who had driven company cars around for months (in one or two cases even years) after they had been made redundant, waiting for them to be called in.

One I heard of – seething with anger at his dismissal – drove his Porsche up the steps of his company, lodging it in the front doors, then, having set off the burglar alarm, threw the keys ostentatiously down the nearest drain. This struck me as a way of achieving only temporary catharsis. Much better to drive the Porsche and knacker it, although since it ultimately belonged to a leasing company, knackering it was not exactly revenge.

Giussi had occupied my desk. I couldn't help thinking that this was indecently hasty – a bit like a widow announcing her engagement to another man before the body of her first husband had cooled down – I was also a touch resentful at being asked to explain my research filing system to her. She seemed surprised to see the three pairs of suit trouser coming out of the cabinet from between 'Chemicals' and

'Consumer Goods'.

Giussi's old place had been vacated. For whom? The Nordic bandit. I hoped that my work station would bring Giussi more luck than it had bought me.

I plundered half a dozen biros, a stapler, a couple of calculators, a ream of A4 and loads of sticky yellow 'Post-Its' for Gen, then got one of the secretaries to run up a CV on her computer. In those days, we didn't all have a PC at home.

After 'work' I went for a farewell drink with Alick. Alick was very honest in admitting that he'd had a hand in the redundancy and he'd been in a very awkward position vis-à-vis the skiing. At that stage, although the decision had been floated, it had not been confirmed. Obviously he knew that in this professional world I would accept that work and play were separate, so he'd decided, after some agonising, he'd come skiing anyway. He'd tried to fend off the trigger-happy Americans but, when it had been put to him how keeping me in the team would affect everyone's bonus, he had been forced to back down.

Alick, Henry and Charlie had come from Swiss Bank (RIP) on a deal whereby they had got to keep roughly fifteen per cent of the commission and market-maker's credit they had made, which last year had been six million dollars or three million pounds, fifteen per cent of which came to £150,000 each. Because of the Gulf War, this year's business had been slower, so four million-ish dollars, minus the half a million dollars of my salary plus overhead. That left three and a half million, fifteen per cent of which would come to a £90,000 each. I wasn't sure whether the strengthening of the dollar over the period was good or bad for the bonus, but assuming it was bad they were in line for a derisory £50,000 pay out on top of salaries on top of basics of around £70,000. Penury! It was not surprising they didn't quite feel able to keep me on.

I'm sounding bitter. The reality is that the choice was not really in their hands; I suppose they could have come up with some team effort to save me, but it's not as if I had been busting a gut to earn commission. While the Japanese were dormant, I could easily have gone after UK or French clients. In fact I'd had one or two Irish clients. One had promised me that he dealt with a strictly limited list of brokers, but encouraged me to keep on calling. I was his first reserve. He had big funds, so who knows? Had he started dealing, perhaps my career would have been different.

Besides, as Alick said, 'Dolly, with your CV, people will be queuing up to employ you. Fluent Japanese and French, five years experience.'

Yup, I agreed with that.

'March will just seem like a month with an extra big pay packet.'

I suppose so.

'You'll want to get a job pretty quickly. We found that when we left Swiss Bank. Two months out of the market was too long. It gets boring at home, missing all the action.'

Completely wrong.

I never could understand this attitude. When I was recruited by Merrill Lynch I accepted a waiver of the three month notice period I'd had with Phillips and Drew in order to start as soon as possible. I wouldn't make that mistake again.

'Why don't you consider a job in fund management, Jim, or go back to Phillips and Drew?' suggested Alick, who still appeared to think P&D had been sad to lose me – unless he was employing a hitherto unnoticed faculty for irony. Either way, both suggestions were thoroughly patronising. He was revealing his true feelings about my professional abilities. I guess I couldn't complain. I'd had five years on the City gravy train and finally been found out, but I was pretty certain I could work my magic on some new firm, market conditions good or bad.

Being fired by Merrill Lynch is like a badge of honour in the City. No one could possibly hold it against me. And at the personal level, I had to accord them respect for having seen through me.

'Well, Dolly, best of luck. Though I'm sure you don't need it. When I've got my apartment in Courchevel you can drive across and we can ski together again.'

Not sure about that. 'Yes, that's a good idea, Alick.'

The City is a small and incestuous place and who knew when I would need him again; not least because I wanted glowing references when his mates rang him to ask 'You know that bloke you fired the other day, should we employ him?'.

We shook hands and he limped away.

CHAPTER 10

I hadn't realised how difficult it was to process a small child for school in less than an hour. My job had been to tear back from work and pick up Gen from the child minder, feed him and put him to bed – if Saeko was filming. I left the house early, she tended to come back late. So it was a fair division of labour but, if she'd married a Japanese man, she'd have had to do the whole lot. And fix me dinner.

Most people's four-year-olds wake up at six then charge around the house yelling. Ours seemed to have inherited the sleep gene from Saeko and, let's be honest, me. I was discovering how refreshing it was not to have to listen out for that 6.30 alarm, get into my cycling kit and discover no ironed shirt or that the bike had developed a slow puncture overnight. I'd become obsessed with different strategies for getting an extra fifteen minutes in bed; coffee and toast at home, or coffee and a Danish while reading research in the Merrill Lynch canteen, bringing the coffee upstairs to my desk, reading the research at the desk.

Now I was released from all that. Task number one was to wake Gen up. If done too brutally, he'd be too grumpy for breakfast and, if no breakfast, too grumpy for school.

The teacher told me that one of the central tenets of the school's 'Charter for a Bright Young Future', which I had apparently signed last term, was punctuality. I told her I was working on it.

'Long holidays you City types have then,' said my neighbour Mr Gibbon as I passed him on the way back from school. A frail looking man, he was still strong enough to restrain Trotsky from lunging at me too menacingly.

I dropped in on Nigel, similarly redundant stockbroker, friend and erstwhile competitor, and swapped notes. He thought that my redundancy terms of three-months pay, tax free because a severance payment, after only eight months in my company, were not bad at all. Most other people said the same thing. As Alick had remarked, they didn't have to give me anything and so the two month's pay windfall would feel like an extra bonus, especially as I would soon be back in work again.

The only thing that didn't quite ring true was Merrill's uncharacteristic attack of decency in giving me any money at all after just eight months service. I didn't have a solicitor as such. For example, when I bought the house I did the conveyancing myself. But my oldest brother Nick (not the winner of the Pratt prize for Latin Unseens) is a shipping lawyer. I rang him but discovered he was down at the Cowshed, so I couldn't consult.

Nigel was waiting to start a new job at Nomura the Japanese brokerage house, expanding their European equity business to British clients. Paradoxically, I could never have worked for Nomura because they used Japanese nationals to service Japanese clients. They were building a team and were going to pay him twenty per cent more than he had been earning when he was sacked. No doubt something similar would happen to me. Nigel was planning a trip to the Alps with a couple of friends for a few days skiing, would I like to come? Though tempting, having only just come back, it would be irresponsible to go again when I really ought to be looking for a new job. So I said 'No'.

I was late again for school, although this time it was

definitely not my fault. Gen's mother would insist upon his wearing two socks the same – she wouldn't accept a Thomas sock on one foot and a Gordon sock on the other. But I hadn't got round to doing the laundry, so couldn't find two to meet this exacting specification, without either holes in the left sock or Dennis the Menace on one and Ninja Turtles on the other. It was entirely her fault because she rejected my far more pragmatic policy of buying job lots of identical socks, so that they didn't have to be sorted out. All my own were charcoal grey.

'Cushy number you're on, then, all that money…in my day…,' said Mr Gibbon as I passed him on the way to school. Trotsky growled in acquiescence, but I didn't stop to hear about the Jarrow march or the Islington rent riots. I just reflected that he must lie in wait for me.

I cut the grass for the first time since October while I waited for the washing machine to finish its programme.

As I pushed the mower up and down I thought things through. Although I had worked precisely two days in the last twenty-five, I did need a little time away from distractions to consider my future before I really got stuck into the business of garnering gainful employment. I wasn't going to make market-maker Ron's error of rushing into the first job I was offered. I rang Nigel (the redundant) and said, 'Yes,' and rang the headhunters and said, 'The week after next.' I was beginning to lose track of time already.

Saeko could see two sides to the skiing argument. She was relieved that she didn't have to go – indeed was not invited – but I sensed she thought I should be looking out for a job more actively. However, with me in my emasculated can't-even-support-his-own-family-shock-of-redundancy state, she was sufficiently sensitive not to say anything.

On Sunday the darling spouse lay in while I gave the bairn his breakfast. The boys in her film crew were back from Venice (or was it Cannes?) for a bit of R & R in somewhere civilised. She had thus been out until three singing karaoke.

After breakfast Gen and I went to the weekly car boot sale. He pestered me until I bought him – in truth I was buying it for me – a 007 Aston Martin (Corgi c. 1967 – the one from Goldfinger – pre-ejected passenger, sun-roof etc), the same as I'd had as a boy (twenty pence). I bought a folding camera (pre-war? Carl-Zeiss), something of a restoration project now, but in its day clearly an item of quality (twelve pounds). And then we saw it.

'Daddy, buy that train.'

A big black monster with Union Pacific written on the side, it had at least thirty-six wheels, if you understand these things, and I don't, probably an o-o-o-O-O-O-O-O-O-O-O-O-O-O-O-O-o-o. It was magnificent. Pongo Parton gave away our train set when I was about three when we were posted abroad. I had never forgiven him.

'Fifty pounds.'

'Forty,' I riposted.

'This retails at £170 new, mate.'

I looked at it and I believed him. 'All right, fifty then.' A tough bargain was struck. In situations like this I found my predatory City instincts useful.

There was no point in having a non-motive locomotive so we bought a transformer (five pounds); plus for Gen – who would not be allowed anywhere near my monster – half a dozen coaches (a pound each), a diesel shunter (six pounds) and a small steam engine (four pounds). We needed track, so the man sold us enough to go round the living room twice (three pounds), blackened by age, the electric points fused together by short circuits. The brand name Tri-ang struck a nostalgic chord.

Half an hour later the track was indeed going twice round the living room floor. Miraculously all the trains worked. It was difficult to know which boy was more excited – it certainly beat stockbroking. Mum came down for breakfast at about eleven. I made her some strong coffee. She looked at me and then at our trains, a glimmer of despair in her eyes.

It was good to be free of the tyranny of the Sunday papers. I still bought them, but read them for pleasure and avoided the business pages.

I leafed indolently through the appointments section. I owed it to myself to look for jobs outside the City. 'Product manager, Milton Keynes, Attractive Package.' I could imagine what that would be. Twenty-five grand – if that – and a Vauxhall Cavalier. The idea being that you'd be driven to greater things by your aspiration to drive a Vauxhall Carlton. I pictured myself in Vauxhall's TV ad: smooth industrialist (which might be a contradiction in terms) with a touch of distinguished grey, enviously eyes up the other vehicles in the company car park, and plots the downfall of Jones in sales.

I reached for the colour supplement instead.

In the evening, Gen, who loved his trains, couldn't be persuaded to eat his supper nor have his bath. Normally I had trouble getting him out of his bath. I eventually got him into bed with the promise of three *Thomas the Tank Engine* stories. He wanted to know why the toy train I had bought him was Number Six not Number One like Thomas and was red not blue. Taxed for an explanation I told him that it was Percy. Gen was lost in thought, but seemed satisfied and went to sleep. My bluff would probably revisit me because I was dimly aware that

Percy was the green engine.

I was now a week into the awful predicament of unemployment. I have a strange ability, when reading a Thomas book aloud, of being able to put in all the inflections and excitement of the story, while having absolutely no idea what is happening at all. It is almost as if I have two brains, devolved organs and, provided Gen didn't ask me a question about Percy, my mind could be completely free to ponder my unemployment.

The ghastliness of this was overstated, I decided.

The advantages were manifold and obvious:

1. Lie-in every day. (In theory – in practice give Gen his breakfast while wife lay in).
2. The sun was shining.
3. I saw more of Gen (when Rory's parents allowed).
4. I got extra holiday I didn't expect, incl. skiing.
5. I could get the garden sorted out.
6. I could do all those DIY jobs I should have done two years ago when I moved into this house.
7. I could get really good at the piano.

This last was a long-standing ambition. I had spent the golden hello Phillips and Drew had given me (the suckers, I'd been desperate to join them) on a stupendous black grand piano. Saeko was a fantastic pianist but she never played, I'd have killed to be able to play like her.

But I could fantasise with the stereo on full, the pianistic equivalent of air guitar, with the thing stretching out before me. This gave a tremendous sense of power of the kind that other men derive from inordinately long zoom lenses, E-Type Jaguars or possibly big black Union Pacific locomotives configured o-o-o-O-O-O-O-O-O-O-O-O-O-O-O-O-O-o-o.

I was currently learning *Für Elise*. Gen wanted me to play 'The Snowman' but it was too difficult.

I walked Gen to school on time to general, if patronising, approval. There was only one other father – with lank, unkempt-looking hair and a nose ring. Obviously a work-shy dole scrounger.

On the way back I met Mr Gibbon again who was off to get his newspaper. I decided to come clean with him.

'I've been made redundant,' I said.

'That's terrible,' he said, his eyes brightening unashameably. Trotsky gave my shoes a friendly lick. 'Are you getting the dole then? I was out of work for five years once. Of course in those days you only got five shillings a week dole. Couldn't buy a bleeding thing.'

The dole! Me! 'I don't think it's right for people like me to claim social security Mr Gibbon,' I replied.

'Why not?' he asked before evidently realising that the reason was I was probably so rich that I didn't need to. He stopped looking so cheerful and dragged Trotsky into his house.

Later, I clean forgot to pick up Gen from nursery school. The teacher was distinctly frosty because it meant she had missed her lunch.

CHAPTER 11

Nigel came round to pick me up. We were to pick up a farmer friend of his and an accountant chum, both near Dover. We were cutting it a bit fine with regards to the ferry, but just as he arrived the phone rang.

It was she-who-must-be-obeyed-even-more-than-she-who-must-be-obeyed, namely, the mother of the latter calling from Japan. She of the over-dressed flouncy braid cushions on the sofa. Instead of simply reporting that Saeko was not in, I foolishly mentioned that I had lost my job.

'Nani? Shitsugyo desu ka?' (What? Lost your job?)

'Hai.' (Yes).

'Nippon dew kangaerarenai.' (In Japan unthinkable.) Ha! They don't say that in Japan anymore.

Get used to thinking the unthinkable, I might have said, but my Japanese wasn't up to it. 'Well here it has happened. Don't worry, I will soon get another job,' I said, eyeing my ski bags. The conversation was soon out of control. 'Anyway', I said, 'I haven't got time to explain, I'm just off for an interview, right this minute, and I'm late.'

'That's not fair, Jim-san, you have to explain.' In the background Nigel was undermining me a little by thundering out 'Chopsticks' on the piano (well known in Japan but incidentally not known as 'Chopsticks' nor even 'Knife and Fork') and telling me to 'Hurry up with that Japanese crap'.

'I have explained', I said, 'I've got no job.'

'But you can't have no job.'

'Well I have got no job.'

'How can you have no job?'

The conversation was developing a certain circularity.

'Mother', I said firmly, 'I have to go for…an interview… now.' Surely a cast iron excuse, even if a bare-faced lie.

'Nan de isoide iru no? Dare ga piano hite iru no ka?' (Why are you in a hurry, who's playing the piano?')

'Nigel, stop playing the piano you're undermining my case.'

'No, your case is already in the car, get a move on...'

'Why are you talking in English?' said my mother-in-law. I knew from long experience – I'd been married to her daughter for nearly five years now – that when she was aroused she exhibited the pit bull syndrome…even if at all other times she was charm personified. I could appreciate the worry strain she was under at the thought that I would no longer be able to keep her daughter in the lavish style to which she had become accustomed.

'I really have to go now; I'm getting very late for my interview. Goodbye,' I said.

'What interview?'

I slammed the phone down, aware that slamming phones down on mothers-in-law is a capital offence in any country or culture in the world. But at that moment catching the ferry to go skiing was more important.

On the way out of London I stopped at a post box and sent the signed letter to Merrill Lynch, accepting the redundancy payment offered to me.

We stopped off near Dover at Nigel's farmer friend's house. I never discovered his real name for sure, it might have been Giles, but his friends wittily called him Wurzel. His friends found this sobriquet hilarious, just as some of mine find the sobriquet 'Dolly' hilarious.

The other friend was Basil, an accountant to high net worth individuals. In better times that might have been me. He had felt the need to cram in an extra morning's work, so had saved time by coming to Dover by train separately. Basil's pay accrued by the quarter-hour of advice, each such unit being worth the redistribution of fifty pounds of wealth in his favour.

We missed the ferry by five minutes thanks to my pit-bull mother-in-law. These days competition with Eurotunnel would mean the next ferry would be forty-five minutes later, but we had time to kill. We returned to the lovely farm house and drank in the beauty of the Garden of England, while waiting for the next one. The weather was warm, spring was here, summer beckoned.

Wurzel was bemoaning the stress of farming. Two stockbrokers and a City accountant looked at him as if he was mad. Farmers always claim to be up against it, but then you ask yourself the old question 'Have you ever met a poor farmer?'

The Channel Tunnel consortium had compulsorily purchased some of his land, and it was taking longer than expected to sell off another bit for a planned motel near the motorway because of a group of anti-entrepreneurial lefties on the council. The caravan park on some EU set-aside land hadn't been the roaring success he had originally anticipated either, and the CAP beet subsidy was under threat too. He was a Lloyds name. The pathos of it was too touching for words.

The record time to the Cowshed was about seven and three quarter hours, achieved at the dead of night at 135 mph in my stockbroker motor (RIP). The ten hours driving, in a distinctly unsouped-up family car provided by Wurzel, were dominated by Basil sorting out Wurzel's financial problems.

10 hours x 4 x £50 = £2,000 worth of free advice. On such trips Radio Four fades depressingly near Calais.

He ate, drank, but sadly didn't sleep accountancy. Accountancy is supposed to be dull and Basil didn't exactly succeed in making it sound interesting, but I deeply envied him his obvious enjoyment of it. It was like being trapped for ten years in a small space with an endless tape of the BBC2's *Money Programme*. I guess my slight resentment about this form of in-car entertainment arose from the fact that I had no bonus to hide in an offshore trust, and no immediate expectation of one. Just the free spending wife and an outsize mortgage.

By the time we had arrived at the Cowshed, he had created complicated trust funds neatly solving the problem of how to settle a quarter of a million onto Wurzel's toddler and his wife's foetus. Somewhere along the line, a blind trust and the Cayman Islands got mentioned. The farm itself was to be transferred into the name of his Canadian wife, which would somehow achieve a total avoidance of any capital gains tax, if his motel got planning permission and he sold off the land to a developer for a massive profit.

Wurzel looked worried at these suggestions. Personally I would have killed for some of this stress.

The proposal might incur the wrath of the Revenue, which would be powerless to do anything about it, but in any case Basil was scathing about the Inland Revenue; any decent tax inspector they had ever employed was now a private 'tax consultant', having been poached to work for someone like himself. The poor tax inspectors spend their time trying to suck up to said accountancy firms to jump to better paid jobs in the private sector. Deep down, these civil servants were all Thatcherite supporters of the private sector, explained Basil (these days you'd say Blairite).

Unpersuasive, easily dupable, unforceful personality. How do people spot these things so quickly? Which begs the question: how did a succession of employers fail to spot it? With my current companions I guess it was that every time I suggested something like 'Let's go skiing now' or 'How about a slightly cheaper bottle of wine?' or 'Isn't it a waste of time to spend three quarters of an hour in a car to go flirt with Twiddles, Fluff and Zara when we have our own exciting company? Hey, Basil, let's talk offshore trusts...' I got over-ruled. I just couldn't sell my ideas.

Some of my ideas were right however. The expeditions to Courchevel had presented no threat to my father's plumbing (ref. rubber intolerance): Nigel would only be earning eighty or ninety grand, enough to spare fifty pounds a head for a date, but with typical stockbroker's commitments, like an overly ambitious mortgage, scarcely enough to impress these girls. Life is much more straightforward if you are born with money. Nigel should have been looking for a nice grateful girl from the East End.

We ate out locally a few times too, in places where prices are half what they are in the resorts and the food better. Good honest country fare. The best things in life are not free, but they need not be expensive.

The only reason we ever managed to pay more than fifteen pounds a head is because Basil the wine buff insisted on buying good vintages from well known vineyards. I don't know what went wrong in my upbringing – maybe my parents went on too much about how little butter they managed on a week during the war, maybe I hadn't earned lots for long enough in the City – but it seemed bizarre to me to fork out more on a drink than on the meal itself. The interest in knowing about wine is obvious, but too much knowledge, once acquired, has risks. I would hate to lose my love of plonk, so I've deliberately avoided finding out. I preferred to spend my money on something of lasting value (like a train set).

I figured out a way of introducing plonk on to the table in the form of a few interesting local wines. You can only really appreciate them here, they don't travel well. It was quite a good stratagem because, although wine snobs can bullshit about Claret or Beaujolais, the Vins de Savoie are not heavily written up in the Vogue Book of Wine. It worked. Basil was reduced to saying something slightly patronising like 'surprisingly good bite, deep raspberry, crisp palate with an over-bite of tannin' or however you express these things.

It was time to get back to the UK and leave the mountains glinting invitingly in the sunlight. Nigel and I, the unemployed, agitated for another day's skiing but sadly Wurzel had to tend to his lambing and planning application, then Basil had to return to solving the problems of the obscenely rich. For Basil time really was money and the fifty pound units were wastefully ticking by unmetered.

For the first time in years I could just have stayed on holiday and, yet, I was returning to look for a job. How responsible can you get?

The normal 'Condemned man eats hearty breakfast' feeling was absent but, nonetheless, there was a sense of foreboding about knuckling down and seeking gainful employment.

We broke the journey at Beaune, in the heart of the Beaujolais, where Basil loaded up on a case of needlessly expensive wine, because it was so much cheaper than in England. 'What's wrong with Safeway's own brand Bulgarian Cabernet Sauvignon?' I asked satirically.

It must have been the academic joy of avoiding taxes that appealed to his accountant's mind because I still didn't believe that he could tell the difference between a Bordeaux and a Burgundy except by the shape of the bottle.

English weather is a cliché but, like many clichés, contains a truth. As we got to Reims, Calais began to appear on the sign-posts and it started to cloud over. By the time we were on the road to Amiens, the car was being buffeted by wind and, at Calais, it was raining. In Dover there was a knifing cold wind. When we had left England it had felt almost like summer.

We spent the night at Wurzel's outside Dover. I lay in until late (10 a.m.), so that by the time I got up Basil had already caught an earlier train and was presumably already notching up units. He was living proof that it is possible to have a boring job and love it. Let's be utterly candid about Basil. He was a bastard and I hated him. Base envy, I admit.

Wurzel was off attending to his lambing, so Nigel and I went out to witness the agriculturalist's stress at first hand. The farm presented a happy scene. I found myself humming the theme tune to *The Archers*. There were ewes in the field waiting to lamb and mothers suckling newborns indoors. There was the odd carcass dotted around; sheep apparently have a habit of dying for no good reason, so I could see the stressful side of farming (especially for the sheep), but despite the cold wind, I'd rather have worked there than in the City. Nigel agreed, except that he had a rather irritating way of putting it. 'I'd rather work here, but I suppose it's not bad earning more than the Prime Minister.' I had only been earning more than the Chancellor.

I felt more positive again. I had a God-sent opportunity

to sit back, pick and choose, and remedy that particular deficit. (Merrill Lynch are more used to being referred to as 'The Thundering Herd' than 'God', but I don't suppose they minded.)

CHAPTER 12

Back home, the expected fat redundancy cheque had not appeared through the letter box. There was only a somewhat hostile letter demanding the return of the battered Vauxhall Astra ASAP, and a statement to the effect that there would be no redundancy dosh for me until such time as it was given back. It could wait a day or so. I decided to waste a day at home re-habituating myself to my surroundings and psyching up for the job hunt.

Saeko was at home too, organising a film shoot on the telephone, which meant that my job hunting would have to be done in snatches or from a public call box or, perish the thought, by letter. In the City – at my exalted level at any rate – you did not get jobs by filling in application forms, but via introductions from friends, direct telephone calls, followed by faxing the CV (though often you could get away without even doing that) or through headhunters.

Personnel men were to be avoided like the plague. Personnel men were quite commonly women. This balanced the genders up a bit and enabled an employer to head off accusations of not being an 'equal opportunities employer'. Who better than a woman to head off such accusations. Personnel people were the nearest you got to a civil servant in the City. Like people at the DTI, they use the word 'entrepreneur' a lot without having the haziest idea what such a person might do. The personnel woman's role was to dot i's and cross t's on the actual contract. She was a mere functionary, stayed a safe distance from executives such as myself, was paid twenty-five grand – average earnings in the rest of the populace would have been around fifteen at the time – and kept happy with a suitably Ruritanian sounding title like Director of Human Resources (the word 'personnel' was on the way out). She or her assistant was usually being shagged by the Head of Bond Trading whose salary she knew. She'd try to get you to fill out forms, but you ignored her until employment terms had been agreed by the man who employed you.

If this description sounds outrageously sexist, it is not my fault. I merely record things as they were and, by all accounts, still are.

The personnel woman was usually jealous of the power of the company car man and often did not keep him up to date on the latest round of firings.

This man (it is men's work) would be the only person in the personnel department who exerted real power. He would be held in universal fear and respect by everyone in the company. He who controls your wheels controls your self-esteem.

He would collect parking fines more effectively than any policeman or bailiff because failure to do so would affect his cost centre and thus his bonus. He was the only true entrepreneur in any personnel department. One scam might be to flog off cars to mates in the trade for their value as recorded in the company balance sheet, after the accountant's notional depreciation, which would be steeper than actual depreciation. So nice little margin there. Or he might get a bit of a rake-off by doing deals with mates on the servicing 'to save costs'. There was all sorts of room for manoeuvre in charging for proprietary spare parts but using generic ones. For example, a Mini headlight unit fits a Mazda sports car and costs £7 as opposed to £42.

But even without such direct fraud, directing a million pounds worth of cars towards a particular garage had to be worth a back-hander or two.

A good relationship with the company car man could make the difference between a XR3i and a Porsche 911 (if one had just become available because a bond trader had just been 'let go').

(I have already mentioned the bad karma Porsche 911, but how do you sell all those personalised number plates such as A 911 WNK? Saudi al-Qaeda-ites I suppose.)

The company car man himself alternated between a Daimler V12 and a Mercedes 500 SEL sports car, depending on whether he was trying to impress his mates down the golf club outside Romford or some peroxide blonde with big boobs down the pub. He was the most powerful man in the firm.

That power has eroded. Company cars no longer attract tax breaks and those in the Ferrari bracket tend to buy their own these days, leaving the company man with a fleet of Ford Mondeos.

The Merrill Lynch man wanted his Astra back. I felt unlucky. You wouldn't think he'd miss an Astra.

I went in to see my first headhunter.

The Dickensian sounding Mr Crump kept me waiting forty-five whole minutes, which stretched the patience somewhat. As an erstwhile highly-paid and soon to be even more highly-paid executive, I should not be kept waiting.

But while waiting for Mr Crump, a young assistant chatted to me amicably. His name was Donald.

'Camberwell? Three bedroom house in the Georgian part, you get some real bargains down there don't you; what, bought in 1989, top of the market, negative equity, five years in the City; wife works in television, don't get paid much do they; yes, we were thinking of sending our one there, nice school; nice suntan, skiing?; interesting CV, I think we'll be able to place you; Merrill Lynch, yes, absolutely ruthless, great for turn-over, we get quite a few mandates from there, always firing then rehiring when the market picks up...'

He asked me all sorts of personal questions, which seemed to be culled from a psychological assessment paper in the guise of 'getting down a few personal details'. By the end I think he had not only my age, sex, experience, but a good idea of domestic outgoings, size of mortgage, wife's earnings, and a lot else besides. Bloody cheek! I suppose it was to gauge where I came on the psychological assessment's greed rating, which he could then use to assess his likely commission for placing me. He would have discovered that I was still locked in a 1980's mind-set and considered myself worth more than the Prime Minister (well, as much as Nigel anyway).

Mr Crump asked me why I was made redundant and what my ambitions were. Tricky questions. I was made redundant because I was useless and, as for my ambitions, these were things with which my life had remained remarkably unencumbered, beyond a loose desire to earn lots of money whilst avoiding too much work or responsibility.

Perhaps I should have taken him into my confidence and admitted as much. Then together we could have plotted a collusive fraud on some sucker City employer. It would be a victim-free crime. After all, they are the ultimate in bastions of greed, and for a greedy person to rip off a greedy institution is scarcely a moral crime. More a duty, I'd say.

Your headhunter could be like your therapist or counsellor. But I didn't know Mr Crump well enough. I felt I had to make a good impression.

I said I was in no hurry in my job hunt and wanted to take this opportunity to make sure that my next job was a good one, genuinely for the long term, and also I wanted to look at the possibility of working outside the City altogether because, while I understood Mr Crump's outfit worked the City, I believed he had colleagues who covered other industries. I was quite keen to go abroad too, somewhere warm, Paris, Madrid, Milan, Hong Kong, Manila, perhaps even Tokyo, with fat overseas allowances and tax avoidance scheme out of Guernsey. I was very flexible and so was my wife, I told him, although I hadn't told her yet how flexible she was. In fact, I would consider anything. although it would probably be restricted to sales of some kind.

Management was probably out, I mused. Despite my salary I had somehow failed to become even Assistant Director at P&D, or Assistant Vice-President at Merrills, a title dished out to virtually everyone with more than a few years' experience. At Merrills I had been a mere Financial Consultant.

Any non-City job would probably have to be some kind of sales or marketing, I said, without having the first idea of the difference between the two. Marketing only existed in the City in firms with large bureaucracies like UBS Phillips and Drew with its philanthropic policy of providing employment for people called Ruedi.

'Do you know what people in industry earn?' I was asked abruptly.

'Well, no, not exactly, but I realise that it's less.'

'How much did you earn?'

'£65,000 a year,' a slight exaggeration, but I had decided to add on £5,000, then make myself believe the lie for negotiation purposes.

'A good widget seller earns £20,000 a year. A top widget seller makes £30,000 a year, maybe a bit more. You have no experience of widgets. Who will pay you anything like what you need? What's more, you might have to live in Manchester. Or worse, Birmingham. Do you have any idea what it's like to live in Birmingham?'

He treated me like a little boy and, as for what I needed, I thought that he was assuming too much. What I 'needed' was a difficult concept. Did I really 'need' £1,500 a month after Saeko's phone bill?

'I am afraid that I cannot recommend your candidature to my clients when you don't even know what you want to do yourself. Come back when you are serious.'

This high-handed, dismissive attitude was unexpected. Headhunters are supposed to be sycophantic and ingratiating. 'Pleased to be of service,' they are supposed to lisp. In the City evolutionary scale they come a long way below stockbrokers for slime and scale. If we brokers were reptiles, then headhunters were bicuspid molluscs, i.e. bottom feeders.

They existed because City firms didn't like to be seen to be ungentlemanly. Historically their evolution is relatively recent, coinciding with the arrival of hire-'n'-fire. They might be the original consultants or source of 'out-sourcing'. The dirty work of poaching talented members of the opposition got sub-contracted. A bit like murder in the Mafia. In the old days S.G. Warburg would never have poached someone from Morgan Grenfell. Just wouldn't have happened. So no headhunter industry existed. Even the term 'headhunter' has a jokey-cum-savage feel to it; this new industry has a touch of the virtual realities to it.

For their pains the modern headhunter gets around a

third of your first year's salary as his fee. A good living can be made at this. Quite a lot of failed stockbrokers become headhunters.

Stockbrokers argue that their function in society is to lubricate the wheels of commerce by directing money towards efficient companies through the medium of high share prices for the good and low ones for the bad. When the company is catastrophically badly-managed no one wants to put money there, its shares can't be sold and it collapses. Give the City credit: they let the corrupt Maxwell Corporation collapse. So they are essential for the good of capitalist society.

Headhunters, too, have a function. As the reptiles swim overhead crapping, the bicuspid molluscs feed on the waste below, cleaning it up. The ecology of the City would collapse without its molluscs. Just like the delicately balanced ecology of any other swamp.

At this point I should mention – like the racist who says some of his best friends are Jews or black – that some of my best friends are headhunters.

Mr Crump had kept me waiting forty-five minutes then told me not to waste his time. The indignity of it. To torture my metaphor further, we reptile brokers were dinosaurs turning to each other and asking 'Hey, did you hear that?' (if you accept the theory that dinosaurs were wiped out by a massive meteor thudding into the Earth and causing the equivalent of a nuclear winter). There was quite a lot of crap and decaying dinosaur to be cleared up in the aftermath of the 1986 Big Bang and the 1987 crash. It was the age of the mollusc scrabbling around for detritus wholesome enough to help them evolve backbones but not nutritional enough to lift them off the bottom of the swamp.

On my way home I needed to calm my anger, so I decided to seek relief by purchasing one of those magazines that one requests to have dropped into a brown paper bag or which one receives by mail order. Before slipping into my fantasy world I made sure that the wife was out. My heartbeat raced in anticipation as I tore off the wrapping, ensconced in a room with slightly subdued lighting lest anyone should look in the window...*Railway Modeller's Monthly*.

It was time to consider how to assemble all the components I had bought at the car boot sale in a more permanent way. Here at last was a text that would unravel for me the secrets of OO gauge as compared to HO gauge and explain to me what was the very best method of constructing papier-mâché mountains, box girder bridges and getting realistic grass or bushes on the Alpine meadows I'd planned or authentic-looking tarmac on the road leading up to the main station for Gen's cars.

My pulse picked up as I looked through the table of contents. 'GUTTERING IN 2MM SCALE' by Mike Stafferton, and 'BRINKWORTH GOODS SHED REVISITED' by Hugh Canaway. 'When Nick Cant dropped round and said, "Hugh, we need a model of a pre-war G.W.R. engine shed, and we need it quick," I was only too happy to search through my box of 4mm scale purlins and trusses and see what I could come up with...I copied the method Mark Smith used in building a Midland coaling stage, described in *Railway Modeller's Journal,* April 1967...'

I read on enthralled, if a little intimidated at the standards required. Perhaps a model of the London Underground would be better. Then no one could argue about authenticity as it could legitimately run in the dark and never be seen.

CHAPTER 13

The job hunt had to start in earnest. I think it was lucky that it was now May and the ski season definitively over.

Saeko would soon be vacating the telephone for a week or so. There was no excuse. Sod the train set, sod the garden. A man is not a man unless he has a job, out hunter-gathering, bringing back game to the cave for his mate to skin and feed to the bairn.

My mate was off to a television trade fair at Cannes (or was it Venice?). She would be manning the Japanese stand attempting to sell the Japanese standard as the world's next broadcasting standard, i.e. High-Definition TV. HDTV looked fantastic; we'd all want it, no question. So it seemed (and so I thought having looked at it). So much for my powers of prognostication; ten years on and it's been a flop, overtaken by digital wide-screen TV (I think; I don't watch much TV).

Nigel suggested that I call his old employers who had fired him, as he still needed replacing. 'But Nigel, you are irreplaceable.'

I gave a man with a funny Eurotrash sounding name at Paribas a call. I began to explain my situation: 'Merrill Lynch, well you know how the Americans are, decided to let me go – not very long term. I talk to the Japanese about European markets…and I gather you might be looking for some new salesmen. Nigel…'

Nigel was not the name to mention – his own departure having been somewhat less than voluntary – although diplomatically he had resigned.

'Absolutely No. No Interest,' he replied. You'd have thought he could have said it less bluntly, spared my delicate feelings. As a salesman, though, I had no right to be disconcerted. Cold-calling new clients was something like this. Never pleasant. I pressed on with my patter until he managed to get rid of me with 'Send in your CV and I promise to look at it'. This was unlikely to mean that I had got my salesman's foot in the door. My CV would end up in the bin. It meant 'Don't call me, I'll call you' or, less politely, 'Bugger off'.

Imagine my surprise, therefore, when ten minutes later Saeko, not yet in Venice (or was it Cannes?), passed me the phone. 'It's for you,' she said, somewhat crossly, as if I had no right to use it. Strange attitude – didn't she realise that an employed Jim meant a Jim not competing for the telephone? Seems rather an outdated family squabble in the era of the mobile phone. More importantly, did she not realise that her Japanese love of consumer durables with names like Louis Vuitton was under threat?

The call was from Mr Crump's assistant Donald. They had a client looking for experienced European equity salesmen and might be able to fix an interview. The poor man with the Eurotrash name from Paribas. To think he could've had the chance to save the thirty per cent of my first year's salary that would now go in fees to Mr Crump. He'd had me on the phone only fifteen minutes earlier. The idle bastard. Pay at Paribas was obviously not linked to costs. I liked the sound of the place. I agreed to see him the next day.

'Are you back at work then, Mr Parton?' asked Mr Gibbon over the garden fence, Trotsky growling quietly at his side. At least Mr Gibbon called me 'Mr Parton'. He was of a generation not to have heard of Dolly Parton.

'No – just an interview – I'm going to play the field a bit before making a decision.' Mr Gibbon and Trotsky snorted in unison and disappeared back into the house.

I planned the interview carefully. I had to be a bit wary because the last thing I wanted was to be offered a job that required me to start immediately. First, I had to suss the market then, ideally, bring the whole process to the boil with three firms offering me jobs simultaneously. An auction for my services might develop. On no account would I mention my secret leanings towards a future in widgets. I would play slightly hard to get, but act as if the City was under my skin, in my blood.

'James – do you mind if I call you James? – why were you made redundant?'

A tricky question.

I assumed that Mr Crump wouldn't have explained the real reason; he'd have been undermining the sales pitch he'd made on my behalf if he had. I wasn't about to admit to low commission numbers either; candour about my business prospects, in the face of an inquisition by Alick's boss, had cost me my job at Merrill Lynch.

I talked about the long term. 'My chosen client base, the Japanese, are a bit short of cash right now, but on a five-year view they will of course come bouncing back, the Wall of Money will return, it will only be necessary to achieve a minute market share of this inevitable bonanza to make the whole business fabulously profitable. Take my client Nomura Investment Trust Management, they have more money under management than the entire Japanese defence budget. OK, so the Japanese may have a peaceful constitution, but that won't last – they've probably got nuclear weapons already and their army is still the eighth largest in the world. You pick up a tenth of a per cent of that business and…wow.'

Nomura had given me the biggest order I ever got – worth £6.8 mill – not bad, but my biggest ever. It was the biggest order I got by a multiple of about six. Most brokers will be unimpressed.

His eyes were already glazing over.

But I'd made a fatal mistake with the first thing I had said; I had mentioned the long term. If the stockbrokers think you can make *loadsamoney* for them quickly they will employ you and, if they don't, they won't. At all costs in an interview for a city job, the conventional estimations of the long and short term should be dramatically shortened. Short term, months; long term, a year at most. Never ever mention five years.

After that we went through the motions.

'Why do you prefer dealing in the French market to the Italian market?'

'There is better liquidity in France,' I answered, referring in my head not to ease of dealing but to the booze. Real answer: 'I am being interviewed by a French firm, stupid.'

This man was not one for going through the motions to excess. He was polite enough to ask me a few more questions but wrapped things up pretty quickly. The interview lasted no more than fifteen minutes.

As we parted he said, 'I'll be in touch.' I knew he was lying. He probably wouldn't even call the headhunter to say 'Who was that lemon you sent me? Do better next time'.

It was a pity, that the Eurotrash man hadn't been more insightful as to his firm's interests as Paribas's offices are off Oxford Street, which would have made a pleasant change from the City. Very near the Steinway and Bosendorfer studios too.

My Yamaha grand did not really have the phallic qualities of a Jaguar E-type. More like a 3-litre Mitsubishi FTO. But really what I wanted was something with both refinement and power – an Aston Martin. In piano terms a Bosendorfer.

Oh well, one interview down, fourteen to go. I had worked out that there were approximately fifteen jobs suitable for me in the City, which could use my skills and experience profitably. If I failed on those I would have to aim lower, perhaps even become a widget salesman.

I learnt another lesson from this interview: if it is all over very quickly or, in other ways, goes badly, kill time in a bookshop before going home.

'That was over quickly,' said Saeko, as I walked through the front door, using a tone of voice normally reserved for an indifferent performance in the matrimonial bed. Talk about kicking a man when he was down.

That evening I drove her to the airport for her Cannes trip (or was it Venice?).

Mr Crump's assistant Donald phoned in the next day to ascertain what the prognosis was for picking up his fee. There was no need to spare him the truth; it had been a disaster.

A succession of other headhunters rang me over the next few days: word gets round. Pickings had been thin for headhunters, few people were hiring but a new prospect for their clients would make them look like they were on the case. Mr Crump had treated me a little dismissively, yet he knew (and I was discovering) that I was in a weaker position than I had imagined...but things weren't great for him either. The bullied often become bullies.

Financial institutions were not expanding in the reckless way they had in the 1980s. Then it would have been easy to lure people into changing employers as a quick way of getting a pay rise, but some were now conscious that job security was worth more than a crazy salary. The accounting term Last In First Out, LIFO, was on everyone's lips. Not many would shift jobs for fear of being LIFO'ed. Gone were the days when headhunters could move all four members of the Citicorp Scrimgeour Vickers star retail analyst team to Goldman Sachs at salaries in excess of £100,000 each and pick up a fee of 30% x £100,000 x 4 = £120,000 just for setting up a few interviews.

Most headhunters were suitably ingratiating. For the sake of narrative simplicity I will call them all Donald and treat them as if they were all the same person, which they may as well have been, with the exception of Mr Crump, and of course my excellent friends at the Bloomsbury Group who had got me three of my five City jobs. The ones they didn't get me were the internal swap at Citicorp and the ill-fated trade-up to Merrill Lynch. So they must have judgement. Actually I'm just giving them a bit of product placement – it's the trend in modern literature – in exchange for a drunken lunch. Call them on 020 7xxx xxxxx for all your personnel needs (City ones, not widgets).

Donald had a suitably ingratiating inflection in his voice. 'Hi Jim, how are things with you?' There would be a hint of infectious chuckle built into the 'Hi' so that you'd get the impression that the act of talking to you had improved his whole day. Not dissimilar to any self-respecting broking technique. Easy familiarity, laced with respect.

I'd go into Donald's office. Typically, Donald would be an ex-Army officer, Old Radleiean (or Old Haileburian) who had made it into the City, but through ignorance or mischance had ended up helping others to earn a fortune rather than earning one himself. He wasn't so professional that he'd worry about presenting an unsuitable candidate to his client as Mr Crump had done. Come to that, when the chips were down, Mr Crump had secured me an interview even though he said he wouldn't present me to anyone until I knew what I wanted. But times were hard.

Donald would come up with the same list of fifteen suitable posts as I'd worked out for myself, plus a few unsuitable ones, usually at third-tier Japanese brokerages I'd already rejected. I was a sucker for an interview however, so I would generally agree to any proposal, such as meeting with small start-up brokers of the kind that describe themselves as 'research boutiques' – a euphemism for not having many analysts or ones that can deliver better research. And code for not having many clients either. Perhaps I am being a touch hard on these research boutiques but, to resurrect my reptile metaphor, they can perhaps best be likened to the small, furry, warm-blooded creatures that in the long term were more adaptable and spelt the end for mighty dinosaurs. Rats. Don't knock 'em. Immensely adaptive, successful species. Did and do the Darwin thing most effectively.

Rory's mum had heard of my plight, so we were invited to dinner again. A genuine victim of the recession would create a talking point. Her husband's law firm had recently laid off some mergers and acquisition lawyers, so she said she knew what it was like. He himself was an insolvency lawyer, so his business was picking up. Employment lawyers – now they do well when times are hard – even when running a hopeless case they have the blackmail card: it's cheaper to pay me off than go to court.

Rory's mum had invited the usual assortment of guests.

When asked what I did for a living I somehow found myself unable, in public at least, to admit to 'nothing'.

'I am an investment banker,' I said.

'Oh, how interesting,' said the lady sitting next to me. 'I have a cousin who's only twenty-six and he is a director of S.G. Warburg. Who do you work for?'

'For nobody.'

'You work for yourself – how enterprising.'

I found the lady irritating and thought it would be fun to embarrass her. 'No, I was made redundant last week.'

The silence was indeed an embarrassed one. You might have got a similar reaction by telling someone you had AIDS and had only three months to live. Redundancy was not all that was bad about capitalism, but it was embarrassing nonetheless, not something that should happen to someone you actually knew…certainly at the beginning of the recession.

To fill the silence my interlocutor said, 'There's been a lot of that in the City recently, hasn't there? Were you one of a whole lot of people?'

'No', I replied, 'I was the only one.'

Another awkward silence, then I added, 'I guess it was a question of Last In First Out?'

Ha, ha, she even knew the LIFO joke.

'No', I said, 'I wasn't making much commission, so they fired me and hired someone new to replace me.' Which was true, Giussi the former intern was already doing far better than I'd done and, in addition to Giussi, there was the new Nordic bandit hired to open up the frozen North, my efforts directed at the Far East having proved that bit too permafrost.

'You're looking very healthy on it, where did you get that suntan?' She attempted to steer the conversation into safer waters.

'I have a lot of time on my hands at the moment, as you can imagine, so I try to take my mind off things by doing a bit in the garden.' Really it was a skiing suntan, but it was fun to discomfit her further.

'How much did they pay you off?' asked Rory's dad. I indicated to him the amount in months rather than figures.

'Is that all?' he said. 'They should pay out lots more than that. They poached you from Phillips and Drew, didn't they? That means they persuaded you to leave a secure job, where you were doing well, for an insecure one. I think you should sue them.'

The lawyer had spoken.

I took a bit of persuading, it would cost a fortune and it might easily backfire. It wouldn't do to be preceded by a reputation for litigiousness. In the City, in principle, the last vestiges of a culture of gentlemanly agreement existed still. *Verbum est meum pactum*, my word is my bond.

On the other hand, just as being fired by Merrill Lynch could never be held against anyone, suing Merrill Lynch could scarcely be considered as infringing any code of honour. They extracted what they could from their employees (nothing in my case) and would expect their ex-employees to extract as much from them as possible. It was the American way.

It was true, they had been indecently, you could say suspiciously, decent about the redundancy offer they'd made, saying 'We don't have to offer you anything, James', which had struck me as uncharacteristically altruistic at the time. Now, from what Rory's dad was saying, it appeared like a straight lie.

'Go for it,' I said to myself. There was nothing to lose.

My resolve was further strengthened next day by the

arrival of another letter demanding the return of the company car or else no redundancy payment. In addition, it requested that I pay an outstanding parking fine.

CHAPTER 14

A few days on Donald rang. 'Hi, Jim,' he said with that laughing inflection of his. He had arranged an interview at the broking arm of a small merchant bank.

We were now several weeks into redundancy and the garden was beginning to look considerably tidier – it was spring and lots of interesting things were coming up. I'd been down to the garden centre to get some bedding plants and planted a book on gardening in the loo so that I could multi-task while crapping and identify what emerging plants weren't weeds.

The train set too was settling down into a complicated lay-out, fulfilling various objectives: it had to have a tunnel long enough for the entire train to disappear into, a through station, Alpine pastures, a turntable, a viaduct and sidings for shunting goods. Quite soon I would feel confident enough to start nailing the track down to the base board on top of the scale model stone ballast that went between the railway sleepers. This I'd bought from a model shop I'd discovered nearby – a wonderful shop run by an enthusiast. He had bits of kit, like switches wrapped in grease proof paper, which he'd evidently had in stock since 1963.

My piano playing, too, was giving me lots of pleasure, even if painful to all around.

Life was rather pleasant. Sod it – who wanted to work anyway?

Donald's interview was thus something of an imposition; I would have to tear myself from a busy round of weeding. I was just getting the hang of weeding; quite a lot of weeds turn out to be plants, so much of my time was spent with nose in gardening book. The interview would be a rude interruption because the company concerned was small, a boutique, and realistically, they'd have little use for me.

On the other hand I could take the train from Denmark Hill to Blackfriars and resolve a problem I'd been having. When trains are on bridges, do the rails run on ballast or on some other surface like concrete? Important to know for the authenticity of my train set and I'd had a devil of a job finding out, because bridges tend, by definition, to be in the air so you can't look down on them. *Railway Modeller Magazine* appeared to assume such knowledge, so it couldn't tell me either. Too basic.

I arrived about ten minutes late, which didn't matter especially as the other side in an interview are always about twenty minutes late. Incidentally, the rails on bridges do run on clinker.

Donald had told me whom I was to see but I was buggered if I could remember. Susanna something. 'I've come to see the head of research, Susanna...' I bluffed at reception. The surname Rosewall was supplied.

Ms Rosewall was quite tasty, not that such observations should detain a married man for a moment. Or a professional stockbroker. We ran through my life history while waiting for a colleague. When he arrived we then ran through his. It always amazed me how interviewers would talk about themselves. The last thing anyone discovered was something worthwhile about the candidate.

'We work on low basic salaries' (= poverty), 'with a large commission share' (= pressure). I could feel my enthusiasm for this particular job waning.

Ms Rosewall, on the other hand, was decidedly comme il

faut, with her deep swimming-pool blue eyes and blonde hair paying carelessly on sculpted shoulders of the heave-in-ecstasy variety. The nose was slightly squiffy, but with legs like hers, who cared?

'What do you understand by return on capital?' she suddenly asked.

This was a faster, straighter ball than most. Return on capital is a fairly crucial, indeed, basic concept for a stockbroker to grasp, any businessman really, but I certainly didn't expect to be tested on it or, for that matter, anything else theoretical. It was a measure given in all company research; along with PE ratios and figures for sales and profit would be one marked 'ROC'. If ROC was improved by a couple of points, surely that was all the client needed to know. Capital was being invested more efficiently. You didn't need to how or why.

We were there, surely, to establish what a good chap I was, not test me on my knowledge, which should be taken as read. Had she not read my CV? A bloody career woman…Mrs Thatcher, too, was said to have been a bit of a stunner in her youth. I digress. It was a fair question, but surprising. Aside from economic competency, there was my claim to be fluent in Japanese. Only two of the five companies I worked for in the City had put me to the test. Back in 1986, with the Japanese bubble market floating ever upwards, it had been more: 'You can handle a pair of chopsticks? What useful insights you must hold into the inscrutable Japanese psyche and how to get a bit of action with the Wall of Money. Here, have a job.'

In these hard times employers were taking more care. Return on capital. Tricky, I thought. Obviously I had a rough idea of what is meant by this measure, having done several

Stock Exchange accountancy courses, chiefly as a means of getting a break from the office.

Broking firms rarely bothered with training. Fair enough, in a way; if you were motivated enough to earn all that money you'd employ your own intelligence and curiosity and find out for yourself. Those who can, do; those who can't, teach. What could a teacher possibly know?

Vickers da Costa sent me out to do a series of exams but mysteriously never asked whether or not I'd passed. In truth I failed the accountancy one. Any boss worth half his salt ought to have had me splattered against the ceiling for my indolence. It's not an especially hard exam. If I'd been my boss I'd have sacked me for that.

'Return on capital,' I looked at her as if she was mad. 'Well it's quite straightforward, it's the return you get on the capital you invest, expressed as a percentage, but obviously there are different ways of measuring it, I could talk for half an hour if you wanted.' I like to think she looked impressed and my bluff was not called, possibly because I had called hers, but more likely because she'd already marked me down as a phoney.

The job they had in mind for me was to talk to UK clients, something I had never done before. I didn't like the idea of working on a low salary for a high commission share, selling to sophisticated Brits, it sounded stressful. Sophistication implied that they would want me to explain the ROC column. I could get this from any research report, but they might want me to be able to explain whether the analyst should use a different calculation from the one the company used, say. And if so, why? And how it compared to other companies in the sector.

At the end of the meeting it was left that I would get

back in touch if I was interested, when more discussions would take place. I didn't think I'd be calling.

Two jobs down, thirteen to go.

I had promised myself that I would investigate alternative, lower-paid careers in widget sales or whatever, but when the crunch came I couldn't be bothered. My previous experience of being interviewed for industrial jobs was that the industrialists were picky about whom they employed. But I doubt very much that they are any better at selecting. Indeed, the British transition from manufacturing industries to financial industries suggests that the City's more relaxed attitude to recruitment works better. Whatever misgivings someone like me had about the City lifestyle, you had to admit that – a few booms and busts aside – the place worked impressively well.

I had interviews with Shell, for example, when I came back from Japan. To get through their competitive recruitment, there would have been three or four interviews, followed, if successful, by two years on a training scheme. I might have got to use my Japanese in year three, by which time I'd have forgotten it and would have needed to go on a refresher course. So, only by year four might I have been working productively for them.

Colonel Arthur at Laurence Prust, by contrast, had filled me with a bottle of Port and made sure I knew how much everyone looked forward to employing me. If I cared to start, come in tomorrow. The personal touch and commendably un-bureaucratic. No ugly talk of contracts and personnel departments; with Colonel Arthur there had been that old fashioned feeling that 'my word is my bond'. Which is how the City used to operate.

If British industry wants to attract bright people (and I can still use the present tense for this assertion), they would do well to drop all the bureaucracy and form filling, take a few risks with their people. The City gobbled up people in the late 1980s, then again in the 1990s. They aspired to the City partly because of the money, of course, as much as the chance of real responsibility within a couple of years for anyone with a bit of oomph. And from any background…Alick, Etonian, barrow boy Bernie…as long as they weren't black or female.

But, as Nigel had said, you're better off with the job you know. It was not all bad being paid more than the Prime Minister (in his case) or a minor functionary like the Chancellor of the Exchequer (in my case). For now, forget widgets. I would stick to what I knew.

I had a series of interviews with City firms. Interviews definitely needed more thought and planning than they had even a year before, as I'd discovered with the question on return on capital.

Nonetheless, quite a lot of the interviews were a complete waste of time. Their main purpose seemed to be to gather market intelligence. All had noticed a sharp drop-off in Japanese commissions and were aware that this sector had never fulfilled the promise it had seemed to show only a couple of years before. The Japanese were not putting money abroad into shares. I could supply corroboration of the dawning perception that the Japanese as an investment power, certainly in equities, were in deep trouble, and that the Wall of Money would be dashed on the pebbles of disappointment.

At one leading merchant bank's broking subsidiary, the salesman plaintively asked, when his boss was out of the room, whether he should chuck in the Japanese clients and move on to something else. He had a wife and new baby, was probably feeling the pinch with an overly ambitious mortgage and was worried by the lack of business. I wasn't about to tell him that I thought the Japanese were doomed as it would have made him even more determined to protect his patch and obstruct suggestions of employing new people to attack his own client base, so I reassured him that he should stick it out for the long term. The Wall of Money might be delayed, but it must, will, has to come. When British investment institutions started investing abroad the norm was to put ten per cent or so of funds offshore. This had more than doubled. The Japanese had yet to reach even ten per cent, I pointed out. The macro-economic picture was very positive. I was looking for a job at his side, what else could I tell him?

For whatever reason, I didn't get the job.

He also told me that before I had left UBS Phillips and Drew, he and his colleague had been interviewing for a job there selling European equities to the Japanese, i.e. my job.

When I had been there you had to be uniquely incompetent to be for the chop. My escape to Merrill Lynch had been very timely. Still, it was difficult to believe that P&D would actually have dispensed with me. I might not have been good, but there were worse who were kept on.

I ran up quite a large telephone bill talking to companies in Tokyo trying to get work there. A few years previously, they would have fallen over themselves to employ me.

I had taught English in Japan for three years after university and, as my time came to an end, I had an interview with Christopher Heath, the head of Baring Securities, a company famous latterly for the destruction of the parent Barings Bank (RIP) by Nick Leeson's trading errors.

Back then, Baring Securities was but a small foreign broking house, the creation of Heath, who'd persuaded the blue-blooded merchant bankers of 200 year old Baring Brothers that they really needed a broking arm. After two centuries of doing nice safe things like fund Great Britain with debt issues during the Napoleonic Wars, they got into something they didn't understand, and it killed them.

Heath was not to blame. He turned Baring Securities into the top foreign broker. When I met him they had perhaps twenty employees; by the time it collapsed, some seven hundred. Profit-wise, it had very much become the tail that wagged the Barings dog. 'The Brothers', as they were referred to, were delighted with the fees – dwarfing their traditional revenue – for helping companies merge, make acquisitions or raise funds by advising them on the issue of new bonds and shares.

Heath's management style was hands-on. Hands-on and strangle. He fell out with The Brothers and left when the securities arm he'd created was in a period of losses. Had stayed in charge, however, he would certainly have noticed Nick Leeson's unprotected £700 million position and inquired further. The Market certainly knew about it – even a translator friend of mine knew about it – so the Brothers should have, too. Heath would have been on a plane to Singapore immediately; if the humble and, by many accounts, rather stupid trader Leeson's explanation for all the money he'd been making had been a good one, Heath would have redoubled his efforts to find the truth. He'd have discovered it, too, and realised immediately this could '*rupt* the bank. Leeson would have found himself splattered on the metaphorical ceiling.

For a while Heath drew headlines as the highest paid man in Britain, earning in excess of two million pounds a year. Not that much, seen from a decade later, but in those days it got him a lot of media attention. Being a private sort of man he changed the way in which he was paid, so no one would know that most intimate of things – the size of his wad.

I was just coming to the end of my three years in Japan as an English teacher when I met Heath for a preliminary drink. He told me that I was probably better suited to becoming a journalist. Nonetheless he arranged for me to meet a colleague in Tokyo, Richard Greer. I put Greer at twenty-eight or so, frighteningly successful-looking, with one of those crisp double cuffed stripey shirts made of very stiff cotton, and the close-shaven look of a man who doesn't think it extravagant to use a new razor blade every day. He was charming, but physically of a colourless, bland demeanour, like a plant that had grown up under a flowerpot. He looked like a walking warning that stockbroking is bad for your health. The interview in his office began at 6.30 p.m., a time I considered as properly reserved for the first drink of the evening. This one experience had shocked me into abandoning any idea of working in finance. Though by the time I got back to the UK, I had forgotten the shock sufficiently that I gave into blandishments.

Friend Chris Lawless of the Bloomsbury Group had got Sanwa International (RIP), a bond dealing outfit, keen on me, but I decided that Laurence Prust were nicer. Also, equities are intrinsically more interesting than bonds, which are all about interest rates, as opposed to companies making or selling things or peddling services either well or badly. I only discovered later that the bond people had been offering £25,000 against LP's £11,000. The bond man complained to Chris, 'Why did he do that? I was prepared to offer him a lot more money...' Chris might have explained that to me, although I'm glad he didn't. I might have been successful at bonds, a simpler product than equities. If I'd been a success I'd still be doing it.

But I went for Laurence Prust out of misplaced idealism. And naïvety. Basing a career path on the niceness of the people I was to work for was an attitude soon knocked out of me. A pity really.

Laurence Prust were gentleman stockbrokers in the old – and had one known it – rapidly-disappearing mould. This became evident about six months later when Saeko, then my girlfriend, who had timed her study year in England to coincide with my return had a small slip-up. My boss arranged a 'business trip' to Tokyo for me so that I could inform my future parents-in-law that they were shortly to be grandparents and, far worse, have a white man as a son-in-law. They were Koreans, so apparently I was preferable to a Japanese, but absolutely not as good as a Korean. Besides she was young and still a student, so the meeting was not the smoothest in my life. Add in my own parents' reaction and there's potential there for a whole East meets West novel, but Gen will read this one day, and as he loves both his parents and all four of his grandparents, perhaps best not to write it.

But I shall never forget at one point being chased around a small Japanese kitchen by my future father-in-law with an exceptionally sharp sushi knife. I don't think I was in any danger, but for prudence's sake I fled down the street. In my socks, because there was no time to grab my shoes from the foot well by the front door (you don't wear shoes in Japanese houses). Saeko ran with me. What the neighbours must have thought, one can only guess, because in that polite Japanese way, they all pretended nothing was happening. In England a big crowd would have gathered.

We survived to return to London where, strapped for cash, I stabbed my kind gentleman employers in the back, they who had paid my air fare to Japan. (If you ever read this, Mr Starr and Colonel Arthur, I still feel bad about it. Please call for your bottles of whiskey. It was a boy). I left for Vickers da Costa who never bothered to test my 'fluent Japanese' either. Another decent company destroyed by the bank that owned it.

CHAPTER 15

Confronted with acres of free time, it would have been easy to fall into the trap of doing absolutely nothing for entire days on end. So I fell into it. For me it wasn't a trap; I was rather enjoying it. I couldn't complain: being unemployed in London was better than being from the marshlands of Southern Iraq or a village in Chechnya.

I wrote myself a long list of DIY tasks, the first of which would be to take up the old carpets, hire a floor stripper and sand the floor.

My piano playing was coming along well too. It was the first time I had the time to lavish as much attention as I desired on my E-type Jaguar substitute. *Für Elise* was almost mastered and I had embarked on *The Entertainer.*

Mr Gibbon came round to complain that he could hear every note in every room in his house. Did I always have to play the same bloody tune? Apart from a right to make a noise in my own house, I would have thought that I had a right to expect a man of his age to be hard of hearing. I, the mildest of neighbours, could have complained about Trotsky, who would lean over the wall to bark at me every time I approached my own front door, and about Mrs Gibbon's half-dozen or so champion poodles, which I rarely saw but certainly heard.

Mr Gibbon was full of surprises. He had played the trombone in the London Symphony Orchestra before the war. You would think that he might be in favour of my taking up playing the piano. His acute musician's ears, however, were very sensitive to all the noises emanating from my house, while apparently immune to those coming from his own.

Trotsky was confined to the front yard, whilst Mrs Gibson's six show poodles had the run of the back. Any noise in our house, a slamming door or creaking window, was greeted by barks in stereo; gruff and aggressive at the front, high-pitched and yappy at the rear.

I toyed with the idea of liberating Trotsky into the back, where he could father some mongrels. Hybrid vigour is best. Take my son, a far superior specimen to Rory. You'd think the animal rights people would have a go at show breeders for the cruelty they cause and the damage they inflict on the canine gene pool. My mother-in-law had an inbred Yorkshire terrier which had died recently, the most positive thing it had done in its short wretched life. Inbreeding had left it neurotic, incontinent and only able to breathe in bronchitic wheezes. Perhaps, after I'd liberated him, Trotsky would show the same sense of mercy to the effete poodles. There was something that appealed to my innate sense of goodness and charity in the idea of Trotsky trotting around the back-yard with a couple of poodles' wind-pipes hanging gory from his mouth.

You can live next door to someone for years in London and find out nothing about them. But I with my new leisure discovered another odd thing about Mr Gibbon. His house was divided in two, with an ex-wife living in an apartment upstairs. The front garden had been divided in two with a sort of Berlin Wall down the middle. I spotted Mr Gibbon one day with Trotsky held by the paws, sitting on one of his master's shoulders, peeing over the fence into wife No. 1's garden. Quite how you train a dog to do this, without it peeing into your own ear, was a matter of wonderment.

Mr Gibbon was a compulsive DIY fanatic. Eighty or so years old, he could still wield a hammer, if no longer a trombone. He was continuously taking delivery of building materials. Having finished off the Berlin Wall and concreted over half the lawn ('easier to hose down'), he seemed to be constructing poodle powdering bays. Very soon there would be no garden left, which was something to look forward to. One wondered if there were more ex-wives under the concrete.

Occasionally I'd catch a glimpse of the older Mrs Gibbon hanging her bloomers on the washing line. She looked around eighty, much the same age as Mr Gibbon, whereas the current Mrs Gibbon was, relatively speaking, something of a floozy, probably around sixty.

Seeing Mr Gibbon in action inspired me to attack various projects I'd promised to tackle, such as stripping old carpet and varnishing floorboards. For this operation I chose a time when Saeko was in Venice (or was it Cannes?) because I knew it would be noxious, dirty, carcinogenic boy's work.

She should be pleased – it was her idea. In Britain, we wear our shoes indoors, which is disgusting if you think about it. Sensibly the Japanese take them off. Britain's Axminsters are riddled with portions of dried, congealed dog turd, gob, chewing gum, brought in off the nation's streets on the bottom of the nation's shoes. I dealt with this by not thinking about it. I was too lazy to take my shoes off each time I went inside.

Saeko had an obsession with dust. She could have employed a cleaning lady, but found English ones too slapdash. Paradoxically, this lead to us living in complete squalor as she was not herself into housework. I did a little cleaning, but preferred the creative side of things, making food for example, as opposed to clearing and cleaning up afterwards.

I was often asked about cultural differences dividing us and dirt was one. In Japan, if you leave a saucepan to soak overnight because you can't be bothered to wash it up, by morning there will be trail of ants and half a dozen cockroaches having a party on it. Outside of occasional headlines about our National Health Service or some posh restaurant, I don't think I've ever heard of a cockroach in England. There is no doubt that the English are dirtier than the Japanese, but then we can afford to be. I reject any suggestion that cleanliness is either genetically or culturally encoded. It is a function of climate. When it doesn't matter, the Japanese are amongst the filthiest people in the world. Visitors to Ben Nevis take their rubbish home. The path up Mount Fuji is strewn with litter.

A people beset with contrasts. Saeko once quoted me a Japanese proverb: 'You don't get good food out of a clean kitchen.' I thoroughly agreed. A sterile kitchen, replete with gleaming white surfaces implies nice sterile warmed-over ingredients from Sainsbury's. Ready cleaned mangetout or prepared sauces.

Serious activity in the kitchen implies wispy garlic shells falling into the cracks between the dishwasher and the cupboard, dirty walls from the smoke given off, if you really do cook the steak in a minute, evidence of home-made jam having boiled over when the telephone went. When in trouble, I would quote the proverb back at her.

I set about removing the manky Axminster, the estate agent's vaunted 'fitted carpets' that came with the house. Beneath was underlay on top of hardboard and only below that did floorboards present themselves. The hardboard came up easily enough but at approximately two centimetre intervals it had been held down by tiny tacks that remained stubbornly in place.

For their removal two strategies presented themselves. One was to pull them all out. The other was to knock them all in.

Hardboard sheets of three foot by three foot held down by tacks spaced every two centimetres equals around 140 tacks per sheet. The living room was 10ft x by 34 ft = 240 sq. ft i.e. twenty five hard board sheets. 25 x 140 = 3500 tacks. Actually the problem was considerably worse than that, once you took into account the fact that 10 foot divides by 3 foot more than three times, giving a 1ft x by 3 ft fiddly bit, plus all the fiddly bits in the hall, landing, three bedrooms, round the loo = 10,000 tacks. And that would be a 'conservative forecast', as a bullish stock analyst might put it about his favourite equity.

A time and motion study – it takes a lot of time and a lot of motion to hook out a tiny tack – revealed that pulling out took twice as long as knocking them in, so I decided to knock them in, which should take two well aimed blows of the hammer. Missing would put the average up, and being a Jermyn Street be-shirted executive unsullied by experience of physical travail, I missed quite a lot; so we were talking 4 x 10,000 = 40,000 blows or so of the hammer to prepare the floor for sanding.

Saeko would be absent in whichever Riviera it was for a few days so I had to get the job done quickly or face evisceration with a ceremonial sword annealed in a forge after the most ancient Samurai tradition or whatever the Korean equivalent was. A sushi knife, I seemed to recall. Saeko's dad would probably have claimed these traditions originated in Korea anyway. A historian of some note, he liked to say that incontrovertible evidence had been found in an archaeological dig at some tomb that proved the Emperor was Korean. The tomb had been rapidly resealed. The Japanese are very much into the uniqueness and purity of their genealogy and didn't like this suggestion one bit.

The hammering took until late into the night. Accuracy was the key, but with 40,000 hits to make, misses were bound to happen, either of the bend-the-nail or the whack-the-finger variety. It was not long, say 1.30 a.m., before a pyjamaed Mr Gibbon arrived to complain.

A soft answer turneth away wrath, but no amount of honeyed words would placate Mr Gibbon. He was relentless, wouldn't let go. He'd have been like a pensioner version of his dog if he'd remembered to put his teeth in. I hadn't been enjoying smiting these microscopic tacks any more than he enjoyed hearing them smitten, so the relentlessness of the verbal maiming caught me in unreceptive mood, even though he did have a point about the noise. After about ten minutes of spurned apologies and promises not to do it again I told him to bugger off. 'I'd expect a jumped-up yuppie like you to say something like that to a poor old bloke my age,' he said as he took my advice.

In retrospect I can see that he had a point. As a retired member of the London Symphony Orchestra he knew the principle whereby naked wood suspended over a body of air resonates more fully than wood clothed in carpet, underlay and hardboard. My whole house was like the inside of a violin and was in the process of being struck 40,000 times.

I was glad of the break anyway. My most adored personal possession, the grand piano, was too big to have been moved from the scene of action, so I had lovingly wrapped it in 150 metres of Safeway's own-brand cling film to protect its gleaming black casework and 2,000 precision-made moving parts from flying dust. A musical phallus in its very own condom. Human nature and the heat of the moment being what they are, such prophylactics sometimes fail to stand up to what is demanded of them. Indeed, Gen owes his existence to one such failure.

A slash of the fingernails and I had the keyboard open. Sod it, I had been slaving all day, it was 1.30 in the morning, I was in a bad mood and Mr Gibbon had made it worse. I needed some relief. I could do a passable imitation of Vladimir Ashkenazi hitting the dramatic chords marked 'fff' in the first two bars of the *Pathetique Sonata* (purists and pedants may point out that Beethoven suggests 'ff', but that is only two-thirds as much fun). Thereafter, there were too many notes. About ten minutes of *Für Elise* later, Mr Gibbon was back, leaning on my doorbell.

He could hear every note in every room in the house.

'Couldn't you get a job?' He hissed through his gums.

'Do you mind not leaning on my doorbell?' I asked. 'There's a child asleep upstairs, you know. You'll wake him.'

A few days later Mr Gibbon was back on my doorbell again. Having knocked the tacks in, I then made an infernal din with the floor stripper I'd hired. I'd been looking forward to playing with this machine. If he was a pit-bull pensioner, this machine was a pit-bull hoover, a device that dragged you across the floor, spitting tacks.

A few days later he was back again, this time to complain about the poisons I'd had to apply to the wood to inhibit death watch beetle, woodworm and dry rot. The fumes, he told me, spread through the wall and were making both the younger and the older Mrs Gibbon 'poorly'. Not to talk of putting the menagerie of show poodles off their feed.

He could smell every whiff in every room in the house.

The situation had created tensions between the two Gibbon households, Mrs Gibbon the elder blaming him for the fumes. Any construction work in this neighbourhood was generally done by Mr Gibbon. Although she had – unlike her ex husband – the virtue of being hard of hearing, she was good of smelling.

'Why don't you get yourself a bloody job?' became his refrain.

'I am trying, but in case you hadn't noticed, there is a recession on,' I replied, but soon learnt to avoid such comments, as they would stimulate a long discourse about the Jarrow March and how we young people didn't know what suffering was. True, of course, but we didn't want to be told.

Mr Gibbon was at home with too much time on his hands for anything except moaning twenty-three and a half hours out of twenty-four.

CHAPTER 16

I interviewed with half a dozen more firms and began to get rather skilful. My expertise proved academic as no one would offer me a job in my speciality.

I grew adept at fielding certain questions.

'Why were you made redundant?'

True answer: 'My chosen client base, the Japanese investor, is doing absolutely no business at the moment and won't be for the foreseeable future and so my company sensibly sacked me as I was of no economic worth to them whatsoever.'

Interview answer: 'My chosen client base the Japanese are going through certain short-term difficulties, but it is only a matter of time before they have spondulicks like you have never seen spondulicks and will rule the world. You know, the Wall of Money.'

I'd ceased believing in this myself by now, but it remained axiomatic that the Japanese were hell bent on dominating not just the market for Van Goghs – a Japanese insurance company had paid a record £80 million for his 'Irises' – but every other market too. Yamaha had even persuaded Sviatoslav Richter to play their pianos and not a Steinway, Bosendorfer or Bechstein. There was still a belief in the Wall of Money, but with business volumes low back in the UK, almost all companies were prepared to wait and see. That is to say, to take a disgustingly short-term view and not employ me.

'I see from your CV that you have worked for five firms in five years. Why have you worked for so many?'

The fact that three of them no longer existed was a

good excuse, though it didn't augur well for my stock selection capabilities.

There is something called the Curse of Parton. The first three companies I worked for in the City had all been effectively closed down. At the time I was made redundant I reckoned the writing was on the wall for UBS P&D which had recently changed its name to UBS Ltd. Wags were already making the obvious joke that the emphasis was on the second part of this exciting new name.

And in due course the parent saw the joke too. They bought Sigmund Warburg's old outfit to form UBS Warburgs, and 'merged' P&D with it, but few can have been fooled – 'merge' in this context means 'close down'.

Merrill Lynch is the soul survivor among my former employers. I wonder if there is a correlation between their survival and the fact they were the only firm with the good sense to fire me. I respect them for that. Though at the time of writing this they were in trouble in the USA for only putting 'buy' recommendations on stocks to which they were the in-house broker.

I resolved not to get caught with the over-busy job-shifts question again and quietly removed two companies from my CV. CVs are never checked anyway.

The true answer about my many moves was that I hated confronting bosses about pay and it was much easier and more exciting to change companies to achieve a pay rise in line with the bull market.

Occasionally an interviewer saw straight through me. A Mr James Shaw was one such. 'You speak fluent Japanese, French, are obviously very intelligent', – OK, so he got the odd thing about me wrong, he didn't realise I had inherited Pongo Parton's brains – 'what on earth are you doing being a salesman? Soul destroying. Smile-'n'-dial. You must have some kind of plan, a strategy to be somewhere in five years' time. What on earth have you been doing with yourself? Why do you want to waste yourself on this job?'

Good question. What had I been doing with myself? I'd never even liked my job. In truth I had no strategy, I had drifted into the City without the first idea of the difference between an equity and a bond, between a stock salesman and a stock analyst. More recently my strategy had been to pick up a couple of those famed hundred per cent bonuses (never did manage that), pay off the mortgage, then pack it all in. Plenty start off with this idea then develop such financial outgoings that there is no escape. I was one such. A further burden in my case was the need to nurse a wife who had been diagnosed HAV+ (Hermès Armani Vuitton), a chronic condition for which no cure has been found.

I interrogated Mr Shaw in turn. He had left County Natwest (RIP) during certain upheavals a few years before and gone to work in industry, which he had hated. 'Lazy, dishonest and doesn't deserve to succeed in this country.' So he had done the natural thing, which was to go back to the City to help these lazy, dishonest, undeserving people to raise money to run their industries.

I had limited experience of industry myself. I worked very hard on my student holiday job during the Saxby's Pork Pie Christmas rush. My mum was a Saxby, so I felt a sense of duty. You'd develop life-enhancing skills, like being able to cut exactly ten pounds off a hundred weight lump of short pastry, such that when you weighed it, you were only a couple of ounces out. Or you'd get to sit next to people with thirty years experience on the pork pie machine and they'd say things like, 'You know, that Mr Saxby, he even looks like a pig.' Then I'd reply, 'Mr Saxby is my mother's first cousin. But don't worry, I won't say anything.' The pork pie factory had been fun, and if you were family you'd get privileges. They might let you do creative stuff like hand-crimp the pies or assemble the six pounders that went to Harrods. An ordinary person would have to have worked years to get so far, yet I was given the privilege of crimping, aged just nineteen. The worst job was squirting molten jelly into the newly baked pies; not even family connections got me out of that.

But it was unfair to call City people lazy. Nor were they, apart from the usual exception, dishonest; my word is my bond, still had some lip service left in it. As for the 'deserving of their salaries?' issue that was more difficult to answer. I had been unquestionably undeserving, even of my relatively modest salary. I think I was – am – capable of hard work…as long as I am not distracted by something more interesting.

Another standard interview question was 'What motivates you?'

Friends at Baring Securities told me that if you were being interviewed by Christopher Heath, erstwhile most highly paid man in Great Britain, there was only one answer. Crap about job satisfaction, desire for responsibility cut no ice. You had to answer, 'Money, lots of money, then still more money, but most of all getting really rich.' But he had the reputation of weeding out dodgy applicants. Nick Leeson post-dated Heath. Perhaps if he'd interviewed and put the motivation question to Leeson, he'd have responded 'I want to travel and see the world'. Heath would never have employed him if he'd said that.

My ambition of paying off the mortgage, funding a smart education for Gen and three more putative children, then, with no debts, establishing a pleasant lifestyle in an attractive Georgian rectory in Somerset required only a low-ish income to make it work. To admit this would have been fatal to my employment prospects, unless the interviewer was bright enough to see that my aim was so naïve he'd have me working for him forever. But then he wouldn't want to employ a naïve person.

Other answers:

1. Ambition for authority. This needs phrasing correctly: 'I want to be sitting where you are in X years time' can sound bold, can sound threatening, but more often is silly. It has a neat element of flattery if the interviewer sees himself as a bit of a role model. Many interviewers do. But if the guy is insecure, he'd worry at the consequences of hiring someone who could be a threat to themselves.

2. The satisfaction of a job well done. Aaaaahh! Sweet. But 'puh-leeze', as we say nowadays. You'd be laughed at for the claim that simply doing your job well was motive enough.

3. Providing a professional service to clients. As above: idealism is not what you are paid for. In some cases good service will produce good commission, but in others it is good tickets for Lords, Wimbledon, Cup Final or Twickenham – preferably all four – or good flattery or some other form of human chemistry. Even unattractive blondes do well with Arab clients. There are some great gay salesmen.

4. Success and the respect (preferably envy) of your peers. This might appeal to some narcissists but is a bit too abstract to impress, despite being the thing that most drives most ambitious people.

I remember the grandfatherly head of sales at Merrill Lynch remarking that the best salesmen were self-confident but slightly insecure, a bit chippy perhaps. Profound, I thought, at the time. In Alick's case, for example, he'd gone through

Eton, no cause for a chip there, except he'd been treated for much of his school career as thick. Being head of a group of salesmen at Merrill Lynch was a good answer to that.

In the City the interview answer prescribed for Christopher Heath was probably the safest. Everyone knows that no one enters broking as a means of enhancing one's spirituality, so money can be the only motivation. Or at a pinch, excitement, but where does the excitement come from, other than from the money?

Unless you could bullshit about some variety of rocket science: 'I've modelled the software data needed to develop a measure for calculating spreads between the decay values of synthetic equity warrants, feeding in different variables, together or separately, like compounded putative interest rates if Alan Greenspan dies tomorrow, spread over time, if the underlying equity out-performs underlying market momentum.'

Sounds good, better hire him in case it is.

Brainy academic types like this frequently get ripped off, although the smart ones do the ripping, knowing that few people know anything at all about the codes of a computer programme. This was especially true in my time, when expressions like 'spreadsheet' had still not been invented. Even more so now, perhaps, when there is so much mind-boggling software out there. And geeks writing code. I think the words 'geek' and 'nerd' may be new, too.

Blinding with science can be sustained for quite a long time. Some clients like it because they in turn can blind their colleagues with it and more importantly their funds' trustees, if it's a pension fund, or the investor himself. A trustee really feels he is getting value for money if he doesn't understand how the money in his trust is being invested. And because he doesn't understand, he is in no position to question the huge profit margin hidden in the depths of the software. Being good at maths and computers is a far more useful skill in the City than speaking Japanese. I know several unprepossessing trainspotter/computer hacker types who earn truly dizzying sums of money (and still wear nylon shirts).

This may explain the contemporary rash of hedge funds. What are they? I dunno. After my time. But they sound too good to be true. Very high risk, except for the fund manager, who takes a massive tithe in fees straight off the top. And the 'high net worth individual' punter falls for it. A kind of socialism: the only real type of wealth redistribution, which is from the rich to the wannabe rich .

If a fund's trustees don't understand, what chance has Joe Public? Unit trusts are bad for your wealth. As are most pension funds. City professionals do not buy unit trusts, knowing the proportion of the fund that goes on admin and also knowing how hit and miss investment really is.

The other question unfailingly asked is, 'What do you consider your greatest weakness?'

There is no choice but to lie in answer to this one. In my case an honest answer would be:

1. Bone idle.
2. Disorganised and inefficient.
3. Incapable of arriving anywhere on time.
4. Not particularly interested in the job.
5. Very forgetful – particularly names, faces, events. (OK at pub quizzes, except the show-biz bits).
6. Weak, easily manipulated personality. (This might just be a positive to an employer who is weak and easily manipulated himself.)
7. Lack of motivation; if only I could pay off my

mortgage (it was an era of high interest rates, 12% or something) then I would happily jack it all in.

Most people who love their jobs are good at them, though difficult to know which is the chicken and which the egg, being good at the job or loving it.

The word at Baring Securities for those facing this question was to think of a mean and nasty weakness, although I was told that Christopher Heath had got a little tired of 'Don't tolerate fools lightly'.

In my speciality he also asked people whether or not they were 'having a love affair with the Japanese'. The correct answer was 'No', otherwise you didn't get the job. At Baring, they didn't like the Japanese.

I could see the eminently wise intent of this question. It was designed to weed out all those dreamers – a surprising number – who mistakenly believe that Japan is the land of Zen, of haiku, of graceful Geisha girls tending to your every need, of the peaceful contemplation of moonlight, of man's harmonious interaction with nature. If I was interviewing someone who, having lived in Japan, claimed to admire these qualities, I'd worry about which planet he'd been on.

Newly returned to London in 1986 at an interview with Barings' Mr Andrew Bayliss, I'd asked if they had many Japanese in their London office. 'We try to have as few as possible,' he replied.

'Is it hard to find suitable ones?' I asked.

'No. We don't like them.' Such refreshing honesty and lack of hypocrisy from a company that made nearly all its profits from Japanese stocks.

Baring declined to interview me this time. They remembered me from five years before, when Richard Greer, the young walking warning that stockbroking is bad for your health, the one with the grown-up under a flowerpot complexion had, insiders tell me, found me a bit too flippant.

Had I been interviewed I would have claimed that my greatest weakness was arrogance, because it implied self-confidence, or perhaps impatience, thus a desire to get things done, with overtones of dynamism. I would hope that 'flippancy' could somehow be re-marketed as 'wit' or that they might overlook my unfortunate trait of not taking anything much too seriously. In any case the best humour is deadly serious.

When asked your strengths there is a nice balance to be struck between being too modest, failing to get your strengths across and claiming too much for yourself. There are weak strengths and strong strengths.

Weak strengths:
1. I like people (= wimpy liberal).
2. I am honest (= naïve).
3. I am a nice chap (naïve, wimpy liberal).
4. I work hard (everyone says that).

Strong strengths:
1. Personal following from cast-iron, provable client base plus commission record that will move with you to whomever you work for. And get two clients to guarantee to follow you and no broker should refuse you.
2. Instinctive, unforced clubability, i.e. as good with the lads down the pub as boozing out of the back of a Range Rover in the Twickenham car park, can adapt to the three Es with equal ease. Old Etonians, Essex boys, not excluding the chippy, lower middle-class fund manager from Esher who used to read *The Guardian* but has self-

consciously switched to *The Telegraph*. Etonian Alick would take Bernie the barrow boy from the Kuwait Investment Office to watch the dogs (I don't think Alick was interested in the dogs), and could make the chap from Surbiton feel at ease shooting at some toff's estate. Even though Alick and Charlie used to laugh behind Charlie's back because Charlie had bought an 'over and under' shotgun, rather than a 'side by side'.

3. Intelligence. (Useful, but street-wise better).

4. Conscientiousness. (Of course, but difficult to prove. Could imply dullness.)

5. Driving ambition or 'hunger'. This last arises often from innate insecurity. Don't forget: 'Insecure people make the best salesmen.'

Christopher Heath would ask if you were 'hungry'. He asked me this in 1985 when I met him. I said 'Yes'. It was seven-thirty in the evening, and as an English teacher down on his uppers, I fancied some freebie capitalist pig-dog scoff, so I inadvertently gave the right answer, which may be why I progressed to the second interview with the pale man from under the flowerpot. Though he didn't buy me supper.

Ultimately, the greatest strength anyone can have is half a dozen mates, e.g. from your rugby team, who will stick up for you when they are asked for a reference. Get those two clients with decent sized funds to support you with your prospective employer and with those references, you will always get a job. Similar rules of thumb must apply in any business in the world.

Unfortunately my best client was Mr Hoshide, who had very small funds.

CHAPTER 17

Mr Hoshide gave me a call at home to see how I was and ask when he could start receiving my advice again. He invited me to dinner.

He selected a Chinese restaurant in Soho and we had some good food. Mr Hoshide commiserated with me about my position and his own inability to have given me more business. He said he almost blamed himself for my redundancy. The Gulf War and the Tokyo stock market collapse had lead to a panicky head office and left him with permission to do maintenance dealing only – when Mrs Watanabe of Niigata cashed in her units, the fund she owned a part of would have to put in a sell order – so that had been little business for me or, for that matter, his other brokers.

'We Japanese have small', he paused on a mouthful of noodles, 'funds.'

I liked Mr Hoshide, he'd been a good loyal client, but I knew that he operated under more constraints than he let on. Size wasn't the only one.

Another was the necessity to give a large portion of his business to his Japanese brokers, and so – although brokers like Nomura had little proprietary information to offer about Europe – they almost certainly had been getting the lion's share of his orders. Nigel, newly ensconced at Nomura Securities, had told me the mouth-watering commission figures of my direct competitor there, a Japanese with less than two years of experience of the European markets.

Mr Hoshide worked for a very large insurance company indeed. This meant that when things went wrong with its investments, his company was amongst the first to be compensated by Nomura. This was usually done by juggling investments around, usually at the expense of Japan's typical small investor – Mrs Watanabe, the bored housewife from Niigata Prefecture who, throughout the 1980s had been gambling the family finances on stocks and shares, in between visits to the local Louis Vuitton outlet.

It's an old stock market rule of thumb – dating from when just before the Wall Street crash of 1929 even the shoe-shine boys were giving advice on stock movements – that when amateurs involve themselves in a market, it is about to crash. But Tokyo had defied all these rules for about ten years. Mrs Watanabe had thought she was a clever investor. In fact the likes of Nomura made sure that the likes of Nippon Life did far better than she did.

The Big 4 Japanese brokers, Nomura, Daiwa (RIP), Nikko (RIP) and Yamaichi (RIP) were eventually forced to apologise to the world for compensating important clients at the expense of less important ones. A book called *The House of Nomura* by Al Alletzhauser alleged that Nomura had connections with gangsters and also made allegations about the compensation racket. Nomura denied this and sued the publishers in London. Even as Nomura issued denials in London, it was admitting the facts in Tokyo. It's a pity they didn't take Mr Alletzhauser to trial. All sorts of dirty linen would have been washed and the Western public might have understood why Japan's economy got in such trouble and has remained in such trouble.

Endemic, institutionalised, macro-economic corruption is what will stop Japan ever becoming the economic super-power it deserves to be given the energy of its people. At the micro level, the people themselves are incredibly honest. You hear tales of an expensive camera, say, being left on a park bench and still there several hours later or handed into the police. Probably not apocryphal.

Westerners commonly feel sorry for the downtrodden women of Japan, the Mrs Watanabes of Niigata. I've always felt this sympathy was misplaced; she has infinitely more freedom than her poor husband who, when he isn't stuck at the office, has to spend insufferable, drunken karaoke evenings out with his colleagues. Mr Hoshide, for example, candidly admitted to me that because he got pissed in two seconds flat, and his doctor had said this was bad for him, he had to mime his frivolity. After half a glass of beer he would go bright red in the face and say in quaint text-book English, 'Forgive me, it's my enzymes playing up.'

Observations about the Japanese getting drunk are not racist. They are based on medically proven facts. I used to teach English conversation to a group of three consultant urologists at Osaka University Hospital, one of the top medical research establishments in the country. My students told me that the Japanese as a race do not have enough of the crucial enzyme that metabolises alcohol.

Poor Mr Hoshide, miming his frivolity, that was one hell of a burden. I mean, how many people in Britain, say, hand on heart, really enjoy the company of the people they work with? Would choose them as friends? Do we invite our colleagues out to dinner out of anything more than a sense of duty and a desire to enhance our career prospects? After all, what was my motive in inviting Alick skiing? Love of Alick!

A lot is made, by Western observers, of the drinking customs to explain Japan's harmonious industrial relations. While drunk, a man can air his dissatisfaction and criticise his boss with impunity. If drunk, the boss, subliminally at least, takes the criticism on board and reacts to it, but would not hold what had been said against his subordinate. This is, of course, untrue. If Mr Hoshide, while pissed, were to say too many harsh things about his boss, he would be plucked from the elite world of international investment banking in London and his next posting would be selling life insurance policies door-to-door in Niigata to Mrs Watanabe.

The Japanese woman is spared all this. She is more or less barred from meeting her husband's colleagues, some would say, a lucky escape and of course she runs the family finances, issuing him with pocket money. With only 1.3 children to look after, the rest can be blown on Hermès scarves, Armani suits and Vuitton bags. Once the child is at school there would be time for tennis or ikebana lessons, coffee mornings with the girls or other diversions.

The diversion I missed out on – not uncommon, apparently – was an affair with the English conversation teacher, though my urologist's wife used to take me every week for a two-hour lunch and conversation in the restaurant of my choice and pay me 10,000 yen.

The archetypal Mrs Watanabe of Niigata Prefecture was strangely stoical about being stuffed at the top of most market moves. It didn't matter because recovery was always quick and the next bull run followed. It takes a degree of sophistication if your investments go inexorably up to notice that they are going up less than everyone else's. Now they were going inexorably down, her losses looked stark. She was starting to question the wisdom of her local Nomura salesman, some of whom travelled door to door. Ikebana classes must have dropped off, and visits from the English teacher would have suffered, too.

With sources of commission like Mrs Watanabe drying

up, Nomura was calling in some favours and I could well believe Mr Hoshide when he said he couldn't have given me as much business as he'd have liked.

Nice guy, Mr Hoshide. I enjoyed the role reversal, him paying for my dinner, and I was grateful for his expressions of solidarity during my time of trouble. A talented stockbroker I was not, but then neither were my problems entirely to be laid at my door. Some were the fault of macro-economic conditions beyond my control. The crumbling of the Wall of Money. I shook hands with him outside the restaurant and directed him towards a taxi. His enzymes had let him down again and he was a bit drunk, in a benign sort of way. 'I am sorry, Mr Parton, about my size,' he kept on muttering.

It was that part of Soho where men walk in pairs, wearing tight jeans and sporting perfect pecs bulging out of spotless Paul Smith T-shirts. I caught the stares of a few passers-by and wanted to say to them 'This man does not mean what you think'.

CHAPTER 18

I had now been out of work for two months. The job hunt was not going particularly well. No one got close to offering me anything, although I had the odd follow-up interview.

Rory's Dad drew a blank suing Merrill Lynch over my dismissal. Had I not signed that crucial document agreeing to severance terms that the likes of Nigel had advised me were reasonable, I might have squeezed more out of them, if only because the opposition prefer to avoid hassle and a few extra thousand here or there makes no difference to them. The obvious lesson is that if you are made redundant, check with a clued-up solicitor before you sign anything.

The garden was looking better and better, the train set had acquired a few mountains and I had sorted out the vagaries of the electrics. Hostilities between myself and Mr Gibbon had reached a state of uneasy truce, but truce nonetheless.

I compared happy holidays in France with the grey misery of London. Perhaps London was not the place for me, but Tokyo looked difficult: employing *gaijins* was too expensive. The tendency was to send them home and replace them with local Japanese. Various friends of mine were back in Britain as reverse tax exiles. After five years in Japan you were in for Japanese taxes at the full rate, so the aim of many overpaid brokers was to come back and do a year in London, before starting out again tax free in Tokyo. In practice some found the competition for clients too stiff, while back in Tokyo, their jobs had not waited for them during the financial meltdown. Their descent was brutally abrupt, from earning

£250,000 tax free, say, to zero.

I tried Madrid and Milan by phone – fancied learning a new language – but in both places encountered initial enthusiasm countered by a siesta effect. They were all too disorganised to do anything. Paris was a different matter. International broking was more advanced than in other European cities and, even pre-Eurostar or discount airline, popping over for the day for an interview was no trouble.

The light at the end of the Channel for Verona, Xavier, was over in London with his French bosses. This gave the opportunity for an informal 'get to know you' sort interview. I was soon shaking hands with Didier Fauchier Magnan and Monsieur Antoine Durant des Aulnois whose names I supply with the benefit of hindsight, because at the time I didn't quite catch them. When we parted their postcard-sized business cards read 'Societe de Bourse Fauchier Magnan Durant des Aulnois'. Silly me for not having heard of them.

I wondered where Monsieur Durant des Aulnois got all the bits to his surname. There had been something distinctly nouveau about him. His real name was probably Jean Dupont.

Fauchier Magnan seemed to accept my argument that now that everyone was cutting back their business to the Japanese, it was a good time to be getting counter-cyclical and setting one up. Privately, I thought while this theory was probably right in this instance it was wrong.

Going against the cycle can be just the thing to do. Buy when there is 'blood in the streets' as Nathan Rothschild used to urge. He was the man who bought on the rumour that Wellington had lost the Battle of Waterloo. To have bought during the 1987 crash, then again at the start of the 1991 Gulf War, then as the second aircraft plunged into the World Trade Centre in 2001, and again at the start of the second Gulf War would all, by and large, have been smart trades.

Doesn't always work. To have made money by buying the Nikkei index at 10,000 after it had fallen from 39,000 would have required immense patience. At the time of writing, a decade later, it's still 10,000, plus or minus a bit.

If you'd sold your house in 1988 while everyone else was in a frantic buying frenzy, by 1991 you'd have been feeling pretty smug. Especially witnessing the fate of the over-mortgaged, now-unemployed, such as me. If you'd stayed in rented accommodation much beyond that, you'd be feeling pretty stupid.

Messieurs Fauchier Magnan and Durant des Aulnois would have looked pretty stupid, in the context of the time, employing me. And with hindsight too. Anyway, they didn't.

Xavier confided afterwards that the two multi-barrelled Frenchmen had been quite impressed by me. He thought that the interview had gone quite well.

'Are you coming to Paris sometime?' I was asked.

Waste of time, I thought. Stockbroking partnerships like this were increasingly on the endangered list. They cared about costs because it was their own money. I'd have to pay my own flight and already I was beginning to become less careless with cash. Better to work for a brokerage owned by a bank; banks didn't understand brokers, but for some reason liked owning them. Costs spiralled accordingly, costs such as a salesman's pay and expenses.

Donald, the headhunter with the laughing inflection to his voice, rang. 'Hi, Jim, how's tricks?' He sounded over the moon to speak to me again. He told me to ring Cecil Butcher, at the aptly named Societe de Bourse Oddo, who were interested in someone with my qualifications. I vaguely knew

Cecil, he'd been at Vickers da Costa and also at Oxford with my Pratt Prize winning brother and future sister-in-law. She said Cecil was best known for the amazing ability to unclasp a girl's bra through the shirt with one deft flick. She found this supremely irritating. How you acquire such a skill is a mystery – hours of practice on a tailor's dummy, I suppose.

On the phone Cecil explained how he'd been out of work for three months. 'By the end of that my balls were burning. I was constantly told I was too old, too senior – at thirty-seven! I wouldn't fit in with younger people in a junior position. I wouldn't be satisfied, they all said. To me it wasn't a question of satisfaction, but one of survival. Are you coming to Paris sometime?'

I wondered which of the interviewing companies I would get to pay for the flight or, much better, whether I couldn't get them all to pay.

Verona's chum Xavier agreed to put me up for the night.

Coming in from the airport I had been struck by how clean and efficient the trains were and, in the Metro, how much better the buskers. No desultory Dylan-dirgers here. Am I the only person who thinks Bob Dylan is over-rated and a bit of a prat? Leaving London would be no wrench.

Xavier's flat was on the sixth floor of a building, more broker's garret than penthouse. About twenty-six, good looking, doing well and, despite his name, English. He was five years younger than Verona. He was clearly loving Paris. I thought it likely that Verona's trans-Manche link was doomed, being a combination of young man having fun in Paris and professional girl in her early thirties, hitting worries about the ticking of her menopausal clock.

In the evening we went to a party of young expatriate

Brits with a token French person or two and plenty of vying to affect the best French accents. Everybody seemed to love Paris and I decided, as if I needed persuading, that I wanted to live there too, away from London and its filthy streets, inefficient tubes and over-taxed booze.

I was all for staying at this party until the small hours, but Xavier was anxious about his early broker's start the next morning, so we left early. My attitude to such things had changed starkly. Getting out in the evening to escape my own company was becoming the most important part of the day for me. Previously, it had been to get home in time for a bit of play with Gen, then into bed by around ten so that I would not be falling asleep onto my screens at work the next day.

I got up at 10.45 for an 11.30 interview, followed by lunch chez Oddo. I would have liked a vat of good strong coffee to get me going, but remembered to hold off. My weak bladder and high metabolic rate had nearly been the death of my employment chances at Merrill Lynch. In fact my impatience had made me seem like a sharp negotiator, but I couldn't count on that a second time. Coffee was a substance that gave me a brief buzz before racing for freedom. Combined with interview nerves it could be quite disruptive. I also remembered not to drink water for the same reason. I badly needed some, because my head hurt from the night before, but knew that there was enough unmetabolised poison in my blood system for several trips to the pissoir and that it would be better if it remained unmetabolised.

The interview with Monsieur Oddo went quite well. Cecil was on my side because he knew me from Vickers da Costa days – fortunately not well enough to know how little I had done in business. I might have been similarly rumbled when he introduced me to another ex-colleague – a dealer from Scrimgeour Vickers – but we didn't recognise each other. I only twigged later.

In France I would be able to restart the whole cycle of selling myself, followed by selling the idea of my client base to the French (le Mur d'Argent arrive) right down to the point where it was discovered that le Mur d'Argent n'arrivera pas.

Monsieur Oddo was a pleasant enough fellow, who had just inherited his firm. He was about my age.

'Combien est-ce que vous gagniez?'

'Soixante mille livres.'

'Vous pouvez baisser un peu?'

Was I to have female clients only, I found myself wondering, before remembering that baisser means 'lower' not 'fuck' (that's baiser). As a partner in the family firm, he had a real interest in paying as little as possible.

I dodged the issue of pay by saying I had no idea of what people got paid in Paris or about the cost of living. Pay was the only serious question he asked me, there was nothing on my weaknesses or why I was made redundant, actual names of clients, how much business I'd bring in. It is strange how such people focus on what you should be paid but hardly ever ask what they would get for their money.

This 'interview' was followed by a very pleasant lunch with Cecil. Cecil talked entertainingly through the lunch and, although exposed for over an hour and a half to the possibility of saying something stupid, I was rarely given the chance.

Cecil, like Xavier, loved Paris. The cost of living back in those days was similar to London, some things more, some less costly. As Cecil put it, 'Cars, smoking, drinking, eating out, sex, anything enjoyable, cheaper. Groceries, clothes, petrol, housing, anything boring, more expensive.'

I was in Paris to get a job and, on the off chance someone might actually offer me one, there were things to weigh up. Saeko would like it. She'd no longer be able to torture me by making me watch her buy frocks at Joseph's in Sloane Avenue, but there'd be more than enough substitutes. This was the home of Vuitton and Hermès and no doubt others too, though 'Vuitton' and 'Hermès ' are roughly the extent of my French designers vocabulary.

I paid little attention to what I wore, clothes just didn't interest me. I was happiest in an old sweater riddled with holes and trousers that didn't show it when you wiped the dirt on them when cooking or gardening.

There was a danger, too, that I might not fit in France. A French girlfriend from my teens would always accuse me of wearing scruffy clothes on purpose with the aim of drawing attention to myself. She couldn't bring herself to believe that my protestations of innocence on this point weren't a fabrication. The truth is I that I'd been ahead of the fashion curve, unknowingly foreshadowing 'grunge' by a good fifteen years. I got it from Pongo Parton who'd been wearing combat trousers for years for his carpentry and gardening. Then the Spice Girls, All Saints, and stars like Robbie Williams copied him.

So would I be able to fall in with the Paris dress code? I had just about learnt to tolerate the City one, learnt its rules, sometimes the hard way. I once flirted with checked shirts, for example, as opposed to stripey ones. Perhaps my investment in a checked shirt was an act of sub-conscious rebellion deep from somewhere within. Just like I used to listen to classical symphonies instead of Genesis or Pink Floyd concept albums when at school. Never been a good sheep with peer pressure.

Though I succumbed to it sometimes. It was quite

common on a Friday afternoon for girls of the ilk of Fluff, Twiddles or Zara to come round City offices hawking (on commission) brogues and double cuffed shirts. After a good lunch you were always vulnerable and, given that these girls were always the sister of somebody on the dealing floor's best friend, peer pressure did the rest. They did a very healthy trade indeed.

One day I bought a checked shirt with double cuffs. I mentioned to a colleague at Phillips and Drew that I would wear it to the office. He said that if I did he would never speak to me again. This threat had no sanction – he wasn't someone I admired or was part of my sales team – but, even so, he was voicing what everyone else thought. I despise myself for the fact that I never did dare wear my checked shirt with double cuffs to the office.

Paris would be worse. At least in Japan, you're a foreigner, a *gaijin*, and by definition weird, so you can get away with a lot. I used to feel a duty to instil rebellion in the Japanese. One way was to jaywalk if the pedestrian light was red but no car coming. Until one day I did it in front of a little old lady, aged at least ninety. She was of a kind you see often in Japan, roughly half my height, small even without being diminished further by a lifetime of becoming bent double by sitting cross-legged at home or reaching down to plant rice seedlings in paddy fields. As I walked she gave me a dumb, trusting but confused look. The confusion must have led her to pause because by the time she went she almost stepped into the path of an oncoming car, before retreating back to behind the line where you are supposed to wait until the light goes green. She said nothing, but had a look of hurt and confusion, like a rabbit that has just been shot, is still alive and is trying to work out what went wrong, just before the eyes finally glaze over and the creature dies.

Disgusted at myself, I never jaywalked in Japan again.

The French and the Japanese have more in common than is realised. The French may not even obey traffic lights when driving, but their dress codes are as rigid as Japanese ones.

They have always had a closer affinity to the Japanese than us, whatever people say about island races. This dates from when the Impressionists were impressed by *Ukiyo-e* wood block prints, often carelessly used as wrapping paper round imported ceramics in the late nineteenth century. They love Japanese fashion houses like Comme ca Du Mode (with its modishly incorrect gender; it should be 'de la mode'), and the films of Kurosawa do even better in Paris than in Tokyo where everyone thought he was mad.

So Saeko would like it. She seemed to like Cannes enough (or was it Venice?). She'd resent my superior grasp of French, for a while, but she'd catch up, and Gen could become tri-lingual. Enough to satisfy any pushy parent. Rory's parents might struggle to deal with this.

I suppose my theory that the Japanese and French are slavishly conformist – while we British, starting with me, aren't – has its shortcomings. Go see all those creative media types in Soho; where before they used all to sport ponytails, now they all have shaven heads. Either look differentiates them from boring City technocrats like me, but are no less of a uniform than a stripey shirt.

Still, if I got a job in Paris, I could play the bluff, slightly eccentric Englishman at the same time as promising great things from my client base. 'Il est un peu fou, ce Rosbif, mais le Mur d'Argent arrive.'

I was careful not to eat or drink to much with Cecil as I still had a couple more meetings arranged for later in the afternoon and, after too much to food and alcohol, sleep and my overly-efficient bladder were the enemies. I said goodbye to him and wended my way.

Fauchier Magnan Durant des Aulnois was quite difficult to find, as had been Oddo. Both companies were behind discreet doors, I suppose on the same principle that the best brothels don't advertise. At neither was there an ostentatious atrium covering five floors, no designer logo, no brass plaque set in expensive marble. As in Japan, broking was a low status profession. The third sons of the aristocracy in Britain, having eschewed the Army or the Church might have aimed to become 'something in the City' but in France, indeed the rest of Europe, that was less likely.

Having identified the right door and walked up to a reception area without a receptionist, I found that the company was ill-prepared to interview me. It was Friday and the various Brits had either already gone for the weekend or were still at lunch, traditions lost in the City with the 1986 Big Bang and the arrival of all those lean hungry American banks (and the fat hungry Swiss ones). Encouraging. The fact that the weekend still started at about midday on Friday in Paris, was another persuasive, if not pivotal, reason for working there.

French broking partnerships were gradually going the way of British ones in selling out to banks. Broking used to be civilised; into work by half past nine, a long leisurely lunch, leave for home at half past four. In good years the rewards were spectacular, in bad ones the partners had to dig deep into their own pockets, mortgage their houses, pay the staff, and keep the firm afloat while waiting for the next up-turn in the economic cycle. This last happened in British brokerages in 1974 during the miners' strike and three-day week.

With banks in charge, pay was much more certain of remaining high but bore scant relationship to profitability.

French broking was already converging towards the British and American model. Days started too early and went on too late. But at least the institution of Friday lunchtime was still intact. As in London and New York or, for that matter, Tokyo, the extra hours would not lead to extra business, it was just a conformity thing, a further example of *Extraordinary Popular Delusions and the Madness of Crowds.*

This is the title of a seminal book by one Charles Mackay. Published in 1841, it demonstrates that collective lunacy and greed is no new phenomenon. He described the 17th Century Dutch speculation in tulip bulbs (Tulipomania) where a single rare tulip bulb got to be worth more than the farm on which it had been cultivated. Mackay would have recognised the phenomenon of Japanese stock and land speculation, as well as the dotcom wipe-out, though inexplicably he doesn't mention the contemporary fall in the price of Australian sheep from 60 shillings to 1. How did he miss that? The chapter on witch-hunts is as meaningful today as when written, as is that on the spread of popular expressions. One that he reported had caught the imagination in nineteenth century London was 'Has your mother sold her mangle?' These days I like the use of 'so', which I think we may have caught from the sitcom 'Friends', as in 'Jim Parton, you are so not a stockbroker...'

A copy of *Extraordinary Popular Delusions*...should be kept in everyone's loo along with the *Bible* (the *Koran* if you prefer), the *Complete Works of Shakespeare*, the *Oxford Book of English Verse* and a few tattered volumes of smutty jokes or limericks.

I digress (again). I was waiting for an interview at Fauchier Magnan Durant des Aulnois. Eventually someone arrived, we had a brief chat, I shook hands with one or two people whose names and significance I instantly forgot, said

'Hi,' to Xavier, exchanged greetings with Monsieur Durant des Aulnois and Monsieur Fauchier Magnan, and that was that. It scarcely merited the accolade interview.

At about four I squeezed in one more meeting with J.P. Morgan's Paris subsidiary. This was more like it. I travelled up seven floors of glass atrium in a restored Art Deco lift, just off the Place de l'Opera. I was kept waiting thirty minutes. It was now 4.30 in the afternoon, Friday, Paris, and they were still working. This was not the firm for me.

A sharp-suited Frenchman of the kind with degrees from both the Harvard Business School and the LSE grilled me for quarter of an hour, before visibly losing interest, and I was back on the street by five.

Never mind. The trip to Paris certainly appeared as though it might net me two jobs, and J.P. Morgan had looked far too much like the broking subsidiary of an American bank.

Back at Heathrow it was the usual story. Sunny in Paris, cloudy over the Channel, which only looks lovely from an aeroplane, raining at Heathrow, horrible from all angles. My mind was made up: Paris it would be.

CHAPTER 19

Money was holding out, although I was beginning budget a little more carefully. Not that I had ever been a big spender. Not interested in clothes, interested in cars only if they were company cars. Saeko didn't seem over-burdened with such considerations and conspicuous consumption remained the order of her day. Returning from her latest trip she was equipped with a new purchase of Charles Jourdan shoes. She was earning and I could hardly criticise. I was the one without a job.

I reckoned that I could visit the dole office without losing too much self-esteem. Alick had once remarked that he would never claim the dole, it would affront his dignity. My moral backbone was less stiff. I didn't exactly need the money, but what is National Insurance for if it doesn't actually mean insurance? Besides the forty quid a week would be a handy adjunct to my play money and maybe I could get the mortgage paid.

The Peckham DSS was a piece of 1970s council architecture surrounded by vandalised buildings. It was in a nicely laid out courtyard, but the flower beds were filled with weeds; the saplings planted in the late Seventies had clearly died in the early Eighties and not been cut down by the early Nineties.

A sign directed me upstairs to where I would be interviewed. A callow youth with a curtain ring through his nose – a 'client' I think, though he could have been staff – made it plain I was not to be allowed upstairs until he had barged me back down again with his mountain bike.

It looked a nice mountain bike and I could see why he had taken it upstairs with him rather than chain it to the saplings outside.

I joined a queue resembling a UN High Commission for Refugees' poster. Richard Claydermann-like Muzak tinkled softly overhead, which I would have thought would make the underclass more aggressive, not less, but then I don't manage the Peckham DSS office. I was unsure that was uglier, the music or a white woman with a shaven head and the obligatory nose ring. There was the odd older white man, with the resigned look of someone who has been there before: London Docker 1960s, car production line worker 1970s, Greater London Council cleaner 1980s. As a young man I was near the beginning of the cycle: stockbroker 1990s.

I was interviewed by a Ghanaian lady who, once she'd established I didn't need an interpreter, asked me accusingly why it had taken me a whole two months to start making my claim and warned that it was unlikely to be backdated. She asked me if I was doing any part-time jobs. There was paint on my fingernails from colouring in the mountains on the train set, so she probably thought I had been moonlighting. I was feeling generous, so I didn't really mind. In any case, she ought to have been able to tell me apart from her usual customer. I might not have shaved for five days but that was because I was an idle sod and not because I wanted to blend in with the surroundings.

The bald girl must have spent a considerable amount of time attacking her bald head with a razor every morning. One wondered why she didn't bother with her armpits. Don't understand the male head-shaving fashion either. Doing my face is bad enough without having to do the head as well.

I was given forms to take home and fill in to claim

community charge relief and income support. The deal sounded better and better.

Back home there turned out to be a little more small print than I had at first envisaged. My savings were still too great for me to qualify. If I paid off part of the mortgage to reduce the savings it would leave me with no money to pay the mortgage. Tricky.

A few days later several letters dropped through my front door. One was from the company car man, demanding payment of that outstanding parking fine.

20th June, 1991

Dear Mr Parton,
We are still waiting for payment of the outstanding moneys on your parking fine incurred on 19th December, 1990. Please send by return of post. We would warn you that unless you pay you will become liable for bailiff's costs (£90).
Yours sincerely,
The Nasty company car man at Merrill Lynch.

I binned it immediately.

There were also two letters from Paris. Both jobs had fallen through. At Fauchier they were unwilling to have their incomes diluted for the sake of the long term.

At Oddo they were just too disorganised to make a decision. A few weeks later I got a phone call from Cecil Butcher announcing that he had been laid off again and was back on the streets.

CHAPTER 20

I answered an ad in *The Times*. 'Career at a Crossroads? We will find the right job for you whether you are redundant or merely seeking a change. No obligation – first consultation free.'

I arrived at the door of a smart West End address and was ushered in to see a Mr Philip Tenison, mid-fifties, bug-eyed, domed head, well-spoken, smooth. We started with a discussion of my life so far. They had already ascertained what I had been earning from my telephone call and how much I'd been paid off, thereby, I suppose, working out what I could bear in the way of fees. I was amazed at how easily I – and presumably lots of other people – gave out such private information.

He glanced through the CV to establish my pedigree. 'Of course we will produce a more professional CV for you. We only take on clients where we are sure there is a future – it is a waste of our time and their money to take on no-hopers,' he said sanctimoniously. The fact that his business was booming, with guilty employers paying out-placement agencies to 'counsel out' staff they were trimming, presumably helped them to be so selective. 'In your case, James, I emphatically believe that you are the kind of person we can help fulfil his potential.' Flattery – a standard sales technique. I had often used it myself.

I wondered why a well-spoken man of fifty-five like himself was doing a job like this. Presumably his own career had been at a crossroads in the not too distant past.

He had all the answers, without really saying anything.

It was a bit like reading your horoscope in a mid-market tabloid. Whichever star sign you read, it is drawn broadly enough to apply to virtually anyone.

'What you need James, I can tell, is a charismatic leader.'

My God, how true, I thought, how did he work that out? It was like saying, 'On Thursday the moon will be in conjunction with Mars and you will experience an event to disrupt your domestic tranquillity.' Well quite, I had an argument with my wife virtually every day. Even if I didn't, because she was in Venice (or was it Cannes), some other catastrophe was bound to happen, like dropping my toast butter side down.

Some of what he said did make sense.

Only twenty per cent of jobs are advertised and a good proportion of those only because statute or company rules say they have to be; even so, often somebody has been lined up for them already. The advert is just going through the motions. His promise was to help me target the unadvertised jobs market. He would also help me develop my networking skills.

Networking skills? What are they? You ring up acquaintances, even distant ones, and ask their advice. You don't say, 'I'm redundant, can you help me get a job?' Which may not even incite sympathy, because you become an instant burden to the person you are talking to. Or, if they were sympathetic, it would be the wrong kind of sympathy, the pitying, patronising kind where they couldn't look you in the eye. The kind you might get if you told someone you were fatally ill.

On the other hand, if asked advice, they are flattered, and although the acquaintance may not be able to help, he may know someone who can, so you string him along until he introduces you to someone nearer your Target Area (definitely said with capital letters). By the time you are onto the third person in the chain you are probably within your T.A. and talking to someone in a position to interview you for a job. If you are introduced, even as the friend of a friend of a friend, it is much more likely they will agree to see you, even if it is only to give some kindly advice as to where it would be better to look.

A further advantage is that you have by-passed the personnel department. I had always thought it important to miss out personnel departments in the City and Mr Tenison explained that it was just as important outside the City. Personnel or Human Resources or Executive Search departments or whatever you want to call them have the job of filtering people out rather than in. Filling in the application form, he said, is delayed as long as possible, preferably only completed once the job is in the bag. Job application forms are negative documents designed to weed you out, not weed you in.

Mr Tenison was talking my language. Personnel people are not at the coal face, doing a proper job. Good ones (from their own point of view) create bureaucracies round themselves. Soon they hire themselves an assistant, if not two, with a view to being at the top of a pyramid. It's Parkinson's Law in action (*Parkinson's Law* is the best business book ever written – should be in everyone's loo next to the *Bible* or the *Koran*, the *Oxford Book of English Poetry* and *Railway Modeller*). Professor C. Northcote Parkinson observed that there were more civil servants in the War Office than ratings in the Royal Navy. The current exemplar of his law is the National Health Service, where there are more bureaucrats than doctors and nurses. Can't last.

Partnerships are relatively immune to the Law – it's the

owners' money – but at banks that have bought brokerships you can build a nice little empire.

Parkinson's Law is actually several laws. One that applies to the City, indeed all business, is the one where institutions that acquire a big show-off headquarters – these days it would be glass atriums filled with incomprehensible sculpture or bits of rain forest – are at the start of terminal decline. 25 Ropemaker Place, Merrill Lynch's HQ – where I'd worked – had rain forest. As you went up the glass lifts in the atrium and looked down at it, you reflected that what the trees needed, above all, was rain. The leaves were choked with dust, and whilst from below the large *ficus benjaminus* trees looked great, from above they looked as if they'd been uprooted from a favela in Sao Paolo.

Hector Sants at UBS Phillips and Drew once told me they'd costed real plants against plastic ones and gone for plastic. 'Saves about £10,000 a year.' I wonder what job title the personnel department had given the person who worked out this important fact.

The managers who think they can save themselves work by farming out recruitment to personnel soon discover that they spend just as much time filling in forms and answering memos. If they are not concentrating, they will be taken in and get the impression that the personnel department is doing really good work and thank their lucky stars that they have one to save them so much labour. The skilful 'human resources' director will tread a fine line between over-loading managers at the coal face, and creating work for them to demonstrate how indispensable he (or more likely she) is. Perhaps that's why we didn't see much of Hector.

Mr Tenison and I had been talking for forty-five minutes. This level of service, in this level of premises from a professional man only a little short of twice my age could not come cheaply, that was for sure. I asked myself how many sales he needed to make a week to justify his existence and what his cut was. He would have to be working on commission, not salary; I could tell that from the intensity of the spiel.

I was not being pressurised to make up my mind there and then, however. Indeed, Mr Tenison assured me that he didn't believe in the hard sell: 'That would be very unprofessional.' Now was not the time to make a decision, he told me. I should sleep on it and, above all, consult with my wife and explain to her how the Tenison Method (more capital letters) would work for me. I could see the logic behind that; nagging wives would have been an important part of his commercial equation. He'd pick up a lot of business from men pressurised into 'doing something' by wives fed up with having them moping around the house.

If Mr Tenison had known my domestic set-up, he might have suggested I got Mr Gibbon in on the act too. Saeko – he'd picked the name up from somewhere, and, consummate professional that he was, was pronouncing it correctly ('psycho') – and I were also to discuss together what breed of dog I most resembled as an aid to the analysis of my character. Mr Tenison said that he would do the same and that almost invariably he would come up with the same breed as us.

The next day a bit more was explained. The first ten days would be spent with a psychologist and a counsellor who between them would work out my strengths and failings and come up with my Key Unique Abilities, My Ambitions, My Opportunities, otherwise known by the somewhat unwieldy acronym, as my K.U.A.M.A.M.O. list. This sounded to me more like a Central African anti-colonial guerrilla organisation than the key to a successful career, but I was prepared to listen. I think the more usual acronym is U.S.P. (unique selling point) but I guess K.U.A.M.A.M.O. gave a bit of brand differentiation.

A jolly little flow diagram was produced with arrows leading to various boxes centring on 'YOU'. This would yield information, which we would use to Target (this word was used rather a lot) certain areas of human endeavour that suited me. We would conduct an Examination of the Total Job Market and then devise a Marketing Campaign. It sounded splendid. We would use my networks and also we would be aware of which newspapers carry what job adverts on what days.

He had started saying 'we' rather than 'you'.

Ultimately we were going to find my Ideal Job and negotiate a high salary; once the Target Company had recognised my Key Unique Abilities it would not want to lose me and would cough up large to retain me. Wunderbar!

What dog had I decided I most resembled? The train set, garden or piano had intervened and I had clean forgotten to engage in this fun little exercise and not given the matter any consideration at all. I was also supposed to have asked Saeko. If I had ever got her to answer she might have said something like the offspring of an Old English sheepdog and a passing stray, which nobody saw, ten brought up on a very muddy farm.

If I were to do the same exercise in reverse, because Pekinese and Chow would have had unfair racial overtones, I would say something like King Charles spaniel.

Was the congress of two such disparate animals likely to be a success? This is what these days is called a F.A.Q., (fuck-yous, I call them) a Frequently Asked Question. 'Do you experience cultural difficulties in your marriage?' Well, you had to feel sorry for the King Charles spaniel, but on his day – not many lately – the farm dog of uncertain provenance had had a ball. Phwooar!

Mr Tenison had decided that I was like an Afghan. Sleek, smooth, physically energetic.

Surely some mistake. Unless he was trying to tell me that if I wanted to get a job I had let my standards slip a bit and should get a hair-cut first. I wondered if he ever described potential clients as pit bull, Chihuahua, poodle, Rhodesian ridgeback or Yorkshire terrier. Physically energetic maybe, sleek, smooth never. Flattery – standard sales technique.

The meeting was winding down. It had all been terribly upbeat. I would achieve my Long-Term Objectives. I would love my job, operate at my Full Potential, be stretched and challenged, be recognised as a High Achiever by colleagues, be self-motivated, Implement or Affect company policy, be proud of my organisation, be surrounded by intellectually stimulating people, socially and culturally (which would make a change from the City), and best of all my wife would adore me because I would come home so satisfied that I would be in a permanent haze of contentment and become an (even more) wonderful husband. My satisfaction would enable me to satisfy her.

Phew, what could this job be – personal sex therapist to Madonna? These days I'd say J-Lo. When could I start? How could I use my network to get this job?

I thought about it. I have a cousin who is cricket correspondent on the *Daily Mail*: he'd have a mate on the pop pages, who'd have a chum in New York intimate with Madonna. All I then would have to do was prove myself the possessor of an enormous organ of inexhaustible tumescence and I'd be away. On second thoughts…am I alone in thinking that Madonna is not even slightly sexy and a grotesquely uninteresting performer?

Now Kylie, on the other hand...

A bit short for me probably. Said to be under five foot. Great bum, though.

Mr Tenison leant back in his chair, the orbs in his sockets bulged, hands were rubbed together. He then leant forward again, a column of ash was knocked off his Panatela. We were getting down to the nitty-gritty. There was not much he could say to disguise the fact that this one would cost £5,500, in instalments, with no money-back guarantee if I failed to get a job.

'We don't offer a guarantee; if you are prepared to pay, it means you are serious and you are more likely to be committed. As I said before, we don't deal with no-hopers,' he said, making it sound as if not offering a guarantee was for my own good. 'But remember, there is no need to make up your mind now. We do no hard sell here. That would be most unprofessional.' He was beginning to repeat himself.

Doing no hard sell must have been tough for him; the fundamental rule of salesmanship is that having Created the Desire, you have to Close the Sale. Perhaps he had spotted that desire was not something with which I was over-burdened. Or perhaps 'professional' products like these have to be left with the potential client for a bit. I don't know; I never was much good at sales.

And yet, as I have discovered, life is sales. For me, they're no fun, yet it is hard to get away from them. There now follows a sales pitch: please recommend this book to all your friends. Indeed I will send a signed copy with bespoke dedication for just £xx.xx inc. postage and packing (see inside back cover for details).

For the first time Mr Tenison looked slightly ill at ease. He squeezed his hands together and hunched his shoulders as he said, 'I want you to go home and discuss this with Saeko,' giving me the sheaf of glossy papers with 'K.U.A.M.A.M.O.' and 'YOU' written on them, dotted with expressions like Full Potential, High Achiever and Personal Life Goal Attainment.

'The question is', he continued, 'not "Can you afford it?", it is "Can you afford not to do it?". You have some redundancy money, do you have any savings?'

I was buggered if I was going to admit to savings, so I answered, 'No, afraid not.'

'Would Merrill Lynch pay for it?' I think that the abortive attempt at suing them had put paid to that one.

'We can also help you with a government interest free loan. They ask you to chip in something yourself, but will pick up the rest. We usually find that our costs are comfortably met by the extra salary we help you to negotiate', he was looking more comfortable again now, 'and we also find that our clients get back to work quicker than people who don't use us. Often by several months.'

What a ghastly thought, I thought.

Nonetheless, I could see it was quite a compelling sales line. He was making out that, although the service cost £5,500, it was free really.

As he like saying 'We do no hard sell here. That would be most unprofessional'.

Mr Tenison wouldn't quite let his Marty Feldman-like orbs meet mine as we shook hands on parting. I thought that he suspected he'd lost his man, which, I reflected, as I walked away, he probably had. £5,500! With all my spare time, if I couldn't supply £5,500 worth of job-hunting effort myself,

I was a hopeless case, besides which, he'd pretty much told me how to do it.

Saeko was of the same opinion. 'Don't waste your money, Jim', and was kind enough to add, 'because you haven't got any.'

I would have been happier if she'd said 'we' like Mr Tenison. His cut? 20% on £5,500? For two hours of spiel. There was a recession on, big banks were feeling guilt, out-placement agencies were booming, he'd bounce back. If he made just two sales a week and otherwise wasted his time with people like me, it was still not a bad living really. Almost as good as a stockbroker.

CHAPTER 21

The sun was shining and the weather in the month of May was promising a good summer. It was the time of year when cricket starts to come back on the wireless. The train set was absorbing and growing. Gen and Rory, a bit of a handful when together, were still delightful in their way. I picked up a brace of long-range water pistols for them from the car-boot sale to encourage in them a healthy interest in boyish things like guns, and to help undermine Rory's mum. Try as she might, she'd never get her son ever to play with a Barbie doll.

Cowboys are good, Red Indians are bad. Such life certainties had gone out of the window. Now it was cowboys are bad because they kill good Indians. Native Americans are a protected species and Manhatton should be given back to the Algonqui.

I taught Gen and Rory how to choose which of them was the baddy. 'Eeny, meeny, miny, mo, catch a ...' a pause was forced on me as the enormity of what I was about to say dawned. '...rabbit by the toe,' said Rory, completing the rhyme.

Saeko, I think, would have liked to see me getting out of the house more. She was not someone given to short phone calls and I was getting under feet, but the money was holding up reasonably well – she was earning some – so redundancy was not too bad. I was doing most of the child-care and thinking I could handle being a houseworking husband.

Against this idyllic background were those intrusive visits to the City for interviews. The City's mediaeval street plan permits little light penetration into its orifices, still less its offices. Those buildings that do benefit from the direct incidence of the sun's rays shield them out with Venetian blinds, and modern architects for some reason have a preference for recycled air and windows that don't open. I am sure that Sick Building Syndrome really does exist. All that recycled air and artificial light, it can't be good for you.

Two large IRA bombs had given the City fathers an exciting planning opportunity that they seemed to have passed over. For a period after each bomb you could walk in certain City streets and hear the sound of footsteps as opposed to traffic. Rather nice, and something that Londoners had not experienced for nearly 100 years. (This was before the introduction of the congestion charge.) In the morning the clip of feet on pavement was more purposeful, with no one talking, as the owners of the feet headed for another day's wage-slavery. In the evening, the steps were slower and people would be talking to each other on the way home. Some permanent large open green spaces with no cars would not only have made the City more pleasant but also might have helped the commercial property market by creating a space shortage.

Gen called me across to corner in the garden, where he had turned over a stone and discovered a lot of slithering fauna. 'A good metaphor for the City,' I murmured.

'What's a metaphor, Dad?'

I was now roughly three months out from under the stone and had already begun feeling like a bit of an outsider. Meetings with committed, hard-working potential employers continued, but such people had no sparkle in their eyes. If you look at someone's eyes it is always a give away; City people, even as they tell you, with genuine enthusiasm, about dynamic thrusting strategies for opening up such and such a market, say it with joyless eyes, no sparkle. The only sparkle is in their champagne glasses.

I knew this and my spell of redundancy was waking me up to LIFE. 'What's the point of working in the City if you don't get paid obscene amounts for it?' My failure to get a job so far was making it clear to me that the amount of money I was going to get was getting less obscene by the moment. No longer would I be vying with the Chancellor of the Exchequer on the pay front. Maybe only a mere member of parliament.

Money can't buy happiness, I reflected. Many of the rich are unhappy, whilst carefree alcoholics loll in cardboard boxes under Waterloo Bridge, foot-loose, fancy-free, have no responsibilities, pay no rent, mortgage or tax and are beholden to no one.

On second thoughts, this somewhat romantic view that the rich are not happy is nonsense. One over-paid executive of my acquaintance, who was in the Japanese warrant market (hope he got out in time – that market is now defunct), put it as follows: 'I'd far prefer to be rich and unhappy than poor and unhappy. Of course, best of all is being both rich and happy.'

Almost everyone in the City starts with the idea that they would do the job for ten years, say, then, fortune in hand, jack it all in and do something worthwhile and life-enhancing, using the vast sums of money they have put aside for that very purpose. Few start off as 'lifers'. The problem is that few of us managed the discipline of saving for the early retirement fund. Once you have a stock-broker's mortgage, kids in private schools, ex and current wife with chronic HAV+, a taste for sitting next to celebs at smart West End Clubs, you are trapped in a gilded cage. I consider myself lucky to have had the choice forced on me – I'd never have had the courage to make it for myself.

In the mid-1980s, just before I entered the City, the British government had decided to allow the barriers between different types of financial institution to be relaxed. Banks had not been allowed to be stockbrokers and stockbrokers themselves had either to have been agents (that is to say advisors on commission) or jobbers (dealers who got to own the shares briefly while buying and selling).

The Big Bang, as it was called, happened in 1986, when I'd been in the City about six months. Prices were generally not on screens but had to be obtained by ringing up your man down on the Stock Exchange floor. Laurence Prust sent me down there for a month or two as part of my training. I had to wear a blue badge to denote my lowly status, a humble 'Blue Button', only allowed to run errands and ask prices from the jobbers, not authorised to deal.

Mainly East End barrow boys, the jobbers would see me coming, detect a certain polite public school nervousness and say the price so quickly that I'd have to ask it again. And again. That would give them the excuse they needed to insult me for being slow and stupid.

The worst thing was ringing up for prices early morning from the Laurence Prust box. You'd get a stream of twenty prices, read out at top speed. Having missed half of them you were confronted with the dilemma of admitting as much to your hardened dealer colleagues or ringing back the jobber to hear them again and enduring impatient mockery. At LP there was one kind officer class sort of man who took a paternal interest in me, he was known as 'Bungalow' by all the jobbers, on account of having nothing upstairs. This may or may not have been fair but at least he was kind.

The Stock Exchange floor died a year or so after Big Bang. Prices moved onto screens – thank goodness you didn't have to ask for them – and the jobbers, now all working for integrated broking houses owned by banks, sat in offices and did their 'Buy, Buy; Sell, Sell' routine into the phone and are now called 'market-makers'.

In the run up to the event nearly all London's broking partnerships had sold themselves out to the likes of NatWest and Barclays. Culturally, such banks were prudent and entirely risk-averse, but with Big Bang they had been sucked into the loadsamoney Thatcherite boom, creating an unseemly rush to buy even second tier brokers like Laurence Prust (acquired by Credit Commercial de France).

This should have been a leading indicator of future trouble, like the 1987 Crash. You have to acknowledge that when it came to selling themselves out, the brokers timed it beautifully and sold for a fantastic price.

One of the few partnerships left, the American house Goldman Sachs, waited more than a decade before selling themselves out. They were right at the top of the market when they floated. There was a hiccup that made the market dip briefly but they held their nerve and, again – leading indicator – did it beautifully.

I know of a former partner at Goldman Sachs who used to get £20 million bonuses. He has a big house with swimming pool in Knightsbridge, and a castle with private beach frontage in Tuscany. So why does he still work? 'I couldn't possibly afford to stop,' he says. 'Have you any idea how much it costs to run a Learjet?'

Well, there's afford and afford. I've huge respect for the few who do make the decision that they can get by on a lower income. One of my closest friends in Tokyo, Hugh Canaway, did throw it all in a little after I was made redundant. A stock analyst at Baring Securities, he had spent the whole morning with a client who was fund manager to a portion of the Sultan of Brunei's billions. This fund manager having, as stated, billions at his disposal, was a Very Important Client. Just a small part of the business he could dish out would have a big impact on Hugh's employability and Baring's profitability – then suffering from such foolish decisions as the flashy move into an excessive amount of prime office space in a new building right at the peak of Japan's property bubble. (You'd think that these brokers – who make their livings advising everyone from Scottish Widows to the vast United Nations staff pension fund or the Sultan Of Brunei on how and when to invest – would avoid mistakes like this).

The man from the Sultanate had scant understanding of the principles of investment, recounts Hugh. In addition, he was monolingual, and that language was not English or Japanese, which Hugh speaks very well. Hugh began to ask himself what he was doing with his life, going through the motions, but not understood at all by this financial troglodyte to whom he was trying to explain the intricacies of the Japanese property market. ('Very simple, sell everything you've got, you git.')

Lunchtime came. Hugh left the fund manager in the hands of the salesman and went off to do his daily workout in the gym.

It must be something about all those executive treadmills. There is no scenery, beyond, if you are lucky, the bum of the girl on the machine in front, nothing to do on the treadmill but think. Hugh thought.

'Life is passing me by. Dear God, can I have another

one, please?'

'No mate, that's yer lot.'

An actual parting of clouds and accompanying thunderclap was not necessary to convince him of the truth of this.

Like everyone, Hugh had resignation fantasies and had even had thoughts as to how he might cope. 'The grass is greener' syndrome is met by the balancing fear that, over the hedge or the hill, the greener looking grass might conceal a bog or a nest of snake. Then there's that Learjet to maintain (not in Hugh's case). Good sense, or more accurately, cowardice, usually stops the leap into the unknown. At least in broking there is the compensation of being rich whilst unhappy.

Hugh, on a whim, returned from lunch and resigned, just like that. He resigned to Richard Greer, the same bloke I'd met six years before, the one with the grown-up-under-a-flowerpot pallor, who had assessed my character (correctly) as flippant, and wisely not employed me.

Greer was surprised at Hugh's action, but made no attempt to stop it. Hugh had been in Tokyo five years and was, thus, expensive to employ. It was not just the salary, but the sumptuous apartment in a *gaijin* enclave, the fact that the company was paying his income tax, the whole sought after 'overseas package'. That awkward gap between revenues and outgoings, created by market slump and the move into the new office building, would close fractionally.

It would be reassuring to think that I, too, had shown Hugh's courage to put your life and health before greed and money and just chucked it all in. Then I could look the world smugly in the face, replete with a feeling of manly, sanctimonious virtue: 'I am a big man, I have conquered material desire, I am a survivor.' I would like to think that Hugh, out of sheer admiration, took his lead from me. But he didn't.

The truth is that I was done first. Done by the commercially astute people of Merrill Lynch, who realised with commendable rapidity that the high hopes that had been pinned on me had been a mistake.

I had been indolently casting alternatives around in my head, but in my heart of hearts, I knew I did not really want to become a widget salesman, anymore than I had originally wanted to be an equity salesman when I drifted into the City upon my return from Japan.

OK, so I could speak Japanese, which had to be worth something to somebody. It is a sad fact that most people are dissatisfied with their jobs, in all walks of life. Most people have jobs, not careers. I once met a household name BBC presenter, in a job for which many would kill. She was bored and looking for something new but couldn't find it.

Completely opting out of the rat race, perhaps by buying a yacht and sailing around the world, is one solution. As a student back-packer I made several three-month trips to places like Peru, India and China. On these trips you'd meet people who'd opted out and gone on the road. They became objects for admiration, emulation and envy; I, too, would never get caught in a rut, life was too short, I would be like them. They had spent their time visiting uplifting places, seeing colourful people, eating interesting food. If they came across something particularly diverting, they could settle down for several weeks, even months, and get under its skin. Perhaps have a searing beach romance with a mulatto maiden before moving on.

The trouble is, though, that after the brave decision to be beholden to no one, few of them became a Paul Theroux or a Bruce Chatwin. The others somehow manage to become bored by the cycle of beautiful sites and peoples and teaching English to hopeless foreign businessmen to finance the next trip.

Dharamsala is one such place, the home of the Dalai Lama, where there is all this white trash, left over from the 1970's hippy trail, the ones who opted out and never went home. Quite a sad bunch.

Occasionally there is one who has kept his dignity; I met an Englishman in Bolivia whose 40kg pack contained two lead crystal wine glasses. He groaned under the weight of his belongings, but he could lay them round his room (or tent, he had one of those in there too), put up a picture or two and call it home.

But in general such people develop mean-spirited obsessions with finding the cheapest hotel, the best exchange rate, where to sell your whisky on the black market, and not being ripped off by the dirt-poor natives. They become arrogant about tourists as opposed to travellers, as well towards the locals. In short, intolerant of their fellow man. They become bored with their freedom, which is surely a worse corruption than being bored with your highly-paid City job.

Saeko got obvious enjoyment from her job. If the Japanese were lashing out on a documentary overseas, the team would tend to be top-notch, so she'd spend a lot of time with people at the summit of their professions not only in TV but also in the subject of the documentary she was making. Thus, one evening, she might be out at dinner with the director of the British Museum, having spent the day filming artefacts that the public don't see, and having them explained by the world's leading expert. The next day she could be hobnobbing with Kurosawa. More interesting, some would say, than being Merrill Lynch's market strategist.

I confess to a ferocious envy of her job satisfaction, but was not too keen on the attitude towards stockbrokers that went with it. Media types, writers, artists, actors somehow manage to occupy the moral high ground, both believing and being believed that what they do is more worthwhile than what stockbrokers or advertising execs do.

I remember being taken to see a play, in which real homeless people acted alongside actors. The homeless were trendy at the time. Saeko and a photographer friend dragged me along. It was good, moving even. But somehow I was made to feel guilty, as if their homelessness was my fault.

The photographer asked whether the experience might change the way I voted. One or two assumptions made there, I thought. She was a young and apparently an up-and-coming arty photographer, with an acclaimed exhibition of photos, predominantly of scenes in Albania, where she'd snapped peasants stacking hayricks. I couldn't myself see what moral high ground she felt she was occupying. Taking pictures of Albanian hayricks is not obviously more worthwhile than helping shunt capital around the globe.

Somewhat the reverse. All that capital shunting has the effect of rewarding efficient companies with higher share prices, so they can raise more money more cheaply to invest in new factories or offices or whatever to create jobs, some of which could be filled by unemployed and homeless people.

An imperfect system that goes spectacularly wrong sometimes, but if the shunters of capital were not doing the job with reasonable efficiency, there would be no spare cash in the economy for people to go off and do things of no economic value whatsoever, like photographing Albanian hayricks from picturesque angles (or write books).

People who make their living out of photographing Albanian hayricks are every bit as parasitic as brokers or advertising execs or consultants (or writers). Not that I mean to criticise her for being a parasite. Nothing wrong with that. Just the 'holier than thou' sanctimonious attitude that goes with it.

If my thinking was moving away from not only stocks but also widgets, it had nothing to do with any rejection of my loadsamoney values. I like money, preferably loads of it. If I could find the option whereby it was possible to be both well paid and content, I'd go for it. The two are not mutually exclusive as the hayrick person seemed to imagine.

The thought that life was slipping by was naggging at me. Can I have another one? 'No mate, that's yer lot.' The reader is bound to guess at some point that part of the denouement of this book is that its writer solved his dilemma by becoming a writer.

The inspiration came to me as I drove back from a game of cricket in which I had scored my usual three runs and taken my usual no wickets (as well as spilling a humiliatingly easy catch). My mum had recommended to me a book by an advertising executive who'd cashed in his chips and gone to live in Provence, thereby doing what every City worker would have liked to have done. Peter Mayle's *A Year in Provence* became a stonking great best-seller.

Most of my great thoughts occur to me in the car, which is awkward for a writer. People stare at me talking to myself at traffic lights or they used to before the advent of hands-free mobile phones, since when everyone has appeared to be talking to themselves. Being in the car and thus away from paper, most of my great thoughts get forgotten in the car, too, but this one remained with me.

Life isn't like that. Virtually no one sells out at the top and moves off to live a fulfilling life of bucolic simplicity and contentment in Provence. In fact, if you read the cover notes carefully, you realise that Peter Mayle had given up advertising some fifteen years before and had been writing for that long before the big bestseller. Long out of print and best forgotten titles like *The Wicked Willy* books.

Not that there is anything wrong with being out of print. Perfectly respectable, as I have subsequently discovered. But I thought that I would tell it as it really is. How it is really rather pleasant actually, floating around home and garden doing nothing very much at all.

There is another book which gives an incorrect impression of life as it really is or was, with a City angle, called *Liar's Poker* by Michael Lewis. It is a slightly maddening book, because Lewis seems genuinely to have lost the need to earn millions and settled down to write a book. And wrote a bestseller. You'd think that one bout of success would be enough.

Hugh once introduced me to another Baring Securities stock analyst called Mark Coutts-Smith who had thrown it all in to do what he considered worthwhile – in his case to help manage the overseas tours of a troupe of Japanese drummers, while indulging a passion for photography. This involved living on the Isle of Sado, off Niigata in North East Japan, being paid very little, getting up even earlier in the morning than brokers do, one way and another living the ascetic life. Not my cup of cha (a Japanese word, incidentally), but I can happily plug his book, *Children of the Drum* which has some spectacular photos in it.

The drummers are the practitioners of Kodo – which loosely translates as the Way of the Drum, just as Ju-do means The Gentle Way, though it never looks gentle as they twist each other into the do-ho (the place of The Way). These drummers have amazingly muscled torsos, which make Linford Christie look weedy, and wear a traditional form of Japanese jock-strap, the name of which escapes me.

Before he had made his life-change, Mark had had the task of ushering Michael Lewis, in his post-broking shackle-free existence, round Tokyo, while he researched his latest book. To Mark, Lewis was just another boring client, rather pleased with himself, which scarcely made him stand out from other clients or visitors from head office in London (like Nick Leeson). Such visitors come to Tokyo once or twice a year and expect to be shown a good time. But if, like Mark, you have to show a good time to two or three of these people a week, the all-smiling-package-tour-guide act palls, particularly if you are just hanging on for that final bonus before heading off to Sado.

When Leeson did his little tour of the Baring Tokyo office, on his way from London to Singapore, from where, of course, he single-handedly wrecked the bank, his passage was barely noticed. When he brought the bank down it was 'What? Him?'

Followed by 'Who?'

Then 'You know, that little chap with glasses...'

'Which one?'

'Well, him anyway.'

To Mark, Michael Lewis was getting in the way of a potentially productive date with a Japanese girl. Mr Lewis kept on dropping remarks like 'As I said in my book...' or 'I think I identified that problem in my book'. Mark was thoroughly used to clients having their own theories about things and equally used to taking no notice of them. He failed to ask 'What book?' and then go on to say 'Are YOU the author of *Liar's Poker*?!?' with suitably more explanation marks, which I can't bear to print. The author of *Liar's Poker* became visibly more irritated by the moment, imagining himself to be – one can only speculate – the victim of a piss-taking exercise.

In fact this was far from the case. Normally a man with a lively sense of humour, Mark was so jaded by his profession he could not even be bothered to take the piss out of it. About to join his troupe of jock-strapped drummers, he had long given up reading any remotely business-oriented books, however funny, and had not therefore read *Liar's Poker*; moreover, his broker's antennae were so ill-tuned (because switched off) that he had failed to hear of it either. (Mark tells me has now read *Liar's Poker* and enjoyed it, as you can't fail to do.)

Much of this was going through my mind as I approached home in the car on the way back from my cricket match. Being out for a duck and taking no wickets was forgotten. I would write a book to put the record straight: most City and Wall Street types are thoroughly run-of-the-mill chaps like you (or me). Television images of young men in bright red braces snapping 'BUY, BUY…SELL, SELL' into three telephones simultaneously give a false image. If only it was like that, then it would be fun.

More crashes, that would be excellent. I might still be a broker.

Most of the time, like war, it's bloody boring. There is even a photo of me in the 1988 Citicorp worldwide company report looking young, fresh-faced, poised over my screen, talking into a phone. Don't remember the picture being taken, but I must have been posing. A friend spotted another one of me in *The Times*, striding purposefully in my pin-stripe past letters cut into a granite wall, reading *Stock Exchange*. Late for my lunch-time sandwich, probably.

That young man in a stripey shirt and Armani shades in his convertible Porsche next to you at the traffic lights. OK, so he's doing well for his age, earning a multiple of what you earn and not worth it. If you are the envious sort, then to be told his job is boring and he'd like to chuck it in is no compensation. Better to be rich and unhappy, than poor and unhappy. The way to deal with it is to reflect that his good fortune or rather great fortune is not your bad fortune, it is just the way life's cookie crumbled. Envy is a pretty unattractive trait. Though I envy Michael Lewis his success with *Liar's Poker*.

If that sounds too much like a sermon, then content yourself with the thought that if the man needs to flaunt his success he is almost certainly compensating for a tiny willy or some personality defect, which is why he is doing so well.

Saeko had been in Venice (or was it Cannes?). When she came back I told her that I was no longer going to look for jobs – I was going to write a book. She affected delight. 'You always hated broking,' she said. 'I am glad you have found something you want to do.' What else could she say, with all those friends taking meaningful pictures of Albanian hayricks? I would be becoming one of them.

CHAPTER 22

I volunteered to become a house husband. Although she treated the idea as a joke, that wasn't the way I meant it. I could look after Gen while she visited Cannes (or Venice). For some reason the idea didn't appeal. These days, post-Lady Di, a new syndrome has been identified and specialists can make a diagnosis. But in the early nineteen- nineties the word 'shopaholic' was yet to be coined, so I wasn't conscious of my redundancy constituting any threat to Saeko's mental health`?

Redundancy had its compensations: the garden, the lack of the daily grind, the tyranny of the Sunday business pages or that terrible feeling on Sunday evening of what I had failed to achieve in the too short weekend. Who wants to read about merger and acquisition activity on their day off? I had always been in a BAD MOOD of a Sunday night, tense about getting to work on Monday to spend a week being unfulfilled.

But I was getting under Saeko's feet, no question. I was not too despondent about my redundancy, being by nature an optimistic kind of person, but may well have been less fun to have around than I might have been. It is probable that in similar circumstances not a few marriages bite the dust. Also, the financial noose was beginning to tighten, and just as the alcoholic has his secret gin bottle, Saeko had her secret Hermès catalogue.

We were having the odd row and a lot of stony silences. At one point I did feel induced to make the jibe, 'This is not such a bad time to get divorced: I'm not earning any money.'

Saeko was a lovely girl. Intelligent, funny, beautiful but, to coin a word, *foibled* she was, too: intolerant, tempestuous, a bloody nightmare to live with.

I reflected on how we had met. It was on a train, a forty minute hop between Kyoto and Osaka, in about 1984. An attractive girl of about nineteen sat next to me. I would have been twenty-four. I was impressed because Japanese girls tend to be a bit shy of sitting next to foreigners on trains. The seat next to the foreigner is nearly always the last to fill and sometimes remains empty even on crowded trains. Not racism, just social awkwardness. Handy for big foreigners who like to occupy two seats.

I looked over the girl's shoulder at her Filofax (Britain's great fashion export of the era), in which she was checking something. She had a date to see a film called *An Office and a Gentleman*. As English teacher and cultural ambassador I felt it a duty to point that it should be 'officer'. We got along famously and at the end of the journey exchanged telephone numbers.

We saw each other once, but nothing came of it. She was too busy, or couldn't be lured out and subverted by a foreigner on the make. I never quite forgot about her, though.

Then, by chance, I met her again in a book shop. We chatted for a while before she disappeared from my life for a few more months. But I kept on meeting her by chance, found her enchanting and, in crowded Osaka, with its ten million or more inhabitants, the odds against such chance meetings were so great that the relationship somehow began to seem 'meant'.

We began to meet on purpose. There was the odd hitch, like she got adult chicken-pox and I thought I was being fobbed off, but anyone less ardent than me would have realised that no woman wants to be seen by a suitor when covered in spots. It wasn't long before I was completely in love.

Who knows, she may have been too.

She came to live in England, where we eventually got married at Brixton registry office when she was three months pregnant. Both sets of parents had been appalled and tried to dissuade us from marriage. My parents thought she was too young and also that I was more in love with her than the other way round. Her parents knew me well from my Osaka days. In their ideal world she'd have married a suitable Korean, though they said I was better than a Japanese.

In retrospect both sets of parents were right about our incompatibility, but they made a big mistake trying to talk us out of something that we had decided on. As a kind of protest we resolved that as we couldn't celebrate the occasion properly we wouldn't celebrate it at all.

Our witnesses were two people plucked from the bus stop. One was a heavily pregnant black teenager. When I look at the wedding photos, I see her clutching a half finished bottle of Lucozade. She looked as bewildered about her condition as Saeko did. The other witness, an old lady, refused at first to be recruited, but was then quite amused by the idea. I got the impression that, after a few moments reflection at the bus stop, she got caught up in the romance of this unusual, anonymous young couple getting married alone. The Registrar said he wasn't going to ask any questions. I think he thought we were doing a deal, so she could get a passport.

Saeko, it must be said, was looking very beautiful in a fabulous deep pink Korean *Choguri* (I think that is what it is called).

And so we were married. Brixton registry office is not quite Gretna Green, but romantic enough in its way.

CHAPTER 23

In about June, Saeko and Gen made their annual trip to Japan to see the grandparents. In my redundant state, I balked at the cost and stayed at home. I still went for the odd interview, played cricket, fiddled with the train set, drove Mr Gibbons bonkers with my piano playing and DIY.

When you are not working or are self-employed as I had now become, and when the wife is away, despite the leisure and freedom, weekends and evenings become if anything more important. You get fed up with your own company, plus all those dull people with proper jobs come out to play.

I began to discover a few of the pros and cons of being self-(un)employed. The pros are obvious: complete freedom and mastery of your own destiny or, at least, you think they are obvious. The difficulty arises when you come to the actual mastering of that destiny. Many self-employed people are self-(over)employed and involved in an undignified scramble to get enough money to survive. This often means working far harder than you ever did as an employee, and usually for far smaller rewards.

Writers are notoriously skint but, perhaps more than other businesses, it is like holding a lottery ticket. You could hit the jackpot unexpectedly. Your little column in *The Independent* newspaper could suddenly become a best-selling book followed by a block buster film, as per *Bridget Jones*. Could happen. Of course it helps if it is good, but the way a book suddenly becomes a craze is very similar to the way certain shares suddenly gain popularity. Or tulips. Or dotcoms. Or everyone gets hysterical about the fate of unemployables quarantined in the *Big Brother* house. Or the habit illiterate teenagers have of texting each other in electronic pictograms or smileys instead of learning to read. Or the spread of epidemics, or non-epidemics. For example, the panic about eating beef, even though there is no solid scientific proof whatsoever that the tiny number of new variant Creutzfeldt-Jakob deaths (only a 100 or so of our population of 55 million) were caused by eating a burger supposedly infected with putative bovine spongiform encephalopathy fifteen years before. It's just not logical to draw a causal relationship from the association between the consumption of burgers and an illness until research substantiates the link. Yet, long before this link was established, fear of the disease resulted in the slaughter of millions of cattle.

The latest one was SARS, an epidemic with very few victims, reportedly a hundred or so in China where they have a population of one billion and where they routinely cart off fifty people at a time to execute them in public stadia after peremptory trials. Even in a place where life is so cheap, the whole of Peking was wearing SARS masks.

Mathematicians and epidemiologists say that the spread of crazes and panics is similar in whatever field. As I've said before, everyone should go out and buy *Extraordinary Delusions and the Madness of Crowds* and keep a copy permanently in their loos.

So it is possible that one day I'll luck out and have a *Bridget Jones* or *A Year in Provence* or even a *Harry Potter* on my hands. The worst thing about not rolling in cash is that it makes you mean. You hesitate to buy a round in the pub…you're not as generous as you'd like to be with your nieces and nephews' Christmas presents. If you're time rich but cash poor and someone asks 'Fancy a long weekend skiing?', you can't go because you just don't have the dosh. I don't know about the happiness but money definitely buys freedom.

There are other hidden costs of self-employment, such as the need to go out in the evening if you work from home. If you fail to do so, you can contract a form of cabin fever from being on your own all the time, and go slightly mad. Madness is probably quite a good thing, in the correct quantities and the right professions: sane people = Dullsville.

You only have to look at a picture of Einstein or Beethoven, for example, to realise that these two people were off their heads. But once you examine their records in, respectively, quantum physics and music, you realise that without a touch of madness the human race wouldn't achieve much at all.

Madness is not, however, a quality to be prized in accountancy, say, or what I ended up doing for a while, translating Japanese forex manuals and the like into English.

'Concerning verification of Deutschmark/Dollar Interest Rate Arbitrage trades, attention must be paid to the Interbank Late Trade Rule 01-03-002.' That was one of my more polished sentences.

But such polish in the translation is not achieved without tearing you hair our, so one's appearance does pass through a Beethoven or Einstein phase. I found, unfortunately, that cultivating wild hair did not seed any creative genius, but all a translator needs to be is right, not wrong…end of story.

The daily exposure to cabin fever makes it essential, though, to get out in the evening and at weekends, because mad creative accountants or translators simply are not tolerated. And going out is expensive.

As Saeko was away I would ring up an old friend from teaching in Japan days, Flick. She was head of Canadian bond dealing at some Canadian Bank. I don't know how much she used to earn but, if I could have her earnings for £150,000, I would have bought large.

Digression: City people make markets in anything, e.g. 'She looks old, what do you think?'

'Thirty-three to thirty-four.'

'I'd buy thirty-four large', i.e. she looks about forty or 'I'd go short at thirty-three', translation: you are being a bit harsh, she's only about thirty.

Flick wouldn't mind me saying that many would have made a price on her age of thirty-three to thirty-four. With the benefit of insider knowledge, I would have been a seller at thirty-three (real age thirty). But the market-maker would have had no difficulty jobbing my stock, sold at thirty-three on to a buyer at thirty-four. The fact is, she looked knackered and haggard.

We would meet for a chat in a restaurant somewhere (eating whilst gabbling inconsequentially is one of the things I do best). I would complain that I couldn't get a job, while she would complain that she hated hers and, incidentally, couldn't get a boyfriend.

'Looking like that', I would say to her – and without detracting from my opinion that she was a very attractive girl, 'it's not surprising.'

I know Flick very well and could say such things after not that much wine.

Well before the coffee, she'd be showing signs of somnolence. 'Supposing, Flick, a nice boy does ask you out on a date, he is scarcely going to be impressed by your lines and grey appearance, particularly if', I would pause theatrically to look at my watch, 'you are falling asleep at nine-fifteen. This is a turn-off to men who want at least to think that their conversation has been dazzling, and that they have a small chance, even if not this time, next time, of getting lucky. Stress related chain-smoking is no good either. You have got to make a decision between earning a quarter of a million a year and getting laid. In this life, short of sleeping with your Kuwaiti clients, it is often not possible to do both.'

Many people who get sex regularly might ignorantly opt for a quarter of a million, but I am glad that Flick gave up bonds and got one of her passions out of her system. She went off to drama school, did a bit of fringe acting for a year or two and is now settled with a nice bloke, a fellow down-shifter, and two kids. They run a small business and, unlike me, have some dosh stashed away.

I'd had the house to myself for close on a month. While Saeko was away, a letter arrived from a friend of hers, a German called Hermann. I had met him, he'd been on her linguistics course at University College London, didn't know him well, thought him a little dull, though pleasant enough. He wanted to bring his fiancée to stay, and show her the sights of London. I had no particular enthusiasm for him, but Saeko's friends were Saeko's friends. I wrote back and said, "By all means make yourselves at home."

I wasn't all that sure when Saeko and Gen would be back. They were due at some indeterminate time the next week. Indeterminate because I had tried to get in touch to no avail; she had been in Seoul on a business trip, and it was around August, the time of the *O-bon* festival, when the Japanese come home to visit the family grave, so getting flights was a problem. By the time I did catch her – and found out when she was returning – I had committed myself to a weekend away that I didn't feel like cancelling.

I had learnt over the years that her passages to and returns from Japan were always very tense times. She would have an entirely predictable fit about something unpredictable within a week of departure or arrival. I had just survived, so I thought, my life crisis – Hooray, I'm no longer a stockbroker – but she went through one every year. Part of it may have been that she couldn't handle jet lag, but I guess that each time she came back she started to ask herself what on earth she was doing here. Rather as I did every time I came back from a holiday in France to English weather, bad manners, dirt and inefficiency, somehow overlooking French dirt, bad manners and inefficiency. When she left Japan, even as a member of the unpopular, discriminated against Korean minority, she left a world of certainties, Mum's cooking, her own futon on her own tatami, familiar smells, attitudes, the right brand of dried seaweed.

It took quite a man to bear the brunt of all these feelings. I was not such a man, so I decided that while I would meet her at the airport I would not cancel my weekend.

I wondered what stunt she would pull this time, but as a minimum I steeled myself for some or all of the following:

1. An accusation of being unfaithful. Fat chance. If only. There I was lonely, effectively single, vulnerable. Who knows what would have happened if one of the mums from Gen's school had said 'Come to bed with me'. I might easily have succumbed. I shall never know. Perhaps because I exude natural fidelity, no one ever did.

2. A new disciplined child-rearing routine – this the hallmark of an overly-fastidious mother-in-law. There would be new stringent standards of hygiene that would be impossible for me – a dirty Englishman – to conform to. I was

brought up to eat my toast if it fell on the floor, even if it had conformed to Sod's Law and landed butter side down. This teaches one not to drop the toast on the floor, but even if you don't learn the lesson you do get to load your immune system with anti-bug T-cells. The Japanese as a people are appalling hypochondriacs. This is not a racist statement. Its veracity can be ascertained by reference to the volume of antibiotics they consume per capita. More than any other people on earth (Data: Merrill Lynch. The French are second).

3. Gen would also be dressed to the nines in fancy clothes, a bit foppish for my tastes. I didn't care what they cost, so long as I didn't pay for them. As the main handler of Gen, my main consideration was that they be suitable for trailing through mud, playing football or climbing trees, without then having to send them to the dry-cleaner.

4. Her employers, having been reminded of her existence by a personal visit to Tokyo HQ, would besiege her with faxes and telephone calls in the middle of the night and make unreasonable demands on her time. They, no more than her parents, could never remember whether to add or subtract nine hours when calling England. This could have devastating impact on domestic harmony and make her even more prone than usual to grumpiness and caprices.

To pick the pair up from Heathrow, then disappear for the weekend, rather than lavish attention on my returning wife may seem uncaring, but it was obviously in both our interests. Best to avoid her for a few days: her body clock time-shifts were like a triple dose of PMT.

When I went to the airport, Gen was delighted to see me and jabbered away at me in Japanese about his holiday. In England he would usually stop me speaking Japanese, I think he found it socially embarrassing.

'Baba and Jiji (Granny and Grandpa) can't speak English, so I have to talk to them in Japanese,' he said proudly. 'You can't speak Japanese, so I have to speak to you in English,' he went on in Japanese clearly not noticing what language he was using.

The lucky little bastard. Able to pick it up like that without any effort. I am often asked 'How did you pick up Japanese?' This is a specious question because it is not a language you can just pick up. Although it's easy to pronounce, has only two irregular verbs and has no future tense or cases and genders, it is totally back to front and, if your English, offers you no reference points. If you're stuck for a French word you try out the English with a Frenchie accent. The equivalent doesn't work for Japanese. No, I swotted very hard for three years, paid for lessons from a teacher out of my hard-earned English teaching wages. Seemed a bit unfair to earn 10,000 yen an hour teaching English, then only pay 3,000 an hour to my Japanese tutor, but that's market forces for you. Even so, I am still at a level that would never be tolerated as 'fluent' in a translator of French.

There are more and more children like Gen. Much of his later schooling has been done in Japan, so he can do the spiky writing and everything. He will be able to make a fortune replacing people like me, if he wants to. But then, who wants to be a translator?

I wanted to take Gen away for my weekend, it would protect Saeko, and she could work through all her funny moods on her own, including the annual appraisal of whether or not she had messed up her whole life in marrying a *gaijin* like me. Small children don't appear to suffer jet lag in quite the same way as adults. With no concept of time, they don't have the built in expectation that they won't be able to sleep.

Saeko wouldn't let me take him and, as I have already mentioned, I knew there was no point in arguing when her body clock was resetting.

I spent an agreeable few days away. I decided I might as well not rush back, but allow Saeko to adjust to her new bedtime and the horror of being in England. I tried to ring her a few times but only got my own voice on the answerphone.

I returned home from my weekend on Wednesday evening. There was no one there, which was a disappointment and also a bit strange; I had been looking forward to seeing them both fully recovered. In the sink there were unwashed mugs and plates, and there were toast crumbs on the table. Proof, if I needed it, that she was back and that not all my mother-in-law's standards had rubbed off or, if they had, had not survived re-entry into our home. Always a relief.

An empty wine bottle or two was evidence either of an attempt to ease adjustment to a new time zone through alcohol or revelry. I listened to my answerphone messages, which shifted the weight of evidence towards revelry, as did the contents of the bin – more wine bottles…and evidence of emptied ash-trays. She didn't smoke! What could she have been celebrating?

It was a funny time of day to be out and to have left no messages. Upstairs the mystery deepened. The bed was unmade, of itself not that unusual – as I say, I'd more or less dragged her down to my level where it came to housekeeping – and there were a few dirty clothes dotted around the place. But the usual array of Clinique, L'Oreal, her favourite Diorissimo was not on the Victorian armoire. The fax machine didn't have five feet of Japanese characters spilling out of it. Indeed the fax machine had gone. In its place was a new

£6.99 telephone. An envelope was Selotaped to it with 'Jim' written on the outside.

Dear Jim,

I have decided that it is time to face up to things. Our marriage is not working. I have decided to go away for a period to think things over. I will be in touch shortly. Be patient and don't worry. Speak to you soon,

Lots of love,
Saeko.

What, go away again? My first reaction was that this time she had excelled herself on the stunt-front, even allowing for the fact she'd just returned from Japan, when homesickness and jet lag did weird things to her. Perhaps I shouldn't have stayed away for so long, but been on hand to wait and serve, and endure the slings and arrows of outrageous time zones.

It was true that we hadn't been getting on that well. I'd been under her feet for several months, and I was not the greatest exploiter of the acres of free time available to me. I might, for example, have studied for and taken those Stock Exchange exams or other qualifications I had successfully avoided acquiring when I was actually working. Moping indolently around the house, playing *Für Elise* too often, always getting stuck on the same bit, bashing tacks into the train set or the floor or suddenly deciding to re-design the kitchen, writing the first few chapters of this. With hindsight, I can see that I may well have been infuriating to live with.

But she'd just had a one-month respite from that and, in any case, trips to Venice and Cannes and evenings out with visiting production crews meant we were like passing ships in the night. We hadn't been seeing much of each other at all.

I racked my brain to think where she might have gone. She had a million and one acquaintances from work, of all nationalities and in all countries, to whom she might go, and I didn't have the faintest idea where to start looking.

Address books, diaries, important papers, the majority of her underwear, charcoal-grey and mattress-ticking Issey Miyake sack dresses, Chanel suit and other favourite clothes were all gone. Gen's drawer didn't have any foppish clothes in it either. The only remaining Hermès scarf had a dribble of red wine down one corner (i.e. was unwearable). I started to become more worried. This was looking serious.

Perhaps my first thought should have been for Saeko, but in fact it was for Gen. Once in Japan extracting Gen would be very difficult. Japanese law is even slower and more expensive than English law. He'd be a teenager and I a pauper before I got him out, if I ever did. I had visions of renting a yacht, sailing into Kobe, then bribing a yakuza to kidnap him and bring him to my boat at the dead of night. We'd then sail through typhoons to Hong Kong, be swept ashore on an uninhabited volcanic outcrop, be boarded by Filipino pirates, Gen would be sold into white (well, semi-yellowish) slavery, my message in a bottle picked up by a passing yacht piloted by a girl (James Bond type) with almond shaped eyes and a tattoo, we'd run the gamut of Triad motor launches, sinister Chinese communist drug smugglers, fall in love, blah, blah, blah. I felt a film script coming on.

I remembered an English student of mine whose father had disappeared...divorce was too cumbersome a procedure for her, it was much simpler just to vanish amongst the thirty-million people living in Tokyo and Yokohama. The yakuza then would first have to find out where Gen lived.

I pictured myself putting Saeko's safe house under surveillance. Six foot four, brown European hair. Dark glasses and a bottle of dye would not solve the problems of how to pass incognito. I resolved that I had no choice but to stay calm.

The answerphone messages and the wine bottles pointed to a party. I went outside to the dustbins and sifted through some of the rubbish. Champagne bottles! Bollinger at that. Decaying sushi! Korean chicken and *kim-chee*! Forensic evidence pointed unerringly to some kind of celebration, perhaps a wake.

CHAPTER 24

Several days passed and no message came. Mutual friends had no idea, and so I stopped calling them. In any case it was embarrassing, unmanly even, to have to admit to having mislaid the wife. I racked my brain for the names of some of her friends, but the problem was that I couldn't remember their surnames.

Talking of her friends, Hermann the German rang to say that he and his girl friend Marlene would be leaving Edinburgh and hoped to come and stay tomorrow. Fine, I said. If Saeko phoned in, it might shame her into a reappearance.

To take my mind off things I busied myself with a round of frantic gardening and lawn grooming designed to irritate Mr Gibbon. I mastered the slow movement of the *Pathetique*.

A couple of days later a letter arrived from Messrs Charles Russell, Solicitors at Law, saying that Saeko and Gen were fine, staying with friends and would be in touch soon.

I went through as many of Saeko's papers as I could find. I came across a letter from a friend Jennifer. 'I don't blame you for wanting to leave Jim, if there is anything at all I can do to help, don't hesitate to ask...' I was shocked to see that the letter was two years old. I wondered what I had done to engender such disapprobation.

I had always liked Jennifer well enough or, more accurately, fancied her a bit, but our relationship had been an uneasy one. It was something to do with my having been a stockbroker, probably. She had the knee-jerk disapproval of someone who has money towards those trying to get it – we are the grubby, exploiting capitalists. She was doing a PhD in some branch of cognitive linguistics. I couldn't myself see why that was any worthier than photographing Albanian hayricks, and considerably less worthwhile than brokering stocks and allocating capital across the globe to where it would be the most productive.

When Gen was small, I once rugby tackled him on the drawing room carpet, as one does. 'He'll play rugby for England when he grows up,' I said proudly to the assembled company of student friends of Saeko's, one of whom was Jennifer. This dated back to when Saeko was doing a linguistics degree at University College London.

There was an almost unified bristling around the room. 'Maybe he'll be very good at knitting,' said Jennifer, putting into words a thought clearly shared by a number of those present. Another student, a bloke whom I knew to be vegan, said the thought of rugby made him almost physically sick. When we'd bought the house Saeko had said he was short of cash, so I'd employed him to help with the decorating...he was the kind of bloke you look at and for no good reason just want punch his face in. Does that make me seem unsympathetic and right-wing? Oh dear. Sorry. Perhaps I am.

There's been some encouraging research lately about the impact of soya milk on babies. Apparently soya is one of the filthiest and un-green crops imaginable and those who bring their boys up on it risk inducing a condition known as 'piccolo penis'. I reckon our decorator had been eating soya everyday of his life.

For me, it was of no importance whether Gen's potential lay in knitting or rugby. In due course he would find out for himself, but it certainly wasn't an issue to bristle on.

I continued my search through Saeko's belongings. Not something I would normally do, but this departure was clearly more than the usual bout of jet-lag madness associated with returning to the land of the sinking pound from the land of the rising yen(as they were then).

There was a fairly complete archive of letters going back five or six years, including all my old love letters to her, which I took and hid. There was an account of the birth of Gen, written by both of us.

Saeko: 5.00 a.m: same as usual. Jim Snoring.
6.00 a.m: every ten minutes. Jim snoring.
7.00 a.m.: every seven to eight minutes. Jim still snoring.
8.00 a.m. every five minutes. Jim got up but didn't believe.
8.30 a.m.: Jim in blind panic, but made breakfast, duck egg and sausage.
(I wonder why we had duck eggs in the fridge.)
9.00 a.m.: ate breakfast. Delicious. Every four to five minutes. Jim rang up hospital and go!
12.35 p.m.: start delivering/push. About 12.50 swap Carmen (black) for Rhona (Scottish). Too many students.

Jim: I asked Carmen if this was the real thing, because we had had a few false alarms over the last week or two. 'Yes', she said, 'this is the real thing.'

Carmen was comforting and reassuring. Rhona, sweet, nineteen-ish and needing 'just one more birth to get her certificate', brushed Carmen aside. That's the trouble with teaching hospitals. All was confusion, and, though I say it myself, I reckon I took over; although Saeko might disagree, *I* deserved the certificate.

Saeko: 1.20 p.m.: I began to understand when + how to

push.
1.25 p.m. Head was seen.
1.34 p.m.: finished.
Jim : First saw little tuft of black hair around 11.30 when Carmen searched with fingers.
About 11.30 each push revealed a medallion of head, which then disappeared. At 1.20 the circle of head began to get bigger and bigger. The mid-wife threatened forceps. Whispers of various unpleasant sounding procedures. No one in charge it seemed. Looked around for Carmen but there was only Rhona who was looking tense and didn't seem to know what to do.
Told Saeko I could see head each time she pushed (slight lie.)
1.25 crown began to appear, until soon after half the head was out. The only time Saeko screamed. I encouraged her to push and in a few more goes the head was out. Didn't really see because she had her feet on my shoulders for pushing.
Head slimy, lots of black hair.
Cord around neck, so Rhona, relieved to be doing something, cut it, then pulled the rest of the baby out, or Saeko pushed it, I can't remember.
Blue, slimy baby on Saeko's chest, she seemed a bit bewildered, both crying a bit.

Saeko: Jim gave me a nice rub + kept telling me what was happening + what to do. Jim said, 'It's a boy, Saeko.' I found him on my stomach. Colour is blue and purple. Soon went pink. I saw his big hands in front of my eyes. I could imagine his feet, of course.
(I have size thirteens).

I got on with my life as far as I was able. No point in moping around at home, so I applied myself to gardening, listening to the cricket commentary on the radio, bashing in a few stray tacks.

It wasn't until Wednesday, a whole week after her disappearance, that Saeko got in touch with me and we were able to meet. In the meanwhile, I had to get a solicitor to combat hers.

Saeko seemed in very good humour when I met her in Soho Square. Her manner was slightly euphoric; it seemed to say 'I've done it'. She had leapt the hedge to the greener grass on the other side. I recognised the symptoms. I had felt the same when I finally decided to abandon stockbroking. Her manner was pleasant, sympathetic, kind even, but she wouldn't say where she was staying nor what she planned.

Our hour in the small green in Soho Square drew to a close. Round us sat hundreds of lunchtime sun seekers, secretaries with their skirts pulled up to their thighs, defying warnings about the ozone layer, eating their sandwiches or catching a few end of summer rays or forty winks. Darren the office boy was out with Sharon the office girl, snatching a furtive half-hour of moonstruck rapture. Life was continuing, while our trivial domestic soap opera played itself out.

Saeko stroked my forehead and gave me a kiss before leaving. An onlooker would have taken us for a version of Darren and Sharon, a little love scene between a beautiful olive skinned oriental girl and a tall suntanned man (never mind that the sun tan was from a summer of loafing about), the dawning regret in the man's eyes only there because of their having to part.

Redundancy I could rationalise: it was the fault of the

approaching collapse of the Japanese financial system, Merrill Lynch's lack of commitment to the long term, the fact that Alick my boss was a bastard...any number of factors other than my own inadequacies. When the wife leaves, one has to face up to the fact that one's inadequacies may have something to do with it. Or, if it was her inadequacies, then my inadequacy at not having spotted them.

CHAPTER 25

While I was in Soho, a message had been deposited on the answerphone. Hermann the German would be coming to stay the day after tomorrow, with his new East German fiancée. My troubles had made me forget about these two, and given that they were Saeko's friends not mine, it might have made greater sense to tell them to go find a bed and breakfast.

I had only met Hermann once before. He was a pleasant, clean cut Hun from Berlin, aged about twenty-eight, just finishing his sociology degree. (It seems that degrees take about ten years in Germany.) A typical modern-day Kraut – uncontroversial, sincere, thought seriously about world peace and saving the environment. How anyone would imagine that the Germans could once again become a threat in Europe is beyond me. No doubt there is no shortage of out-and-out fascists in Germany, but we have no right to be complacent about our record of tolerance, just never been put to the test.

The couple arrived a few days later and were a good distraction from my gnawing marital problems. Marlene was from East Berlin. It was typical of Hermann's sincerity to embrace the ideals of the nineties and go for an Ossi. To think that only a few years before their love might have led to their being shot. Forbidden fruit is the sweetest, even when, like Marlene, obviously reared on too much kartoffel salad.

Marlene could speak no English and my German was limited to '*Dass ist eine shone Pickelhaube*' and '*Ich bin ein Berliner*', so Hermann became full time translator. As a gift for letting them stay I was presented with a small marble plinth with a piece of coloured plaster on top, 'Berlin Wall, 1962-

1989.' It sits on my mantelpiece still, a small symbol of optimism for the future.

Over the next few days they embarked on a round of sightseeing, the Changing of the Guard, Tower Bridge, Madame Tussauds, a trip out of town to Windsor Castle and Hampton Court.

Hermann was still the bright, sincere, fundamentally dull Hun he had always been. Marlene, being only eighteen months out from behind the Wall was very different in character. She had wanted to take tea at the Ritz, but they had been turfed out because of Hermann's lack of a jacket and tie, although she had been smartly dressed enough, in a pleated skirt demurely covering her knees.

It was ironic that Hermann the Westerner should be caught in this way, rather than Marlene. I remember a trip to the Opera in communist Prague of 1986. I was the stinking traveller making his way back from Japan via China and the Trans Siberian Express, with dirty Taiwanese tennis shoes, in fact, dirty (and smelly) everything. I had assumed that I would therefore fit in with the proletarian Czech audience, but in fact they were starchily formal, all in jackets and ties, and looked at me askance, much as the Ritz had at Hermann. The only reason I wasn't chucked out was that I was able to bribe the usher a US dollar.

Marlene hadn't completely got the hang of dressing like a capitalist, though. There was something peculiarly post-totalitarian about her hairstyle, the over-bright, we-are-not-communists-anymore lipstick. But then perhaps I shouldn't focus too much on her time warps; Hermann, after all, looked like a seventies pop star.

In the middle of their stay Saeko phoned again and I

went to meet her. The fact that I was looking after two of her friends elicited no more thanks than 'Send my regards to Hermann'.

We met again in Soho Square and I am afraid that we had a humdinger of a row of the kind where an audience of strangers builds up. She pointed out that I had once said that it would be a good time to get divorced while I was redundant, because it would cost me less money. This was true, but I had not been expecting to be taken at my word.

Hermann and Marlene were embarrassed to be staying at the height of our marital discord, but I said that it was not their problem and told them to relax. Like my wife, they took me at my word. They abandoned sight-seeing for a day to unwind at home. Hermann was so relaxed that he was under the impression that it was acceptable to import some of his Northern European habits to the UK and wander around the garden in a posing pouch. He was quite slim for a German plus a little pale and weedy, not quite Master Race.

Marlene had a more Brunhilde-ish build, as befits the product of a country where socialist prudery had been the norm (when bodies are predominantly covered, they are not groomed for exposure). Her expression of liberation was to uncover. There was lots of pink flesh spilling out of an even pinker bikini that like the Berlin Wall was not quite up to the job. I caught a glimpse of Mr Gibbon diving back behind his curtains, having got a pleasurable eyeful, no doubt wondering what the Cold War had been about. There was some nice crumpet out East.

Like her lipstick, the bikini said, 'I-am-no-longer-a-drab-communist and I-embrace-the-West.' Lucky old Hermann, and Mr Gibbon, too. Listing their inadequacies provided a distraction. I hope for the sake of the new united Germany, people like Marlene don't lose their sense of irony and cynicism, and end up as over-sincere but harmless Eurobores like Hermann.

CHAPTER 26

At the end of the third week of her flight Saeko finally came home. The threatened move to a flat had proved more difficult to execute than she'd imagined.

Back too, came the fax machine and the full armoury of other office equipment, plus calls in the middle of the night from Tokyo. Term restarted and I resumed the merry routine of the previous six months, of walking Gen, who of course was delighted to see me again, to and from school.

Slightly wounding was the fact that Gen had been staying with Rory's parents at their holiday cottage in the New Forest. If I'd known I'd have driven down and got him. To be fair to Rory's parents, they had just been caught in the crossfire of someone else's divorce and things hadn't been fully explained to them.

Saeko and I circled each other in the house uneasily, studiously avoiding rows. Gen didn't seem to notice at all. He was used to us both doing separate things, but however foul we were being to each other, he was never happier than on the few occasions when we ate together en famille.

A couple of months passed. When she was not out living it up, she tended to be in her room with the door closed. There were a lot of muffled telephone calls, the Japanese cooking knives (far better than Sabatier) started to disappear and, bit by bit, the office equipment started to shift out again. I suppose I should have seen the writing on the wall, but when you don't want to believe something, you filter out the signs. I think it's a state known as 'denial' and I was in it.

Similarly, I ought to have read the signs of my approaching demise at Merrill Lynch. The interviews with a Danish stockbroker, about whom Alick, Henry and Charlie had been very enthusiastic and for whom, without major upheavals, there would be no place to sit.

A pleasant November morning came. As usual I got Gen up. He'd gone to bed late, so it was a delicate operation. Tickle the feet until the first signs of consciousness begin to appear, then retreat. Saeko stayed in bed, awake but making no signs of a move. Lord knows why it wasn't me agitating for a divorce.

Gen was awake. Once those eyes started to flicker there was no going back. 'Good morning, Gen, did you have a nice sleep? You've got to go to school. Quick. Breakfast.'

We raced up the street. One good thing about Gen was that he liked a race, which meant that he was less late than he might be. Although he would get very upset if I won, so the trick was to allow him to breast the tape fractionally ahead of me. We passed Rory, who was playing up a bit about going to school. As we went past, Rory shot Gen who turned round and shot back. Rory received a welt from his mother. Corporal punishment! Not exactly politically correct.

'We don't like guns, do we Rory?' she said.

'We like guns, don't we Daddy?' said Gen. Mrs Rory looked at me so disapprovingly, I decided to wait until she was out of earshot to whisper my agreement. I think Mrs Rory probably disapproved of racing to school too. Racing = Competition = Bad.

I couldn't see any point in enforcing disarmament because it is counter-productive. As a result of a ban on firearms in Rory's house, he spent his whole time constructing them out of Lego, drawing them, even fashioning sculptures of them out of his fish fingers and rocket salad.

By the time I returned, Saeko was unaccountably up and unaccountably agitated, but then I could never account for her agitations. She left in a hurry, saying she would be back to take Gen out for lunch with a friend.

I busied myself with tearing down the spent tomato plants and withered lobelias. There was no escaping that winter was nearly upon us. The garden was smothered in crisp brown leaves.

Lunchtime came and I had to drag Gen out of Rory's house where the two of them hid on the way back from school. I had to deliver the child to his mother so that she could take him to lunch with the friend.

'Where are you going?' I asked.

'To a Japanese restaurant with Jennifer,' she said.

'Nice,' I said, thinking how expensive Japanese restaurants were and of our steadily accruing overdraft. I had my lunch, did a bit more gardening, but was driven indoors by the cold wind and impending darkness – the clocks had just gone back. It had been a lovely morning, but I find short afternoons depressing. No wonder so many Swedes and Finns commit suicide in winter.

I retreated upstairs to attack a mountain of bills and correspondence that I had been putting off for a while. My filing system had three trays, one labelled 'In', one 'Out' and one 'Procrastinate'. In practice the 'In' tray was not substantially different in function from the 'Procrastinate' one.

Telephone bill, £1,273.58. Final reminder in red. My mother would be in trouble with my father if the quarterly bill reached fifty pounds. The secret of staying married for forty years? At around a quarter to five the front door bell rang.

'Ah, Saeko has forgotten keys or had her handbag stolen again' I thought. She'd twice had it whipped from under her feet in the cafe at Harrods (or was it Harvey Nics?).

At the door was a man clad from head to foot in black leathers, clutching a motorbike helmet. Our street was built in a funny order, with modern semis on one side, a row of nice Georgian stuff, some oddments, like my house, a thirties development on land sold off from the big Victorian house on the parallel street. This meant that the numbers were all out of order. My house, number Fifty-three, was next to Number Six, so although I was not expecting a visit from a motorcyclist, I was not entirely surprised, and readied myself to explain to him how to find his way to Number Twenty-two.

'Are you Mr Parton?' I reeled in surprise at the very suggestion.

'Why, yes, I am.'

'No relation to Dolly?' he grinned.' Motorbike couriers and taxi drivers can never resist it. 'Here mate, could you sign for these, please.' Surely the Merrill Lynch company car man had given up on that unpaid parking fine by now. A fat brown package with my name on the outside and the legend 'BY HAND'. Six months since I had left Merrill's, it seemed to be taking a sledge hammer to crack a nut. I signed and took the papers.

I was right to think it was from lawyers. Not Merrill Lynch's, my wife's. Messrs Charles Russell again.

There were twelve pages or so of tight script telling her life story, with a particular emphasis on her marriage to me with a compelling account of what a hopeless husband and rotten father I was.

I was described as potentially violent. Example: the train set upstairs was proof of an irresponsible attitude that could have resulted in Glen electrocuting himself. *Women*. Saeko couldn't even work out how my stereo functioned, so one time seeing some spare wires put them straight into the electric plug socket. They were the speaker wires. My fancy speakers, cooked. Her excuse was that she'd seen the builders do it with a radio.

Russells I'd heard of. They're one of these firms that crops up in articles about the Royal Family's divorces. Typical of Saeko, even in divorce, to go for a brand name. Typical, too, of those paid by the hour to take statements about train sets.

But going for the train set – that was low; I suppose I might have had passing moments of homicidal funk each time I rerailed a derailed *Thomas the Tank Engine*, though actually Gen got very good at it himself. It takes a lot of touch for a four-year old to do that, and I was rather proud. Rory, by contrast, just used to try and run the delicate mechanisms up and down the carpet.

The penultimate paragraph was a long explanation about the qualities of her new flat and her hunt for new schools. In the middle of this account of graft and suffering was the sentence 'I eventually left the matrimonial home on the 4th November'.

Until this point I'd been increasingly numbed by the 'Affirmation of the Petitioner' and that a relationship with someone I had loved, still loved (for all her faults, and I had mine) could come to this.

The 4th November. Today. She was gone. Gone with Gen. They weren't out to lunch at all, it was a straightforward heist. They were gone and wouldn't be back. I paced the house in a futile, impotent way, angry at being duped.

A court hearing was scheduled for just three days later.

Next day I went to the school and explained the situation. I had bottled my emotions until then, but there was something about going through that Victorian gate marked BOYS next to the one marked INFANTS that set me off. I bit my upper lip, projected it, stiffened it, but it was no good, I cried.

I took some deep breaths, and walked around the empty playground. Children's voices could be heard coming from the classrooms and a more strident one of a teacher, not quite in control of the children. I went into the nursery a bit more composed.

I talked to Gen's teacher, who was astonished to find that there were any problems between me and my wife. 'He seems such a well-adjusted child,' she said. This set me off again and the teacher had to take me outside, while Rory, momentarily distracted from the creation of a plasticine gun remarked to his chums with a child's devastating bluntness, 'Gen's daddy is crying.' I expect they all went home and told their mums. Quite exciting.

That evening was Guy Fawkes night. I wondered where Gen would be watching the fireworks.

A few days later I met my solicitor and barrister – both female – at the Royal Courts of Justice in the Strand, the one you always see on the Nine O'Clock News. A fabulous Victorian Gothic monster, it seemed extraordinary that such ornate facilities could be available to help us solve our menial domestic squabble. Our court was in an annex with a massive vaulted corridor where the other litigants waited their turn. Everyone talked in subdued whispers. You could identify the lawyers because they all looked so relaxed; the female ones – solicitors and barristers – were all dressed in black.

Despite my looking anything but relaxed, a male lawyer

came up to me to ask how long I thought my client's case would take. Rather than tell him that I was a client and not a lawyer, I indicated that he should direct his question to my lawyers. He seemed to turn his nose up at having to ask women. As he sauntered off, my solicitor and barrister chimed a muttered, 'Sexist.'

With the benefit of hindsight, I can add the epithet 'stupid' because I have subsequently discovered that the overwhelming majority of matrimonial lawyers are women. But perhaps he approached me in the hope of finding a fellow-fish-out-of-water.

I saw Saeko on the other side of the corridor with her lawyers. Her solicitor was young, pretty and normal looking – the kind I might ask out a on date if we really did get divorced. It was difficult to reconcile her appearance and the horrors written about me in the 'Affirmation of the Petitioner'. I couldn't believe that Saeko had thought all those things up. Ghastly though I may have been, she must have needed some help from a more creative person to answer more than a few loaded questions. Lots of hours at £130 an hour had gone into the creation of that document (these days it would be more like £200).

I was dying to test the vaulted acoustics, and thought to myself that Gen would have liked this place, he could have yelled his head off like he had in Tutankhamen's Tomb. I wondered where he was.

After waiting all morning, we were told at one o'clock that we could go to lunch without missing our turn in the queue, as the courts adjourn for lunch. I didn't feel like eating so went for a walk on my own down by the Thames.

Back at the court, two o'clock passed, then three. The number of tense looking litigants and their smart, relaxed lawyers dressed in funereal black thinned out. Every so often, the door of one or other of the courts would open and one party would emerge looking upset, and in tears, while the other side would come out looking joyous and exuberant, and embrace waiting family and friends.

The building was overheated and I went for a walk in the courtyard. 'I am just going outside and may be some time,' I told my solicitor. By the time I got back it was four o'clock and my lawyers were scouring the lavatories and the courtyards for their errant client. (Maybe they'd have been better employed at the other meaning of 'scouring the lavatories').

The courts pack it in at four-thirty, so we only had half an hour, but our case was so cut and dried, I thought that any judge would be able to come to the right decision very quickly. I shouldn't have been tense, but I was, as the barristers went through the formalities and the judge read the affidavits while we sat in you-could-hear-a-pin-drop silence for ten minutes.

4.10: Each barrister made a brief submission on our respective cases.

4.20: The other side had said in the corridor outside that if they lost Saeko would move back in with me. This was said as if it was a threat, but to me it was the best solution. You can't just chuck away five years of marriage that casually. She had made her point. I would try harder. I might even look for a job.

The judge looked at her watch. 'I'm afraid you can't expect me to rule today', she said, 'the issues need to be heard, I will therefore adjourn this hearing until 22nd November. Time: half a day.' She ruled that in the interim I should be allowed to see Gen from after school on Fridays and that he should return to his mother at 10 a.m. on Sundays.

I was shocked to be bound by court order as to when I could and could not see my own son, a son I'd been daily accompanying to and from school until just a week before.

I had been confident of winning, would have been surprised had I lost, but a goalless draw was the last result I had anticipated.

Guessing scenarios often fails because there are too many variables in the affairs of men. If I extrapolate my experience in court to cover the City or the BBC weather room or, for that matter, anything else, it should send a dire warning to any would-be forecaster that forecasting doesn't work. Which is why City forecasters and Chancellors of the Exchequer ought to give up trying, and why the entire broking and fund management industry is a rip-off.

At home there was a big void. No more friendly routine of to-ing and fro-ing from school, or visits to Rory's house. I performed some therapeutic tidying of crumpled pyjamas, made Gen's bed – they'd left in a hurry.

Treading on Lego in bare feet on the way to the loo in the depths of the night is one of the pains of parenthood, but the fact that the child who had dropped it was no longer there gave the experience an extra emotional pang.

On the two intervening periods of access, Gen was in good form and obviously delighted to see me. He did not understand what was going on. He had been told that he was visiting 'Mummy's work', and asked me if I wanted to come and see it too. Everything was a bit of an adventure for him.

CHAPTER 27

Two weeks later and we were back in the vaulted corridor with its untested acoustics. Again lunchtime came and went. This time I made a show of being more relaxed, although I was feeling more tense than I ever had in my whole life, a tension made worse by the fact that I was utterly powerless. Everything was in the hands of my lawyers.

The two opposing teams sat at different ends of the corridor, avoiding each other's eyes. Every so often though, the two barristers would meet in the middle for a parley. Each trip to the loo involved passing the enemy dug-out and making a decision as to whether to nod in acknowledgement or look the other way. No doubt Saeko was as conscious as I was that we were employing professionals to do our dirty work for us. It was another measure of the embarrassing failure of our marriage that we couldn't sort this out ourselves.

I ostentatiously affected calm, by reading the newspaper and *Private Eye*. Half past two…half past three…other groups slipped in ahead of us. Some were very quick, just ten minutes or so, but the group of people immediately in front of us were obviously having a real ding-dong.

At about a quarter to four I popped across the road to the newsagents again and bought six toffee bars, hoping that Sod's Law would make the case start in my absence like the last time. This demonstrated an abysmal misunderstanding of the workings of the Law. The whole point of Sod's Law is that its immutable effect only actuates to *thwart* plans not to realise them. The Chancellor of the Exchequer or City economist effect! If you anticipate one thing then something else happens. This meant that when I came back, no one was scouring the courtyards for me.

I kept one toffee bar for myself and distributed the rest to the lawyers. I then sauntered across to the opposition's table and slipped them one each, too, before retreating. I wanted to present them with a dilemma. If they spurned them, they would look churlish, if they ate them they would be communing at the table of the enemy. I wished that I had thought of getting them iced lollies (the building was still very over-heated), which would have made the dilemma more pressing because of the melting issue. I also had images of my wife's young barrister pompously declaiming in court through a bright orange mouth.

Just short of four o'clock the court doors swung open and the previous case came out. A scuffle broke out between the two presumably divorcing parties. I had witnessed a real life court room scuffle as described regularly in the pages of *The Sun*. They were called back in again to be fined for contempt of court.

Yet again it was just past four, and only half an hour before the judge packed in for the day. My heart sank. At this rate we would soon be entering a third replay followed by a penalty shoot-out.

If the previous judge had not had time to make a decision on the basis of the affidavits alone, neither would this one. Sure enough he adjourned the hearing, but with a variation. He sent for the Court Welfare Officer. Not a creature I'd ever heard of before.

Fifteen minutes or so later a kindly looking man in his mid-forties arrived and sat in the witness box, while the judge explained to him the conflicting positions of the two parties. 'Redundant stockbroker...now works from home ... claims he has the time to look after the child...freelance television producer...says she can pick and chose jobs to fit around mothering commitments...'

The judge ordered the man to visit our respective homes and do an assessment of whether it would be in the child's *'best interests'* to stay with the mother or return to the father.

'Surely', said the Court Welfare Officer, 'since we are only talking about interim care and control, shouldn't we just allow the child to stay with the mother until a fuller hearing?'

This was devastating suggestion, fortunately the judge disagreed. The CWO was to visit both our homes, write his report and we would reconvene under the same judge at the beginning of December.

The CWO looked like the kind who might spend his Saturday afternoons jotting down numbers at the end of Platform Four, Reading Station, so I reckoned on influencing him positively. On the other hand, as a social worker, he was certain to be left-wing, with an instinctive dislike of greed-is-good stockbroker types like me. I would use my redundancy to incite sympathy; on the downside, my wife would be able to play the racial minority card.

We filed out of court and the opposition thanked me loudly for their sticky chocolate bars, eating them ostentatiously. For them this result was the run-in to an outright victory. It bought time and more fees (or *disbursements*, as lawyers call them). The case would not be heard for a month after the departure of Saeko and Gen, when the *status* would be developing a *quo*.

CHAPTER 28

I pondered my tactics.

The day before the Court Welfare Officer's visit – two days before we were due back in court – my mum came round and scrubbed the house from top to bottom. She even cleaned around the light switches, something I would never have had the imagination to do – if cleaning round light switches takes imagination. When she'd finished, the house was gleaming. Of course, this tactic could back-fire – there was a risk that the deserting-the-ship, trying-to-be ex-wife would get the credit.

I had kept a load of Gen's washing back, so that when the CWO came round I would have an array of clothing on the line, in order to look both domesticated and caring. City-slicker stripes and double cuffs would be suppressed in case the guy was chippy.

I also stopped buying the *Daily Telegraph* and got *The Guardian* instead. A bit fascist *The Guardian*, controlled as it is by the Thought Police, but it is generally well-written and does have some useful supplements. *Guardian Society* was one and, by good chance, that day's edition had an article headlined, 'Increasingly Fathers Run the Home, While Mothers Win the Bread' by the Social Affairs Correspondent. I left it carelessly but ostentatiously open by the sofa. A subliminal message would be delivered: I-used-to-be-a-stockbroker-but-I'm-all right-now.

I felt confident but was not complacent.

The great day came. I went to pick Glen up from his new school, but he wasn't there. The judge had said I should pick him up there early to settle him down. Eventually Saeko and Gen arrived. She said he had a cold and had had to go the doctor. He looked and sounded perfectly all right to me.

I was now in a rush. My plan of bribing him with a McDonalds to reduce him to a state of childish quiescence before the Court Welfare Officer had failed. I wondered if late delivery of child had been a clever lawyer's tactic or Saeko's own idea.

The kindly looking Mr O'Rourke arrived at the front door a quarter of an hour late. The house was spotless. Gen's laundry flapped lazily in pristine splendour along the clothes line. We chatted amiably for a couple of hours, while Gen played quietly upstairs with the train set. He didn't ask me at all about my relationship with him, which I presumed was taken as read.

Mr O'Rourke took the clothes-line bait – hook, line and sinker. 'Ah', he said, 'I see you have got on top of the domestic side of things...' I felt I had made a good impression. Later he saw the artlessly laid pages of the *Guardian Society* section in various strategic locations around the house. 'Ah', he went again, 'a stockbroker who reads *The Guardian*, how unusual.'

Now there's a man with no prejudices, I thought. 'A redundant stockbroker, Mr O'Rourke,' I replied. 'One's perspectives change.'

I gave Mr O'Rourke some tea and shortbread, slightly conscious that this was a risky strategy. Saeko would have subjected him to a full blown Tea Ceremony. Couldn't compete with that. She had also nicked all the best china.

Gen was at his most infectiously droll over tea. 'Pass Mr O'Rourke the shortbread, Gen.'

'Pass Mr O'Rourke the shortbread, Gen.'

'No, pass it, Gen.'

'No, pass it, Gen.'

'Stop copying me, and pass the shortbread.'

'Stop copying me, and pass the shortbread.' A little grin appeared on his face.

'This is one of Gen's favourite games, Mr O'Rourke, he loves copying me...'

'This is one of Gen's favourite games, Mr, O'Rourke, he loves copying me.' By now Gen was laughing.

'If you won't stop copying me, I'll...' I paused at the looming disaster. Social worker Mr O'Rourke would certainly not approve of smacking bottoms.

'If you don't stop copying me, I'll...' The little swine had the intonation perfectly, right down to the hint of desperation.

Apart from this small incident, Gen behaved impeccably throughout, and the Court Welfare Officer and I parted, I felt, on the best of terms.

There was one small incident, which I should have choreographed better. Mr O'Rourke professed an interest in music and so I gave him a brief rendition on the piano.

His chest puffed out an inch or two as he ventured confidently, 'J.S. Bach?'

'C.P.E. Bach,' I replied, too quickly. You might have thought that I would be immune to such errors, after five years of sucking up to clients in the City. No wonder I lost my job.

His report dropped on my doormat a few days later. It said, that 'Mr Parton, whilst obviously a caring father, is not, in my opinion, capable of looking after the child on a full-time basis...the child also exhibited some provocative behaviour in his presence, which he did not – at any rate while I was there – show with the mother, who handled him at all times with perfect poise, juggling the demands of motherhood with the demands of work...' blah, blah, blah.

So much for New Man. The report also laid some stress on my attitude to safety, appearing to accept what Saeko had told him, namely that '...Gen's ancient model railway lay-out has unsafe wiring, which might result in electric shocks or even a fire, dangers that the father does not seem able to appreciate or anticipate.'

He recommended custody to the mother. If I ever see him crossing the road in front of my car, I fear that I may hesitate fatally between brake and accelerator, probably hitting the latter, hard.

EPILOGUE

In exchange for a bit of product placement in this book, I blagged lunch off my favourite headhunter, Chris Lawless of the Bloomsbury Group, together with his colleague Stuart Clifford. Chris, the reader might recall, had always been willing, whenever I needed a pay rise, to help me find a new job. Thanks to him I'd ended up at Laurence Prust, Citicorp and UBS Phillips and Drew and he was not guilty of the passage to my nemesis – Merrill Lynch.

After 12 years out of the markets I had to ask him: 'Am I still employable in the City? There must be something I can do, maybe I am too old for sales (forty-three), too out of touch to be a front-line broker, but could I be editor, say, of an otherwise unreadable investment research journal? Is it conceivable that some mug would still have me?'

'If you're serious', said Chris, 'there does happen to be a Japanese broking house looking for a Japanese-speaking salesman...'

Aaaarrghh, Chris, no please. No.

Chris himself had decided that his headhunting days were over. In the good times placing a sales team at combined salaries of half a million and trousering 30% commission hadn't been bad, but he'd had enough. A man of appetites, immensely clubbable, three times Oxford University hockey blue, cricketer, drinker, smoker, someone of whom you would say as he arrived at a party, 'Oh good, Chris has arrived.' He was not one to let life pass him by.

He and his wife had just bought the Scottish franchise for a toy company and planned to move to Edinburgh with their three kids. But a few months after that lunch, and shortly before he was due off to Scotland, Someone up there said 'No mate, that's yer lot'. Chris died of a heart attack on his way to the gym. It wasn't one of those mid-life-crisis, must-get-fit visits to the gym. Being a sportsman, he was pretty fit and without symptoms, although three weeks before he'd given up smoking. Maybe that's what upset his system.

He was just forty-one. This book is dedicated to his memory.

Had I put my mind to it, perhaps with the help of Chris, I could probably have got another job in the City and, if I'd stuck at it, by now I'd be thinking of my move out of the rat race into the country and my first Old Rectory with tennis court and swimming pool. So did I make a terrible mistake?

I must be grateful to Alick and Merrill Lynch for forcing choices upon me that I would never have had the courage to make on my own.

I did not find my feet immediately. For a while I translated Japanese stock-market research into English, which may have been even less uplifting than the job I used to do as a smile-'n'-dial salesman. I got into journalism fairly quickly, but it took three years to find a publisher and become an author.

Not an easy profession, though I make it more difficult by giving in to distractions like 'It's a lovely day, do you fancy a game of tennis?'

Why say no, if you can say yes? This is not a dress rehearsal. This is it. At any time Someone might say 'That's yer lot, mate'. Have that game of tennis.

I took up tennis a year or so after the City to suck up to a senior person at a newspaper who'd suggested I join a particular club. I did, even though the entry fee plus first year's membership cost more than I could afford. Plenty of work flowed for a while, then he disappeared off to Canada to edit a paper there and has barely been heard of since.

But I've not wasted my time at tennis, a game which, judging from my tennis club, is generally only played by the young and earnest, and hearties over the age of sixty-five.

I'm in gold letters on the club board – albeit with a doubles partner who is very much better than me. I needn't be defensive: in doubles the weaker player gets more of the ball, I held my own and as far as I am concerned that's my personal Wimbledon. I am immortalised. I am by no means ready to die next week but, if I do, I will die satisfied – a life fulfilled.

Had I still been working in the City I'd be hitting the executive treadmill each lunchtime and never have had the time or energy to play tennis. Jogging or rowing machines may make efficient use of time – but they are sad. Not that I made much use of the equipment. I played a bit of squash at Slim Jim's gym in Broadgate but mainly caught up on lost sleep on the loungers there.

After the City – and the demise of my marriage – I took up rugby again, aged thirty-one. Twelve years on I'm still playing. I nearly died my first outing, a match between two Japanese banks. Not from injury but from the sheer effort of running around the place, being knocked over, then having to stand up and start running again. At thirty-one I was ageing badly.

I am now the longest serving player for the London Japanese RFC. Fast and furious – you can't avoid the word 'nippy' for their style of play. A failing Japanese economy means fewer Japanese in London, but it's still not a bad team. We even had their ex-World Cup captain Hayashi play for us one season.

I am also the oldest regular for the Kew Occasionals RFC. They have also made me immortal by engraving my name on the '"Not" the Yamaichi Trophy' – a cup purloined from Oxford University when Yamaichi collapsed and, perforce, had to stop sponsorship. It was as a sort of Most Valuable Player award, in my case earned by playing every match one season and washing the shirts the most often. I'm very proud of that cup.

Next season is my last season. I say that every season.

The trouble is I love my rugby. The Kews hit demographic shrinkage a few years ago through people getting married or old. There is now an intimidating youth policy: a regular new draft of twenty-somethings down from university starting out in the City or consulting.

There was a period when companies like Accenture – crap name or what, who'd employ them on a re-branding exercise? – were offering them £10,000 not to work but to go on holiday until a position became available. Consulting was having its own little bubble. Those who can, do; those who can't, consult.

So long as these youths tolerate me I shall carry on playing in their team. Rugby must be the only sport where a rank amateur like me, who didn't even get into his school 1st XV, gets to play with the greats. He won't remember me but I've played with J.P.R. Williams. That was as a ringer for the Commons and Lords XV, a team founded by Phillip Oppenheim, then a Tory minister, a friend I met through rugby. I'm now a partner in his two theme restaurants called Cubana.

I once stopped an ex-All Black called Butch Anderson from getting near any line-out ball all match – he was too big to be lifted whereas I'm light and can be sent higher. The new lifting laws have been wonderful for me. In open play I take a pragmatic view towards safety and only tackled him with the assistance of three others. He was playing for the New Zealand parliament; the whole team took it much too seriously.

They were in the same Cape Town hotel as us. At nine o'clock with a match the next day, we were heading out with the Irish for a waterfront bar somewhere. Encountering their coach – yes, they had a coach – we asked, 'Where's the rest of your team?'

'In bloody bed I hope.'

Nothing would be achieved without the world's obsessives, I suppose, but some people need to get a life. In fact, if you haven't spotted it yet, that is the theme of this book.

On the same tour I got in trouble with Ian Davidson, a Glasgow MP, when I took a photograph of him drunk. 'If that gets in the papers...' he said and went on and on about it, even when he was sober again. I wanted to explain to him that if I ever rang up a newspaper editor and said 'Do you want to buy a picture of Ian Davidson somewhat the worse for wear?', first question I'd be asked is 'Ian who?'.

Perhaps his paranoia was correct. Innocuous stories pick up momentum in the same way as rising or falling shares. One year the Lords and Commons did a late summer tour to Catania in Sicily, just below Mount Etna. Phillip had just lost his seat and there was no Ian Who. There was only one other genuine parliamentarian, a young hereditary peer called Dominic, Lord Addington, who has hung onto his position despite being abolished. I can write what I like about him since he's dyslexic and won't read this.

It was August – the political silly season of no news. Some of our players got very drunk one night, in particular a publican from Norfolk and a vet from the Scottish Borders –

'When I put down a dog, the best way is with a mallet.' What about a cow? 'Bigger mallet.'

They attempted to remove the marble angel from the bottom of an elephant statue of great symbolic importance to the Sicilian sense of nationhood. A leg came off in their hands. When they tried to leg it with the leg, they were too legless to escape from the pursuing Carabinieri and were soon caught.

Phillip, Dominic and I had been sharing a quiet bottle of Chianti somewhere. The only indicator we had of having missed out on a massive night of revelry was the dry powder fire extinguisher that was let off in my room, which made my jock-strap itchy for the rest of the tour.

So the next day we hired a car to go see the island, returning to the hotel late in the evening to find a normally exuberant team extraordinarily subdued. We heard the story of the arrest. The Sicilians had taken the vandalism personally. There were reports of a taxi driver saying, 'One person drove the vandals back to the hotel. If I find that person, I *keeell* him.'

If he was prepared to kill his innocent compatriot, the driver, imagine what he'd do to the publican and the vet. Something worse than the latter could do with his mallet I imagine.

Faces were drawn and even the pink lobster sunburn colouring had drained from them.

Next day the local media started to take an interest.

The day after the British media started to pick up on that interest.

As I've said, it was the Silly Season. There was little competing news. Dodi and Di were on Mo's yacht somewhere, Tony Blair and family had done family photo calls in Tuscany and that was about it.

Nominally we were the Lords and Commons team, albeit made up entirely of ringers plus one superannuated ex-MP and a minor peer. Not quite major headline stuff but all in all a reasonable story for desperate newspapers in August.

Phillip Oppenheim manfully lied down the phone to *The Sun* that it was another British team that had committed the sacrilege. I know what it is to be framed by him having agreed to be the Cubana fall guy when Westminster Council did us for fly-postering.

On the Catania rugby festival poster there was, indeed, another English team. They had, however, been a no-show. 'Even as we speak, they are on a plane returning to England in disgrace,' he said. The only truth in this was that they were not in Sicily.

Our captain Dominic Addington, a twenty stone brick shit-house, was shitting bricks about his parliamentary future. Although hereditary, he is not landed, has no art collection to sell to the Getty Museum, and needs the money. Lords get paid for attendance by the day. He has the best attendance record of all peers of the realm and is Liberal Democrat spokesman on disabilities.

Meanwhile, the story had expanded to fill the whole of the front page of La Siciliana and was bubbling under in the national papers, too. In Rome memories of the vandalisation of the Trevi Fountain by a tourist were recent and raw, so the story was very topical. Personally, I found the fuss a little hypocritical since, if you look at the statuary in Catania's park, every single marble bust has had its nose knocked off.

Quite correctly *The Sun* had not completely bought Phillip's spin and began to show signs of being on our case. They would be sending a stringer from Rome.

Then the next day, when we came down to breakfast,

someone said excitedly, 'Have you heard the news?'

Oh no, not something else. Have they peppered the publican from Norfolk? Has the vet from the Borders found a freshly severed pig's head seeping blood into his bed?

'Princess Diana is dead.'

'Tell me you're not joking,' said my Lord Addington.

'No, look at the telly, it's all over it on every channel. She's had a car crash...'

He thought through the political implications for our tour for a moment, then said, 'Thank fuck for that.'

What's that got to do with any of this narrative? Well if I had still been killing myself for wealth and position in the City I'd never have had such life-enhancing experiences. I would not still be playing rugby. 'You're too old, James,' as my mother (wrongly) says.

I wouldn't be involved in the restaurant business. I wouldn't have my name in gold letters on the tennis club board, or on the plinth of the '"Not" the Yamaichi Trophy'. I wouldn't have written four books, including ghosting one for Robbie Williams. As for his quote on the front cover, I just made it up. Which is what ghostwriters are often employed to do.

Writers are always asked, 'Do you have a routine?' and you hear smug, sanctimonious, generally female novelists being interviewed on the radio about their latest Aga-saga or bonk-buster saying, 'It's a job like any other, I get to my computer at nine-thirty, then I work through until...'

Do I have a routine? Absolutely not. For me the whole purpose of leaving the City was to have no routine.

Then they feel entitled to ask 'Do you make a living

at it? I mean can you support yourself? Just from writing?' A question every bit as impertinent as 'So just how big was your bonus?'

Even other authors do it. I met a moderately well-known one called Terence Blacker at an agent's party who asked me that very question.

'So do you make a living at it?'

'I used to work in the City,' I said.

'Ah, say no more.' That explained it. I'd worked in the City. Cash in the bank. No problems. I could afford to be a writer.

Lately I've taken to saying 'I have a trust fund from my parents. I don't need to work'. I enjoy the way it both winds and shuts people up. Wish I had one. I can pass myself off for a trustafarian for a little while – I have no visible means of support, play tennis or garden during the day, dabble in restaurants, and drive an impractical sports car from Japan. (Actually that was a failed business venture. I imported three second hand Mazdas and only managed to sell two.)

I should have known better; everyone was doing it at the time after a period when you could make several thousand pounds per car. When rank amateurs get into a market, the game is over.

Like when everyone you met at a dinner party a few year ago had a mysterious 'internet idea', which they were unwilling to divulge 'I can't tell you, no one has thought of it and you might steal it...' Most of these ideas were worth the same as Ian Davidson MP's photograph (for sale at a modest price if anyone wants it...)

You could be sure lots of people had thought of it. The dotcom bubble was about to burst.

I was never a natural second-hand car dealer any more

than I was a natural stockbroker. My own involvement should have warned me that the market in second-hand cars from Japan had topped out. It's 1929 Wall Street stock-expert-shoeshine-boy syndrome.

Still, I like my car and should any reader want one… There are still bargains, my fee is modest and the Japanese are fastidious, so the cars tend to have been very well looked after, though I'm not stupid enough to offer any guarantees.

A friend called Niwa buys them for me, 'I used to be a green-grocer, so you can trust me,' he says. 'I love cars, they are like cabbages, every one is different.' Niwa knows about cars, so it doesn't matter that I don't, and he really is as honest as a greengrocer. Buy a few cars through me and I might be able to afford to be a writer.

Do I make a living as a writer? Mainly I rub by, sharing my house with paying lodgers, doing a bit of this and that with second-hand cars, restaurants or journalism, and living modestly. I don't have to burn my priceless manuscripts to stay warm. I'd like more money for long trips to Ladakh, Patagonia or Madagascar say. Maybe the worst thing about not being flush with cash is that it makes you ungenerous. In a bad month you feel the pain of a big round of beers and flinch away from paying only to end up over-compensating by suddenly buying too much beer.

If I had a real crisis, I could always rent out the house and go and live in the Cowshed. Not a bad idea, maybe I'll do that anyway...

When short of cash you inevitably end up reflecting from time to time on the person we all know at the other end of the scale, mine is the former partner of Goldman Sachs. Could that have been me if I'd been more driven?

The buzz was that he had been getting £20 million

bonuses. Someone who knows says that he never got anything close to that, knock off a zero – £2 million in a good year just £200,000 in a moderate one and as little as £20,000, in a bad one, to all intents and purposes a zero bonus, the national average wage. It is well known, however, that partners such as he got £60 million for their shares when Goldman Sachs was floated on the stock market. This is not a mildly revolting amount of money, it is obscene. Obscene, however good he was – although one must acknowledge that he can't have been useless.

His £60 million could turn me through the politics of envy into a New Labour-voting-*Guardian*-reader, but doesn't. You never lose your awe for levels of wealth like his – but his happiness is not my unhappiness. Envy at the fact that he has retired aged forty-six? Moi? I retired twelve years before at thirty-one, albeit without the rambling beach house in St Kitts that he's acquired. Still, I've got a share in the Cowshed, win tennis tournaments, part-own two successful restaurants, no longer struggle with *Für Elise* but am in a five-year plan to beat Chopin's *Scherzo in B flat minor* instead, and play rugby with JPR.

Our Goldman's man had taken no personal risk to get this money. All he'd done was pass the Goldmoonies arcane selection procedure twenty years ago – a bit like getting into one of the more exclusive Ivy League fraternity houses – sign along the dotted line like Faust, give over his life and individuality, develop a hard streak to climb the slippery pole (he gives his Filipina maid only twenty-four hours off a week to see her children). His wealth was a fluke. Future City generations won't collect like that. He won the lottery by being in the right place at the right age at the right time (when the City and Wall Street were demutualizing) with the minimum of risk.

That's what makes it obscene; he didn't have to do all that much beyond hanging on in there. He took no risk. It's the same thing that upsets people about fat-cat boardroom pay in other industries. The worse that can happen to these guys is that they get fired, then paid off magnificently, whereas an entrepreneur can lose everything including his house.

Still, it's dirty work that has to be done by someone, and I wasn't prepared to.

Hair-shirted denial of the attractions of wealth is unattractive. I wish I had more. Money can, without question, buy you happiness, even if we all know of rich kids who die of drugs, depression and purposelessness. Money didn't do John Lennon much good either. He's dead. Even if the Beatles were right to suggest that money can't buy you love, it can certainly predispose people to love you. Are we to believe that it was his engaging personality that shrimp Bernie Ecclestone used to get that towering model to marry him? Or that Wendi Deng went purely for Rupert Murdoch's pheromones?

A Sunday paper survey said you needed £5 million to retire without stress. That must be about right. I can't believe that the 6th million makes a great deal of difference to one's mood, unless you really can't get through the day without the thought that a Learjet is sitting on some nearby tarmac for you.

I suppose a decent sized yacht, London town house, country estate, a couple of overseas properties, a helicopter and a stable of fancy cars might make a dent in £60 million and, if you are into collecting Van Goghs, then you need more like £600 million to be at peace with yourself. But if you had all that, you wouldn't have time to enjoy it all, you'd have all the stress of running five different lots of staff and making sure the butler in each house wasn't quietly ripping you off, so I reckon yes, £5 million would be about the right amount to live off comfortably and still be fun, a liberating sum.

Research into the well-being of lottery winners has shown that, by and large, they be well. Writing books is like holding a lottery ticket with much better odds. It could just happen that *Extraordinary Popular Delusions and the Madness of Crowds* might work for you, you could have a *Harry Potter*-scale hit on your hands.

Meanwhile life is enough fun without being J.K Rowling or Dr Atkins (of diet books of prodigious sales), even if it is a correct perception that writers mostly struggle. Get togethers at the Society of Authors can be demoralising events. Authors en masse are a diminished, defeated group – all of them blaming publishers, agents, the public, whoever for their failure. There is an accompanying whiff of desperation that you just don't get in the City.

As a breed, publishers hate authors (but not mine, Artnik loves me). I was playing in the Publishers Tennis tournament, came off court having lost or won, I don't remember which, one of the two anyway, and started to bore someone with an account of my game. I must have lost otherwise I wouldn't have been going on about it. If I'd won I'd have been self-deprecatingly basking in the glory.

'Why don't you write a book about it?' asked a publisher mockingly.

Boy, they hate us.

Around 100,000 books a year are published in the UK and, even if a good proportion of that is represented by specialist manuals, legal tomes, maths text books or local history books written out of enthusiasm and from which no one could hope to make a living, if you're obsessed with being in print – so many people have a manuscript in their top drawer – it seems there are plenty of opportunities.

Making money out of it, on the other hand, in the teeth of competition from the other 100,000 other books plus magazines and newspapers, not to mention pornography on the internet, is not easy.

'How do you get published?' that's the other question. As with the City the best way is not to be a good writer, but to know someone. The agent who first got me into print, Mark Lucas, was my sister-in-law's agent. My current publishers, Artnik, are regulars at Cubana.

Nick Hornby's dad was chief executive of W.H. Smith. That can't have harmed his initial entry into print. But it doesn't explain his subsequent success, including adaptations by Hollywood of *High Fidelity* and *About a Boy*. Hollywood didn't film his books to suck up to Britain's biggest bookshop chain. His success is explained by the fact that people want to read his books. Good luck to him, I say, without the slightest touch of rancour. I lie...I do suffer slight pangs of professional envy. The same sort of low intensity envy I feel for the former partner of Goldman Sachs with his rambling beach house in St Kitts.

Authors do have the right to complain that publishers are pretty hopeless but most wouldn't approve of the cure, which is for those nice chaps with English literature degrees to be shaken up by hard-nosed, unsentimental City business people.

I have a couple of sob stories. One concerns *The Bucks Stop Here*, precursor to this volume, published in 1994 and out of print since 1998. It raced to No. 14 in the Sunday Times bestseller list. Unfortunately they only list as far as No. 10 in the paper and you need to be in that No. 10 to get noticed by the public and to activate *...the Madness of Crowds* effect on sales and have a true bestseller.

I have no special fan base peculiar to Piccadilly so far as I know but there, in Waterstones, was *The Bucks...* filling the No. 1 slot above anything by Nick Hornby or Bill Bryson (J.K. Rowling was still struggling and unheard of). Yet in Hampstead they'd not heard of it at all.

'*The Bus Stops Here*? Let me look it up on the computer.'

'*The Bucks...*'

'Sorry, yes. Ha, Ha! Funny title. Hmmm. We had a copy but it's been sold, shall I order you one?'

'Well, I'm the author. How about ordering ten and putting them on your shelves?' In some books shops the attitude is 'An author? What are YOU doing in a bookshop?' In others they are excited to see you and order five copies, and allow you to sign the one they have in stock (which is good; signing makes it soiled goods, which means it can't be returned to the publisher). If they did order five I'd be back a week later doing the same routine, making sure that next time they really do order ten. I'd soil the five in stock with my signature. Obviously if every author did this it would be chaos. Luckily only Jeffrey Archer and I do.

You can't depend on the publisher's sales reps. They have twenty other titles to push. Even before you compete with the other 100,000 new titles, you compete with your own publisher's list. I've stood behind a sales rep and it's frightening for authors. Each book gets 30 seconds of patter and that's it.

At the book launch party my editor said that my book was 'Our surprise success of the summer'. I think it was due to my own efforts and not theirs that my publisher Simon and Schuster ran out of copies of *The Bus Stops Here* just three weeks after publication. Then they farted around reprinting with a new cover with the nice critiques on it while momentum was lost. I fell like a British tennis player from 14 to 253.

I've always wondered why they bothered publishing a book that surprised them when it succeeded. That's publishing for you – their default expectation is failure, it's the culture and it's rather depressing. For all the harshness of the City, life there is predicated on the notion of success. Even when you lose your job you assume you will bounce back.

So do I make a living from writing? The correct answer is 'Some years'.

From time to time too I shoot myself in the foot. I fell out with my agent Mark Lucas, a Big Agent these days having cleaned up on the Lebanese hostage crisis and the First Gulf War. He represents hostages John McCarthy and Terry Waite and with the help of ghostwriters, turned one Tornado pilot shot down in Iraq and one ex-SAS man into successful 'novelists' who, unlike me, produce one book a year.

He got me a nice job, ghosting for Robbie Williams. Robbie was one year into his solo career and, though I was dimly aware of the band, Take That, I'd never heard of him. So I hung round the twenty-five-year-old pop star for a month or two. It was great fun being on stage at Glastonbury, looking out at 35,000 fans enjoying the mud, while standing next to the gorgeous Nicky from All Saints and Robbie's mum. It's fascinating being at the front, you see all the fainting fans being passed limply over the heads of the crowd to the front and the waiting St John's Ambulance and all the girls with their tits hanging out. *...the Madness of Crowds* indeed. After Glastonbury I went back to London in the helicopter, what a thrill and so quick and convenient! I think if I were an ex-Goldman's partner with £60 million I'd hire a helicopter quite often.

I am always asked 'What's Robbie really like?'

Very good at pool. Not too good at tennis but could be; he's a natural sportsman. Beyond that I am too professional to say. I never signed and was never asked to sign a confidentiality agreement. To my mind, in the old-fashioned My Word Is My Bond place from which I like to think I came, this means I can't say anything beyond what is already well known. The book I wrote for him is pretty honest, I think, though I wasn't fully let into the secret of his drug addictions.

He is a hugely talented entertainer who writes lyrics, sometimes corny, but none the worse for that; they work as well as any opera libretto lyrics, which are always pretty ridiculous. He also has a great ear for what music will go with them. I liked his collaborator Guy Chambers, probably because he came from a classical music background like me. A shame that Guy has apparently been dumped but he must have at least five million and counting by now, so he's fine.

Mark Lucas got me some good jobs until I shot myself in the foot was over the *Official Guide to the Millennium Dome* – a piece of hackwork and a reasonably paid summer job that wouldn't interfere with my tennis too much.

But the Dome suddenly cancelled the job. I was blameless, I'd done a month's research and no one could hold my writing against me since I'd not done any.

They'd not got round to sending me a contract, I'd been working on trust, though they had sent me a Confidentiality Agreement the moment I started. A paranoid piece of paper, I decided, and somehow never got round to signing it.

Mark said he'd get me £800 compensation for the lost job. That seemed very little on a two month project which was supposed to pay me £8,000. So I offered my sorry tale to a Sunday tabloid that agreed to pay me £4,000 to Tell All about the contents of the Dome. The contents were still Tony Blair's State Secret. Everyone had been asking What Is Going in the Dome? and I was in the position of both knowing and being able to say, Nothing Much. But it was an exclusive.

So, for two days work scribbling up a hatchet job on the Dome for £4,000 or, if lucky, £800 compensation? That's what is known as a no-brainer. Not a hard choice.

I made the mistake of telling Mark's colleague Julian about my plan to sell my tale of betrayal. I thought I was being rather clever. Julian didn't. He warned that it would be unwise to go ahead. 'We find you a job and you immediately betray confidentiality...'

I just thought he was being wet. Although even I was not so naïve as to think that their relationship with Harper Collins(the publishers of the guide) wasn't far more important to them than their relationship with me. Mark came in on Julian's side, so I wrote him a pompous letter, complaining that he '...couldn't even stand up for me within his own agency'. I liked the guy and I'd often written him stinking letters before with no consequences. That's what agents are for: to get you deals and to absorb authorly angst.

Anyway, Mark fired me. So I earned the £4,000, but what I lost was the next Robbie Williams book, the one when he was BIG. I met its ghostwriter at a party. He told me he'd been paid £200,000, like a Goldman's man in a moderate year. We were definitely fringing into City levels of remuneration here.

Oh well. I'd had my moment of rage and I felt better for it, especially as one gathers that the New Millennium Experience Company (RIP) consulted lawyers and seriously thought of suing me. So what I wrote must have been good.

But I do miss ghostwriting. It is an under-valued profession, and Mark Lucas is one of the best suppliers of projects around. A feeble creep, but good at his job. He used to complain that he had as much ability as anyone in the City but earned a fraction. His choice. But he could have done very well there.

News reaches me on the wind of former colleagues.

Of the five City companies I worked for, I enjoyed Merrill Lynch the most (or disliked the least). There was a certain Frontier Spirit. If you were prepared to work at Merrill's it showed you were prepared to take personal risks in order to have a more exciting and potentially more rewarding life. Failure to perform meant being hanged from the nearest tree, which is what happened to me. Success meant riches beyond the dreams of avarice, which is what happened to Alick, Henry and Charlie. At least for the period now ended.

Giussi is the one of us who appears to have done best and survived longest. She is still doing well at Morgan Stanley. Nigel – he of the failed attempt to seduce Twiddles and Fluff on the skiing holiday – is one of the great survivors, still smiling-'n'-dialling at Limited UBS. He bought the farm next to Wurzel's. Wurzel manages the land while Nigel weekends in the house and has finally married a delightful Norwegian. There is also a baby on the way, a child that will no doubt benefit from a hands-on dad since it is hard to imagine that Nigel will still be doing the City thing in five years time, he'll be looking after his toddlers. Sensibly, he has avoided management, so his shoulders are not hitting the sides of the pyramid.

Alick, after a period of being promoted sideways into jobs like Head of Information Technology, emigrated to New Zealand. He did achieve his ambition of buying that chalet in the French Alps, albeit not in Courchevel.

Henry was out of work the last time I saw him. All the signs were that his shoulders had hit the side of the City pyramid and that he'd have to think of something else to do, but he bravely claims to be down-shifting.

He remarked to me a decade or so ago that I was lucky. 'Jim, you speak Japanese, you'll always have something to do. All I know is broking. I'm thirty-seven and I have no qualifications, I'd be stuck if I lost this.'

If he fails to find another broking job and, pushing fifty, that moment must be close – sales is a young man's job – then I won't feel sorry for him, because he and Alick are both affable, competent people and once the choice is forced upon them, they will find other outlets for their talents and energies and after overcoming a period of self-doubt will do very well at whatever it is that they turn to.

(Henry is wrong about my Japanese. Even a skill like that is vulnerable to the next generation. I learnt it when few others were bothering. I was in a programme of forty teachers sent to Japan by the British Council and the Japanese Education Ministry. The same programme now sends six hundred a year. I could get away with a fairly ropey standard which would never be tolerated in a translator of French, because I was a rarity. Then there are the Gens coming of age who are truly bilingual and will do my job more quickly, cheaply and accurately than me).

In the mid-nineties, Charlie became head of European equity sales at some bank. This over-promotion went to his head it seems. In his permanent quest to be posh, he developed a polo habit and would leave the office in all his kit, including shiny leather knee guards and riding boots and breeches at four in the afternoon to head for Windsor Great Park. This did not go down well with his superiors.

He now runs a venture capital 'boutique'. Running a financial boutique is an activity popular with those in denial about the end of their City careers. Loads of such boutiques sprung up in the early years of the new Millennium as the City went through exactly the same process as it went through when I was made redundant – mass job losses. The period was so identical there was even a Gulf War run by a President Bush.

Charlie is energetic, hard working and takes no shit from anyone. He is a driven man. But the best salesmen are people who have something to prove. It makes them that little bit more hungry.

Charlie went to a very minor public school and would like to have the plummy accent and the easy manner of Alick and Henry. He is almost there but just tries slightly too hard. This manifests itself in various ways, such as one of the most acute cases of B.R.A.N.D.S (Brand Name Dependency Syndrome) that I have ever witnessed.

He may still wake up one morning and realise that his Five Year Plan to become upper class is doomed. Crossing class barriers is perfectly possible, but is a generational thing: if he can get the kids into Eton – if that's important to him – then the wealth he will have accumulated will mean they'll do just fine. Charlie himself is inescapably and totally identifiably lower-middle class. And why be ashamed of that?

Still, because of his drive, the likelihood is that his will be one of the investment boutiques that makes it. Most won't.

That Georgian Rectory or Holland Park mansion (or both) is beckoning. Michael Lewis in *Liar's Poker* refers to the satisfaction of big wages coming from their being a way of keeping score. I'm not sure. Most people are rather embarrassed about the score and correspondingly discreet, making it hard to compare scores. None of us really know what the Goldman's man earned.

Christopher Heath, as I said earlier, changed his way of being remunerated to avoid the publicity of being Britain's highest-paid exec. We all envied Heath his two million pounds a year, but close friends of mine who worked with him say that what really motivated him was that he found broking exhilarating. If you were to ask him directly what motivated him, he might candidly admit 'money', but possibly he was being less candid than he seemed. By all accounts he loved his job and that is worth far more envy than the money. Having been slung out of Barings pre-Leeson, he has his own boutique brokerage, doing well apparently. He just can't give it up. He must be worth millions and his motivation can only be that he loves it. Not just the money – which I am sure he enjoys – but more the buzz of the markets, of dealing.

There is a nice theory that has people in any kind of organisation being promoted to their level of incompetence. Alick got there quite quickly before making the case-book smile-'n'-dial salesman's mistake of going into management (which, as observed already, doesn't exist in broking firms) and which Nigel so presciently avoided.

When *The Bucks Stop Here* was published all its victims were invited to the launch party. Henry, Charlie, Nigel – they all took it on the chin. Alick, though invited, didn't come. That is the measure of the man. I'm reliably informed that he consulted libel lawyers.

Regrets? Just one maybe. With the job, six months later, went my marriage – possibly unconnected events, possibly not. Losing my job may have precipitated the break-up, but no doubt it would have happened anyway. If something is inevitable it is probably better that it happens sooner rather than later, so that the adjustment begins early. Well, except death.

Saeko totally trounced me in the custody stakes and I regret having had fatherhood taken off me. Gen lives in Japan with his mother and has for the last six years or so. I see him about once a year and we talk over the phone. We have a great relationship, Saeko has never attempted to brainwash him against me or anything like that, but still...

Even that experience has its upside. Being thirty-something and single and now forty-something and single is very good fun, plus there's been the time for all that rugby and tennis. Most people downshift to spend more time with the family, I ended up spending less.

I became involved with a charity called Families Need Fathers, a group for disenfranchised dads and a few mothers too. I turned up at a London Branch AGM and no one wanted to be next year's chairman. I stupidly put my hand up.

Then the national chairman died aged forty-six of a heart attack – not on his way to the gym, he always looked unhealthy. I replaced him as boss; a job I failed to shake off for five years. It has 3,000 members and running it was draining with some quite damaged people whose instinct was to lash out at the people who were trying to help them rather than at the morally bankrupt, lazy family lawyers and policy makers, both of whom think fathers are an optional extra.

A feature of the voluntary sector is the in-fighting that goes on – there is nothing less charitable than people in charities – and if I'm really proud of one achievement it is that I sorted that out at FNF and that my successor runs a harmonious and increasingly influential organisation, giving real help to the parents who need it.

There is still some way to go with the influencing. I occasionally go to family policy seminars – something I hate – that are filled with wringingly-dry, man-bashing 'a woman needs a man like a fish needs a bicycle' types. The men there are wringingly wet. Wring as in, you want to wring their necks. The whole atmosphere is of axes being gently ground to get the next government grant. I'm glad to say we got FNF one.

FNF sometimes helps City people, who have a relatively high marital breakdown rate. Usually they come to us having made the mistake of paying for really expensive West End lawyers who are no better than cheap ones. There is no shortage of people spending a whole City bonus on a divorce. You're better off – and you will certainly be better off – doing it yourself.

I nearly crashed once when I heard my wife's solicitor, someone called Philippa Pearson, on the car radio defending solicitor's fees on behalf of her professional association and justifying the public money spent on them, 'We have to pay rent for offices in expensive parts of town...' She really did say that.

I met a friend of hers who said Philippa claims she has never lost a case. I suppose she did 'win' the case against me. You can't lose when representing mothers and the way not to lose when representing fathers is to counsel them to give up. So probably it's true, she's never lost.

But Ms Pearson is crap, I wouldn't employ her to deal with a disputed parking ticket. Our divorce took four years. Saeko and I laid quiet siege to each other after she'd won custody. When it became apparent I was not going to crack and seek profitable employment in the City we wrapped things up. Possibly for fear that there would be no assets to strip. In fact there were, but Ms Pearson never asked me for an update, low at the time of separation. One holding had quadrupled. Out of compassion for me? That doesn't fit the personality.

Four years of talking through lawyers, and paying their disbursements, did not leave me with much respect for them. It's true the adversarial system is bigger than all the people who work in it, but people who spend their costed-by-the-hour time drafting indignant letters to fathers about bringing the child back at 6 p.m. on the dot and not 6.15 p.m. develop an unpleasant mindset.

I never spotted a sign of a decent person in the barrister she instructed in our case. A man called Nick Francis who told me, accurately, that 'I didn't have a cat's chance in hell of winning' my custody case. I recounted this story in a newspaper article, implying that it was a bullying utterance. That was my way of getting revenge. Codes of conduct are such that family lawyers are not supposed to bully, though they often do. I must have drawn some blood because I got five pages of tightly written angst from his libel lawyer, a Mr Rubinstein. Fortunately, Francis had also written to someone else about the incident and he'd superciliously noted that he'd not said 'cat's chance' but 'snowball's chance'.

That was the end of his case, really.

If any City person is feeling guilt about having too much gelt, Families Need Fathers is a really good cause and your money will go far. You should reflect that every time your soft top Saab gets slit into, the crime was almost certainly committed by a teenager who lacked the guidance of a father.

I had no idea what I was letting myself in for when I went to Japan (having seen a might-as-well-give-it-a-go ad in the university careers room), originally for one year, eventually staying for three. Gen is the delightful result. I took a risk marrying my pregnant Japanese girlfriend. I took a risk joining Merrill Lynch, knowing how unsentimental they are about whom they hire (and then fire). That has forced me into positive decisions.

It is much better to regret doing something than to regret doing nothing. If any doubts surface, I say go for it. Je ne regrette more or less rien (apart from not taking out redundancy insurance – surely the ultimate insider deal). When I was made redundant, I certainly lost sleep rehearsing speeches and strategies that might have saved me my job, what the French call esprits d'escalier: that brilliant sharp word which you could have said but you only think of as you are descending the staircase having been booted out of the mistress's bedroom. Losing my job, though, was A Good Thing.

The matrimonial breakdown that went with it could never be described as A Good Thing. I am often asked whether the marriage broke up for cultural reasons and I don't think so. We were just different people with different interests, different friends.

Rory, like Gen, is nearly grown up. His parents got involved in the New Labour project. Though they could easily afford it, they were not in favour of private education. Everyone should have the same start in life, they piously said. But they weren't sufficiently committed to Camberwell schools for some reason and moved to Chiswick. The big irony is that Rory couldn't get into the school they'd moved to be near and he now goes to St. Pauls, one of Britain's best known public schools.

In *The Bucks Stop Here* I took some trouble to disguise Rory, a mere child. I heard indirectly that no fewer than three different sets of parents of limited acquaintance were offended by the description. I'm proud of that – I must have got the caricature spot on. 'Rory' has turned out well despite his parents.

Mr Gibbon died aged 87, predeceased by both Mrs Gibbons. The dogs found good homes. By the end of his life Mr Gibbon and I had become friends. He was ill for the last couple of years and I used to visit him in hospital and, when he was at home, check on him or go to Safeway for him. Although his hearing never faded, he stopped complaining about my piano playing, to hear it thundering through the wall I think made him feel less lonely. He even left me £1,000 in his will.

I wish I'd ghosted his autobiography for him now. It would have been more interesting than Robbie Williams's. I wrote a *Guardian* obituary for him in which I uncovered all sorts of interesting things. He once flew the Red Flag over the St Pancras Town Hall in place of the Union Jack and was so left-wing, he was expelled from the Labour Party.

His Great War veteran father took ten years to die of his wounds and could not afford a grammar school uniform, so he could not take up the scholarship he'd won. Then Mr Gibbon was orphaned, so he educated himself largely; too much in Marx and Engels for current tastes but you can't blame him.

'Whatever the opposition say, the red Flag will still fly over the Town Hall and, for my money, over Buckingham Palace as well', he said, 'while the Queen could live somewhere quietly in the country so that some rooms could be used to house people who are overcrowded.' Once he spent six months in Brixton for having assaulted a policeman on a march. The officer had been rough-handling a female demonstrator – that was Mr Gibbon's version of the story and I tend to believe it.

I didn't agree with his politics but his views were sincerely held. His Communist mates said he could never bring himself to lie or say things he didn't believe, so he lacked the ruthlessness to make it in politics.

He saw the Soviet Union for the Evil empire it was and involved himself in letter writing campaigns to help free dissidents. He hated anti-democrats like Arthur Scargill.

He certainly didn't waste his time on this planet. He learnt the trombone at the orphanage and ended up playing in the London Symphony Orchestra under all sorts of the greats, like Gustav Holst and Vaughan Williams.

His last few months were spent in an old people's home. The ladies were all over him and he had a wonderful time. Of course, he carried on complaining about the noise through the walls, which was much worse than my piano. After all, he was in an environment where almost everyone except himself was deaf and the television in each room was on volume 9. Still, it gave him something to moan about, which I think he needed in order to be happy. He wouldn't have liked a perfect world.

I met a very nice Japanese girl who was left by her English husband, then shortly afterwards lost her job – a situation the mirror image of my own.

Don't panic.

Reader, I didn't marry her.

She had been angry at the time, she said, but she doesn't mind now. The she went on to say something that I thought was profound in its way, a good motto.

She said, 'Being happy is the best revenge.'

I am.

Other titles published by ARTNIK

All ARTNIK titles can be ordered from any bookshop or, in case of difficulty, from...

SALES & DISTRIBUTION
LITTLEHAMPTON Book Services
Faraday Close, Worthing
BN13 3RB UK
bmr@lbsltd.co.uk
DDI: 01903 828860

ARTNIK BOOKS
341b Queenstown Rd SW8 4LH
ArtnikBooks@dsl.pipex.com
+44 (0) 20 7498 1257

Artnik Books is a patron of The Artnik Foundation (reg. no. 8490/2001), which was established in 2001 to promote literary exchange between Eastern Europe and the West.

Other titles published by ARTNIK

TITLE	**A Right to Kill?**
Tony Martin's story as told to John McVicar	
EDITOR	John McVicar
PRICE	£16.99
PUBLICATION	February 2004
BINDING	Hardback
FORMAT	240mm x 160mm
EXTENT	280pp
ILLUSTRATIONS	12 Colour Photographs
ISBN	1-903906-36-9

When Tony Martin shot and killed one of the burglars breaking into his isolated Norfolk farmhouse, he touched a nerve in middle-England's heart. **He fought back...**

The farmer was convicted of murder, later to be reduced to manslaughter by the Court of Appeal.

A wave of support swept the country and spread all over the world. Martin became the unwitting icon to all those who believed in defending their life and property even if it meant taking the law into their own hands.

This book narrates the farmer's own story, as told by him and those who supported him during 3 years of incarceration. Much local colour is provided by long standing friends in Norfolk.

The book will go behind the scenes of chequebook journalism and explore the complex and often hilarious relationship between Martin and his supporters.

Other titles published by ARTNIK

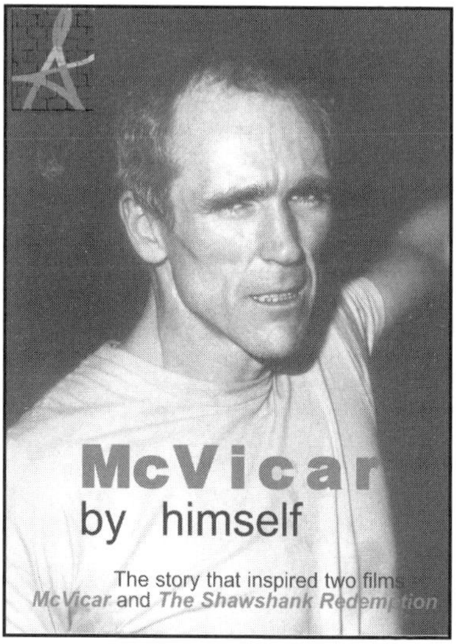

TITLE	McVicar by Himself
AUTHOR	John McVicar
PRICE	£8.99
PUBLICATION	Autumn 2002
BINDING	Paperback
FORMAT	200mm x 130mm
EXTENT	263pp
ILLUSTRATIONS	B&W Photographs
ISBN	1-903906 05 9

McVicar by Himself, a classic in the genre of prison books, was first published in 1974 when the author was serving a 26-year jail sentence for armed robbery. It was to inspire Roger Daltrey of The Who to make the film ***McVicar***[1980], which in turn influenced Stephen King's story of the ***Shawshank Redemption*** [1982] and the eponymous movie.

The first edition was riddled with inaccuracies as the original editor, the ex-KGB agent Goronwy Rees, was denied access to McVicar and he had to work with a barely decipherable handwritten manuscript. Artnik's new version has been completely re-written by McVicar: the inaccuracies corrected, new material included and the book's message clarified.

It includes hitherto unpublished anecdotes about Britain's most savage criminals of the 60s - the Torture Gang boss Charlie Richardson, his macabre hireling "Mad" Frankie Fraser, even Moors murderer Ian Brady and others who were imprisoned in Durham's infamous E-Wing at the time.

Other titles published by ARTNIK

BOOK Two bites of the Apple

Book III of the trilogy **A Plateful of Privilege**

FOREWORD Nigel Dempster

AUTHOR Alexander Thynn, Marquess of Bath

PRICE	£12.99
PUBLICATION	March 2003
BINDING	Paperback
FORMAT	200mm x 160mm
ILLUSTRATIONS	16 B& W photographs
EXTENT	260pp
ISBN	1-903906 26 1

This book follows in the wake of *The Early Years(*Nov 2002, Artnik) and *Top Hat & Tails* (March 2003, Artnik). *Two Bites of the Apple* is mainly about Lord Bath's two-year stint in the Guards as a conscript, but it also covers his period in Paris studying art and women. While he was in the army he became a boxing champion and lost his virginity. It is a very funny book and was serialised in the *Mail on Sunday*.

Lord Bath's public image is that of an indulgent, eccentric, hedonistic, sexual libertine. This trilogy - **Two Bites of the Apple** is the third book in the series - shows that he is all that but he is also a prolific writer, artist, thinker... He has consciously lived his life according to his principles rather than those of his age or kind. Born to a life of privilege, having inherited one of the oldest titles, a fortune and a stately home, he has flouted all the obligatory sexual, social and political conventions... his practice of polygyny being the most notorious.

Other titles published by ARTNIK

BOOK How to join the club of the Rich and Famous

PRICE	£4.99
PULICATION	October 2003
FORMAT	165mm x 130mm
EXTENT	162pp
ILLUSTRATIONS	B&W Drawings
ISBN	1-903906-01-6

How to Join the Club of the Rich and Famous - "a short guide to social climbing" - is the arriviste's little Bible. It provides the reader with the tools for and the inside tips on how to join the most exclusive club of them all - that of the Rich and Famous. The author has swanned around Europe and America in precisely this world, picking up wealthy husbands and discarding them along the way. She knows exactly how this club ticks and the slightly sardonic tone of her check list to what joining it requires suggests it is not worth the effort. But that might be because she has been there, done it and still has the jewellery and the furs to prove it.

Valentina Artsrunik is a Countess of Russian descent who grew up in Bulgaria and France, but has lived in England most of her life. She has travelled widely, attended countless social functions, raced horses, and enjoyed the company of the jet set on each side of the Atlantic.
She launched Artnik in 2001

Other titles published by ARTNIK

BOOK The Book of Criminal Quotations

EDITOR	J.P. Bean
PRICE	£9.99
PUBLICATION	October 2003
BINDING	Paperback
FORMAT	200mm x 130mm
EXTENT	296 pp
ILLUSTRATIONS	B&W photographs
ISBN	1-903906 30 X

The Book of Criminal Quotations is the result of the editor, J.P. Bean scouring virtually every true crime ever written for quotable quotes. Whenever some criminal or someone involved in the criminal justice system has been credited with saying or has written something macabre, funny, insightful, poignant or just worth quoting Bean has selected and included it in this book.

It records from all over the world the words of murderers, conmen, gangsters, jailbreakers, supergrasses, detectives, judges, even public executioners. John Gotti, Ronnie Kray, Pablo Escobar, Ned Kelly, Ruth Ellis...

Meyer Lansky, *Mafia godfather*: "One quarter of us is good. Three quarters is bad. That's a tough fight, three against one."

Cynthia Payne, *Streatham Madame*: "The trouble with men is that for a woman to have a civilised conversation with them they need despunking first."

Other titles published by ARTNIK

BOOK Princess Stephanie

Inside the life and mind of Monaco's wild child

AUTHOR	Paul Donnelley
PRICE	16.99
PUBLICATION	February 2004
BINDING	Hardback
FORMAT	200mm x 130mm
EXTENT	260pp
ILLUSTRATIONS	8pp colour photographs
ISBN	1-903906-34-2

Princess Stephanie charts the story of the Monaco's celebrated enfant terrible. It begins with the tragedy that proved the turning point in her life: the death of her mother, Grace Kelly, in September 13, 1982 when the car they were in crashed. Badly injured, Stephanie had to clamber out over the unconscious body of her mother, who had suffered a mild stroke at the wheel. She nevertheless had the presence of mind to put on the handbrake and move the automatic shift to park.

For two decades Stephanie has denied persistent rumours that she was the driver. In intervening years, she lived it up as only a rich, headstrong and some would say disturbed royal can. She inherited her mother's powerful sex drive and has had a string of highly-publicised affairs with "below stairs" men that have corroded her relationship with her father and sister.

While Donnelley documents the well-known scandals in her life, he always does so with an eye not to sensationalise but to paint a human portrait of this complex, turbulent and fiercely independent woman .